The
Drucker
Difference

**What the World's Greatest Management Thinker
Means to Today's Business Leaders**

Craig L. Pearce

Joseph A. Maciariello

Hideki Yamawaki

New York • Chicago • San Francisco • Lisbon • London
Madrid • Mexico City • Milan • New Delhi • San Juan
Seoul • Singapore • Sydney • Toronto

The *McGraw·Hill* Companies

1 2 3 4 5 6 7 8 9 0   DOC/DOC   0 1 0 9

ISBN: 978-0-07-163800-5
MHID: 0-07-163800-8

This publication is designed to provide accurate and authoritative information in regard to the subject matter covered. It is sold with the understanding that the publisher is not engaged in rendering legal, accounting, or other professional service. If legal advice or other expert assistance is required, the services of a competent professional person should be sought.

> —From a declaration of principles jointly adopted
> by a committee of the American Bar
> Association and a committee of publishers.

McGraw-Hill books are available at special quantity discounts to use as premiums and sales promotions, or for use in corporate training programs. To contact a representative please visit the Contact Us pages at www.mhprofessional.com.

Contents

Foreword

Charles Handy

This book is a celebration of a sort. Not many people can expect to see their lifetime's work entice an entire faculty into a collaborative project that builds upon that intellectual legacy. But then, not many people are Peter Drucker, nor are many faculties like the one at the School of Management in Claremont that bears the Drucker name. To have one's work grow and develop beyond one's death is every scholar's dearest wish. The project that this book outlines is, therefore, the sincerest compliment that could be paid to a great thinker, teacher, and wordsmith in the centenary of his birth.

But it is more than that. It is, or should be, an inspiration and a challenge to other places of learning and teaching. The editors of this volume of essays are too modest. The story behind the book is indeed unique, as they say, but the editors underplay the special institutional culture that made it possible. Could it have happened at other schools of business, one wonders, and if not, why not?

As they tell it, a meeting of the entire faculty of the Drucker School (or the Peter F. Drucker and Masatoshi Ito Graduate School of Management, to give it its full title) decided spontaneously, "without prompting or provocation," to develop a course together. Each week of the course would be taught by a different faculty member, each one demonstrating how Drucker's work was being developed in his or her own area of study. This book provides an overview of these individual contributions to the course.

For 18 professors to work together in harmony is rare enough, but to agree to weld their individual research and teaching to another person's work is even more special. Of course, the Drucker School is not a big school, which can make this easier, but you do not have to be big in numbers to make a big difference, in this case the Drucker Difference, as they term it. Indeed, big institutions, in their pursuit of ever more size and supposed clout, can forget why they were created in the first place.

Graduate schools of management are unusual places. Most graduate schools focus on one discipline, be it law or medicine or architecture. Management schools, on the other hand, bring different disciplines to bear on one area of activity—organizations—usually leaving it to the student to make all the necessary connections between the disciplines. The variety of disciplines makes it even harder to develop a common philosophy or direction. Once, in my earlier career as a professor at the fledgling London Business School, a journalist rang up to ask what the school thought about a recent economic downturn. I heard myself reply, "The school, as a school, does not have a view, although individual professors might." I thought, as I put the phone down, that ideally the school should have a view, or at least a shared philosophy.

The Drucker School does. It is a philosophy deeply rooted in Peter Drucker's humanistic theory of management and government—a view of organizations as if people mattered. Peter Drucker lived so long, was so curious about so much, and covered so many topics in his writings that there is a deep well of thinking for the school to draw from. It was once remarked of a potential British prime minister that he would be a disappointment because "he had no hinterland," meaning that he had a narrow and shallow foundation to his worldview, clever though he might be professionally. It is a failing shared by too many leaders of business today. No one could say that Peter Drucker had no hinterland. Indeed, it was his broad understanding of history, art, and of all the human disciplines, not just of business, that made him so interesting to so many for so long.

Therefore, the book is, in the first place, an excellent way to understand how Drucker's ideas apply to today's dilemmas, be they the problems faced by organizations, by governments, or by individuals. But it also serves as an example of how a management or business school can use a declared philosophy to blend together what are, at first sight, very disparate disciplines. I have been privileged to get to know the Drucker School at close quarters and I know that it works.

Charles Handy is a social philosopher, author, and broadcaster, living in London. He was a Visiting Scholar at the Drucker School in 2008.

Introduction

The Drucker Living Legacy

Craig L. Pearce, Joseph A. Maciariello, and Hideki Yamawaki

The alternative to autonomous institutions that function and perform is not freedom. It is totalitarian tyranny.

—Peter F. Drucker

This book provides a current snapshot of the work coming out of the laboratory that is the Peter F. Drucker and Masatoshi Ito Graduate School of Management, where faculty, students, and staff alike explore the frontiers of management together. Peter Drucker, of course, was a member of our faculty from 1971 to 2005, and he taught courses right alongside us until he was well into his nineties. In fact, many of us took great pleasure in sitting in on his classes. Beyond the classroom setting, most of us had a personal relationship with him—he influenced our thinking, our culture, and our philosophy. What was so striking about Peter was that he was so humble and so magnanimous. He gave credit to everyone around him, and he shared his ideas and his advice freely and respectfully.

Our philosophy of management at the Drucker School is deeply rooted in Peter's professional work and in his personal character. Our approach to organization is keenly focused on the human side of enterprise—the idea that people have value and dignity, and that the role of management is to provide a context in which people can flourish both intellectually and morally. This is the philosophical position that binds our faculty together, it is the message that resonates with us, and it is what initially attracted us all to the Drucker School. Today, we aspire to carry the Drucker message forward through our teaching, our writing, and our consulting, and, it almost goes without saying, through our civic engagement. Peter's devotion to the work of social sector organizations has been an example to us all.

It was very sad for all of us when Peter passed away on November 11, 2005. At the Drucker School, naturally, there was a sense of void. He was, after all, the glue that had initially bound us together in our quest to improve people's lives. Initially, we found many people, ourselves included, asking questions like, what would Peter think? What questions would Peter ask? Or, what would Peter do? Of course, Peter would have discouraged such questions—he wanted us all to think for ourselves, but none of us could ignore Peter's deep commitment to management as a human activity, which is what this book is all about.

We discovered, in our journey, that Peter's philosophy permeated our worldview in such a profound way that he continues to live on through the work of all who walk in his footsteps. One thing we all know so well about Peter is that he did not want us to simply look back at what he had done. He wanted us to pick up the management mantle that he carried so aptly for so long and carry it forward, each on his own path.

During a Drucker School faculty meeting in the spring of 2007, a remarkable thing happened. Spontaneously, without prompting or provocation, the entire faculty coalesced around the idea of developing a course together, in which we could build upon and honor the intellectual foundations that Peter Drucker had laid for each and every one of us. It was to be a new course; a different course; a course that covers the various disciplines of management. It was a course inspired by Peter Drucker, and it was meant to continue to build the

Drucker living legacy within our respective fields and extend his legacy into the future through our teaching.

While the "Drucker Difference" course was conceived in the spring of 2007, it was born in September 2007. The course is unique. Each week, it is taught by a different faculty member. Each class session begins with Drucker's philosophical foundations, and each faculty member then extends Drucker's foundations through his or her own work. The course perpetuates a living Drucker legacy, and this book captures the essence of the course.

To some of us, Drucker's intellectual work can be found traced to his work on pensions; to others, it is to his work in the nonprofit sector; to others, it is to his half-century of work on knowledge work; and to still others, it is in his deep-felt concern for the importance of creating a functioning society. Peter was prolific. His work touched on nearly all aspects of society (including art and chaos theory, which are not included in this book), and each of us draws from the well different lessons to carry the Drucker philosophy forward. Here we briefly review the contents of this book.

The Contributions in This Book

This book begins with "Management as a Liberal Art," by Karen Linkletter and Joseph A. Maciariello. The authors make concrete Drucker's ideas on how management, appropriately practiced, is a liberal art. What Drucker meant by this is that management is liberal in that it draws on the fundamentals of life, like knowledge and wisdom, and it is an art in that it requires application and wisdom to be realized.

Next, in "Drucker on Government, Business, and Civil Society," Ira Jackson does three things. First, he introduces Peter Drucker's philosophy of government. Second, he explores Drucker's perspective on the appropriate relationship between business and government. Third, he examines the common challenges and differentiating characteristics of management and leadership in business, government, and civil society that Drucker was among the first to understand and to champion. In so doing, the chapter lays a clear course for the future of such endeavors.

In the following chapter, "Leading Knowledge Workers," Craig L. Pearce examines the nature of knowledge work, the emergence of which Drucker identified nearly half-a-century ago. Knowledge work is fundamentally different from other types of work: it requires voluntary contributions of the intellectual capital of the skilled professionals doing it. Accordingly, Pearce claims that we need to ask ourselves what type of leadership is most appropriate in the knowledge worker context. Therefore, this chapter discusses multiple forms of leadership and identifies how each is most appropriately deployed among knowledge workers.

Next, in "Value(s)-Based Management," James Wallace examines the juxtaposition of the creation of wealth-based values with human values. The value-based management (VBM) approach emphasizes that the sole purpose of the corporation is to create shareholder wealth, while the corporate social responsibility (CSR) framework emphasizes broader social concerns and multiple stakeholders. Wallace demonstrates that these two philosophies are really far more complementary than they are at odds with each other; when both are appropriately engaged, they can lead to a virtuous cycle in which doing good leads to doing well, which can provide the ability to do even more good. As Drucker stated: "It is not enough to do well; it must also do good." But in order to "do good," a business must first "do well."

Building on Wallace's chapter, in "Drucker on Corporate Governance," Cornelis de Kluyver expands on Drucker's views on the critical role of governance in modern enterprise. This chapter surveys key issues in the current corporate governance debate and links them to Peter Drucker's philosophy and writings.

Then Richard Ellsworth, in "Corporate Purpose," provides perspective on the role of corporate purpose, which Drucker defined as the core concept of the corporation. As corporate purpose is the central element of strategy—the end toward which strategy is directed—it can act as a source of organizational cohesion, strategic direction, and human motivation. Grappling with the fundamental reasons for a firm's existence raises issues concerning the means and ends of corporate performance. Thus, this chapter examines the profound influence that purpose, or the lack thereof, has on the corporation.

Subsequently, Vijay Sathe, in his chapter "Strategy for What Purpose?" provides a powerful framework—the POSE framework—for assessing strategy, the means through which purpose is achieved, and the success of strategy. The POSE framework stands for purpose, objectives, strategy, and execution, and it is firmly embedded in Drucker's work on strategy and strategy implementation. It is a useful tool for managers at all levels.

Next, Sarah Smith Orr, in her chapter "The Twenty-First Century: The Century of the Social Sector," provides a framework for building an understanding of the distinctive features of nonprofit/social-sector organizations by applying and adapting the tools originally developed by Peter Drucker.

Hideki Yamawaki, in his chapter "Economic Environment, Innovation, and Industry Dynamics," then provides a more macro view of the environmental forces acting on firms. In line with Drucker, Yamawaki examines how a country's present business environment is shaped by its historical, political, economic, and societal conditions. By developing a deep understanding of such issues, one is better prepared to understand the shape of the future to come for an industry, for a specific company, and for the global economy.

In the next chapter, "A Pox on Charisma," Jean Lipman-Blumen clearly identifies Drucker's deep concerns about executive leadership. Drucker insisted that leaders must be judged by their performance and character, not by the more elusive and seductive quality of charisma. In this chapter, Lipman-Blumen demonstrates how leaders can remain true to their own constituents, maintaining their integrity and authenticity, while connecting their vision to those of seemingly antagonistic or competitive groups with whom they must live and work together in an increasingly interdependent world.

Following, in their chapter "Knowledge Worker Productivity and the Practice of Self-Management," Jeremy Hunter and J. Scott Scherer explain Drucker's long-established emphasis on the need to manage oneself. They do so by exploring the notion of "mismanaging" oneself—something that is commonly experienced as stress and that has many hidden personal and organizational costs. Accordingly, this chapter introduces basic concepts and practices of self-management.

Roberto Pedace, in his chapter "Labor Markets and Human Resources," then exposes the intersection between Peter Drucker's ideas on human resources and personnel management and the tools that economists use in addressing issues in these areas. Although this was not the primary emphasis of Drucker's thoughts, much of his work described the importance of managerial decisions in employee recruitment, training, incentives, and compensation, and Pedace draws clear lessons for managers in this critical area of enterprise.

The decision an employee makes about motivation critically affects his or her productivity. Jay Prag subsequently expands on Drucker's views of the economy in his chapter "Peter Drucker: The Humanist Economist." In this chapter, Prag shows how Drucker came to understand economic activity through intense observation of human behavior—something that is often modeled away in the mathematical equations espoused by the vast majority of modern economists, which may lie at the heart of the weakness of modern economics.

In the next chapter, "The Drucker Vision and Its Foundations," Richard Smith provides a comprehensive historical review of Drucker's intellectual contributions. He then examines how we might realize Drucker's vision in our organizations today, particularly with respect to the role of managers, the function of markets, and the importance of innovation. Smith illustrates Drucker's deep commitment to the Austrian School of economics and to individual responsibility and freedom and the ever present dangers of losing these freedoms.

In the chapter "Drucker on Marketing," Jenny Darroch examines some of the principles of marketing and innovation that Drucker introduced many years ago. Darroch's chapter emphasizes the need to look at the business from the customer's point of view—perhaps the most important Drucker lesson in marketing. In addition, the chapter examines the ongoing, dynamic tension between serving existing customers and creating new customers.

Finally, Murat Binay gives an overview of the retirement systems in the United States and the rest of the world, in "A Closer Look at Pension Funds." As Binay explains, Peter Drucker envisioned the potential significance of public and private retirement systems and made prescient observations about our pension fund systems. This chapter explores the economic and social impact of pension funds, along with their influence on the ownership structure of U.S. corporations.

Tying It All Together

This book provides a veritable cornucopia of ideas that extends the intellectual fruit cultivated by the master horticulturist, Peter Ferdinand Drucker. As such, it is a living, breathing, organic document. The people involved in this project are deeply committed to the Drucker philosophy, which emphasizes lifelong learning and continual development as knowledge workers and as human beings. We sincerely hope that you find the contents stimulating and provocative. Of course, while we are building on Drucker's foundations, the views expressed are solely those of the specific authors of the various chapters—we are all a work in progress. We encourage you to join us in our quest to make a difference in our lives and work.

1

Management as a Liberal Art

Karen E. Linkletter and Joseph A. Maciariello

We do not know yet precisely how to link the liberal arts and management. We do not know yet what impact this linkage will have on either party—and marriages, even bad ones, always change both partners.

—Peter F. Drucker
"Teaching the Work of Management," *New Management*

News headlines in late 2008 and early 2009 screamed evidence of the public's disenchantment with corporate America. Protestors repeatedly gathered on Wall Street, voicing disgust with the government bailout of the financial sector. AIG executives reportedly received death threats after the firm's bonus payouts became public. New York Attorney General Andrew Cuomo launched an investigation into Merrill Lynch's accelerated payment of employee bonuses prior to its merger with Bank of America. Rick Wagoner, CEO of General Motors, along with fellow CEOs Robert Nardelli of Chrysler and Alan Mulally of Ford, flew to Washington in private jets to plead for taxpayer money to rescue the automobile industry, leading many pundits to note how "out of touch with the real world" corporate America had become.

From bloated salaries and unwarranted bonus payments to outright swindles like that of Bernie Madoff, the public image of American business has taken a beating in recent months. Fueling this populist ire is a sense that corporations have lost their moral compass; who wants to help a bully that doesn't play by the rules? It seems that something is drastically amiss in the boardrooms of America. Do we have the wrong people leading our organizations? Have they been trained poorly? Or is it simply, as many have argued, that our brand of capitalism breeds greed and lust for power?

Peter Drucker had a great deal to say about the role of power in organizations, as well as the selection and training of effective executives. But his most pressing concern was that organizations direct their attention to people; organizations must provide human beings with status, function, and a sense of community and purpose. Viewed in this context, the management of people within organizations involves an understanding of human nature and cultural or communal values and morals—in Drucker's words, with questions of "good and evil."[1] Although most businesses have some sort of ethics code in their mission statements, matters of good and evil are perceived as being best left to the realm of theology or philosophy—not the boardroom. Yet Drucker insisted on the need for values in organizations. This is clear not only in his written work but also was evidenced by his teaching style and philosophy, as both of us witnessed in our years of working with him. And, given the state of business's image in the public's eyes, perhaps it would help to at least raise the question: What do managers and executives value and why? If organizations are about human beings, from where do those human beings derive their values?

One way to begin to address this subject is to take seriously Drucker's statement that management is a liberal art. Although he never fully defined this concept, it is clear that he envisioned a linkage between the liberal arts tradition inherited from Greek and Roman civilizations and the pragmatic, day-to-day operations of an organization. One crucial element that links the liberal arts and management is the fostering and maintenance of cultural values. Historically, liberal arts training emphasized the cultivation of beliefs, behaviors, and opinions that were thought by a given civilization to be of high moral quality (good or right). If management is, as Drucker said, a liberal art, then it must similarly involve the development of shared codes of conduct and beliefs within an organization. The practical implications of management as a liberal art for today's organizations are far-reaching, and may indeed provide a new blueprint for redeeming corporate America's reputation.

The Liberal Arts: A Historical Tradition

The concept of the liberal arts, from which the term *liberal art* stems, has a long history. Although the concept originated with the Greeks, the Romans, notably Cicero, used the Latin term *artes liberales* beginning around the first century B.C.E. The definition of a liberal art was a skill or craft practiced by a free citizen who had the time and means for study; in its classical sense, education in the liberal arts was meant for the elite, ruling classes of society. Liberal arts training, then, meant training citizens to be society's leaders. Therefore, the ideals of an *artes liberales* education were to instill standards of conduct and character, knowledge/mastery of a body of texts, a respect for societal values and standards, and an appreciation for knowledge and truth. As the Roman Empire collapsed, the Church incorporated the classical ideals and curriculum of the liberal arts into Christian education, infusing the old *artes liberales* with a new religious mission.[2]

As centers of learning were established at the great universities throughout Europe, and as the ideals of the Renaissance began to seep into those institutions, the curriculum of liberal arts training changed, but the emphasis on the values of antiquity and the transmission of moral values in order to refine the human being remained. The models of higher education developed at Cambridge and Oxford were virtually transplanted to the American colonies as primarily Protestant denominational colleges, such as Harvard (1636), William and Mary (1693), and Yale (1701). As in England and Europe, these early colleges educated an elite corps of young men in classical literature (in their original Greek and Latin), as well as the Bible, in order to develop their moral character and their suitability for further studies in law, medicine, or the ministry.[3]

Changing attitudes and increasing industrialization fueled a call for an educational curriculum that was accessible to a broader segment of the public and suitable for the practical needs of an expanding economy. The Morrill Act of 1862 provided federal funding to colleges that taught agriculture and vocational subjects, reflecting this revised definition of what constituted appropriate subject matter for institutions of higher learning. The model of the German research university, where scholarly production had replaced teaching as the source of academic prestige and income, laid the groundwork for the new American universities, such as Johns Hopkins (1876). In response to the growing demand for more pragmatic training, several of the liberal arts colleges established the first graduate schools of business.

Yet even within these new professional MBA degree schools, there was an assumption that incoming students would have received a liberal arts education; Dartmouth's Tuck School of Administration and Finance (1900), Harvard Business School (1908), and the University of Pennsylvania's Wharton School (1921) all required either an undergraduate degree or a course of undergraduate study concurrent with business training.[4] The reason for requiring a liberal arts education as a precursor to business studies was to provide a moral foundation for young people: training in religious and classical values and virtues.

The concept of the liberal arts, and by extension "management as a liberal art," must therefore involve a foundation in values, virtues, and character formation. An important point, however, is that there was never a single, agreed-upon curriculum or standard set of disciplines that constituted a liberal arts education. The Church significantly modified the pagan Greco-Roman *artes liberales* tradition, emphasizing those disciplines (language, grammar, and history) that would allow for the study of scripture. Liberal arts training changed again and again to accommodate new information and outlooks. When new translations of Aristotle's texts and other philosophical works became available in the twelfth and thirteenth centuries, logic was more highly valued as the route to knowledge of "the good." The new humanism of the Renaissance, which also embraced classical texts, injected a focus on the worldly realm; liberal arts education aimed to prepare one for a moral life on earth, not just the study of scripture.[5] The tension between "learning for learning's sake" and learning as preparation for a productive life remains today. There has never been, nor is there now, a uniform course of study that constitutes a liberal arts education.

What *is* constant, however, is the attempt to inculcate a set of agreed-upon values, or cultural beliefs. The values and beliefs change over time, but the overarching goal does not. Ultimately, the *artes liberales* and their various iterations strive to define what is good, right, and just in a given society or culture. As the tradition has shifted its context from pagan to Christian to today's secular society, the ideal of instilling shared values remains, but has become increasingly complex. In a diverse society, what constitutes "right" and "good"? Who or what defines them? Where one locates these values is an important question. To wrestle with this question is to wrestle with the legitimacy and universality of certain values. Ultimately, it involves addressing larger theological or philosophical issues: Drucker's concern with "good and evil." Such big-picture questions are not confined to the ivory tower; the overwhelming success of Rick Warren's book *The Purpose Driven Life* indicates that there is a global search for answers to some of life's most important questions, such as, "Why am I here?" and, "What is my purpose?" Instilling a liberal arts mentality, then, involves an ever-shifting search for the best way to foster values based on tradition, even though that tradition may morph over time. It is to take seriously the counsel of Socrates to examine one's life, for "the unexamined life is not worth living."

Today, the *artes liberales* are widely proclaimed to be irrelevant to American society and education. The past goals of liberal arts training seem elitist, culturally insensitive, and totally impractical for today's cadre of up-and-coming executives and professionals, not to mention midlevel managers or entrepreneurs. Liberal arts colleges have radically revamped their curriculum, entrance requirements, and attitude to try to survive, economically as much as culturally. Yet there is much evidence to support the view that the erosion of the liberal arts is in part responsible for our current climate of greed and profit at any cost. In his recent book, *From Higher Aims to Hired Hands*, Rakesh Khurana argues that the business schools' recent emphasis on maximization of shareholder value as the sole measure of organizational success has demoted professional managers to nothing more than "hired hands." With no responsibilities to anything other than themselves, these hired guns lack any sense of a greater moral, social, or ethical obligation to society or the organizations that employ them.

In *Management, Revised Edition*, Peter Drucker, a thinker who was always ahead of his time, called management a liberal art:

> *Management is thus what tradition used to call a liberal art: "liberal" because it deals with the fundamentals of knowledge, self knowledge, wisdom, and leadership; "art" because it is practice and application. Managers [should] draw on all the knowledge and insights of the humanities and the social sciences—on psychology and philosophy, on economics and history, on ethics as well as on the physical sciences. But they have to focus this knowledge on effectiveness and results— on healing a sick patient, teaching a student, building a bridge, designing and selling a "user friendly" software program.*

Drucker believed that management would be the key to keeping the liberal arts sentiment alive in today's society. He saw an important relationship between the two forms of training. The liberal arts can bring "wisdom" and "self-knowledge" to the practice of management, while management can "be the discipline and the practice through and in which the 'humanities' will again acquire recognition, impact, and relevance." And practicing management as a liberal art might, in fact, return management to its original, intended professional status.

Applying Management as a Liberal Art for Today's Executives

If Peter Drucker was right about management being a liberal art, management must return to the original ideals of liberal arts education that were fundamental to the concept of professionalism in business and to Drucker's concept of "the educated person." The difficulty in implementing management as a liberal art lies in the perceived dichotomy between the "ivory tower" of academia and the "real world" of business. As we've shown, the history of the liberal arts tradition involved training for the "real world" of politics, law, medicine, and religious leadership. Furthermore, reconciling the classical *artes liberales* with the everyday world has a long tradition in America. The Puritans established an extremely intellectual society with one of the highest literacy rates in the western world. Harvard College's primary mission was to train ministers in a liberal arts curriculum. But the college also matriculated grammar school teachers and government leaders, fulfilling its mission of instilling cherished values and traditions throughout the Massachusetts Bay community.[6] The Puritans were also remarkably successful in the material realm; historian Stephen Innes has argued that the Puritans' brand of Calvinism propelled their economic development.[7] The Founding Fathers, too, embraced liberal arts ideals in their concept of "republican virtue," believing that a republic would survive only if its leaders understood the importance of societal values and the concept of a common good.[8] Education was considered essential to sound governance of a free society. Thomas Jefferson founded the University of Virginia not only to "develop the reasoning faculties of our youth," but also "to harmonize and promote the interests of agriculture, manufactures and commerce."[9]

The connection between the goals of the liberal arts and those of practicing professionals may have been lost, but it can be restored. In Drucker's view, it was the liberal arts' responsibility to "demonstrate and to embody values, to create vision . . . [and] to lead."[10] Management as a liberal art, then, would require practitioners to do the same.

Peter Drucker codified management both as a discipline and as a profession embodying both *technê*,[11] which he referred to as specialized knowledge or technology, and practice, which he referred to as art. "Practice" is the art of integrating and harmonizing the various specialized bodies of knowledge so that the energy turned out by the organization is greater than the sum of the individual contributions.

And, as Drucker states in *The Practice of Management*, "To get more than is being put in is only possible in the moral sphere." Consequently, the practice of integrity in the management group, and especially in top management, is the cornerstone of management. Executives are exemplars, and their practices set examples for others to follow. Their practices determine the esprit de corps of the organization (i.e., what Drucker refers to as the spirit of the organization). And for the esprit de corps in an organization to be high, integrity must permeate management practices.[12]

In his work *Orators and Philosophers*, Bruce Kimball argues that liberal arts education has historically involved a tension between those who believe that such an education should have as its end the pursuit of truth (the philosophers) and those who believe that it should allow people to be functioning members of society (the orators). Management as a liberal art would effectively blend the two models, requiring not only that professionals function as effective managers, but also that they embody larger values that supersede the mundane, day-to-day operations of the organization. Drucker showed a clear preference for executives who possess integrity and good moral judgment over executives who are more intellectually gifted but who lack integrity. The heart of the rationale for this preference is his passion for the growth and development of the individual:

> *A man might himself know too little, perform poorly, lack judgment and ability, and yet not do too much damage as a manager. But if he lacks in character and integrity—no matter how knowledgeable, how brilliant, how successful—he destroys. He destroys people, the most valuable resource of the enterprise. He destroys spirit. And he destroys performance.*[13]

The practice of management as a liberal art thus involves not only the ability to apply knowledge in the material world, but also a constant reference to higher sources of moral reference.

One of the legacies of business school training in agency theory and managerial reliance on financial models as the sole measure of performance is the absence of any such moral reference. Executives today are not provided with a moral compass by the market system. The market is blind to both good and evil and is thus capable of producing both great good and great evil. Without a moral reference point, executives are unlikely to act in a responsible manner toward their own people, toward their customers, or toward the public. They are especially unlikely to develop the potential of their own people. We are seeing this now (April 2009) as workers by the millions are being displaced and confidence in our nation's financial and regulatory institutions has eroded. It is not too harsh to proclaim that the public is losing confidence in management as a profession.

Without competent executives who abide by strict principles of moral conduct, the very survival of our society's essential institutions is being jeopardized. It is on these institutions that the survival of our free-market system as we know it in the United States rests. The idea that both capacity and integrity are required in society's executives was not new in Drucker's writings. It was firmly established over 80 years ago by Chester Barnard in his landmark book *The Functions of the Executive.* Written during the Great Depression, Barnard's work served as a defense of the capitalist system in the face of massive dysfunction of the American economy. In the 1930s, rampant unemployment sparked a significant movement against capitalism, fueled by such political figures as Louisiana Governor Huey Long and California gubernatorial candidate Upton Sinclair. The perception of inequality, of a lack of commitment to shared values, led to public disgust with what had been a cornerstone of American society. We are witnessing a similar shift today, as people perceive that corporate America does not share the same moral values as mainstream Americans.

Management as a liberal art offers the hope of aligning the values of business with those of individuals and of the broader society. Drucker believed that the organization was the key to aligning individual and societal values. As a social institution, the organization has responsibilities to the commonwealth. As a human institution, an organization depends upon the performance of its people for its success. Drucker was fervent about the role of the human being and the dignity, the growth, and the development of the human being while at work. In the foreword to *Management, Revised Edition,* Jim Collins noted, "To view other human beings as merely a means to an end, rather than as ends in themselves, struck Drucker as profoundly immoral. And as much as he wrote about institutions and society, I believe he cared most deeply about the individual."

One of the primary goals of a liberal arts education in any era was to develop a thinking, virtuous individual. In Aristotle's Greece, the study of the liberal arts depended on leisure time: the freedom to pursue intellectual activity for its own sake. In our modern world, very few of us have the luxury of pursuing the philosophical avenue of the liberal arts tradition; the oratory model of Cicero, of a virtuous citizen of the world, is more realistic to most Americans. A liberal arts approach demands that we connect the mundane world of work with the erudite world of philosophy and morals. Work is instrumental to the development of the person. Management's task is to develop people so that ordinary people are able to perform in an extraordinary way. In *Concept of the Corporation*, Drucker wrote that "the most successful and the most durable institutions" employ managers who "induce in their members an intellectual and moral growth beyond a man's original capacities." This end is embodied in Drucker's very definition of leadership: "leadership is the lifting of a person's vision to higher sights, the raising of a person's performance to a higher standard, and the building of a person's personality beyond its normal limitations."[14]

Where, specifically, have today's managers failed to model the liberal arts ideal of management? One particularly troublesome area is the imbalance between executive and worker compensation. According to the *Wall Street Journal*, in 2007 the average CEO's income was more than 180 times the income of his typical employee. Excessive executive compensation was especially troublesome to Drucker. He saw it as not only unseemly, but immoral. Today we are experiencing a backlash against executives who led their organizations into bankruptcy and then reaped large bonuses. In an obituary written one day after Drucker's death on November 11, 2005, Patricia Sullivan of the *Washington Post* reported that Drucker warned of the consequences of excessive executive compensation. "In 1997, he predicted a backlash to burgeoning executive pay, saying, 'In the next economic downturn, there will be an outbreak of bitterness and contempt for the super-corporate chieftains who pay themselves millions.'" We are now (April 2009) witnessing an avalanche of criticism directed at the executives of American International Group (AIG), who were scheduled to receive $165 million in executive bonuses, after AIG received $182 billion of bailout funds from the Treasury of the United States. AIG was deemed "to be too large to fail." A public backlash did indeed occur, and a number of AIG executives returned the bonuses.

Drucker and his longtime colleague and friend Walter Wriston were like-minded on many issues, including excessive executive compensation. Wriston served as CEO and chairman of Citicorp for 17 years and led the bank to international prominence. He never received a salary of $1 million per year, despite Citicorp's position as the world's largest bank. He noted that his annual salary of $950,000 was a far cry from the $200 million compensation that some lesser lights in banking were earning in 2006. In an interview conducted by A. J. Vogl, editor of *The Conference Board Review™ Magazine* (just weeks before Wriston died), Wriston called for a new breed of corporate statesmen, like those of the not-too-distant past, who would be willing to speak with authority against executive abuses. "Where are the business leaders? My mentor George Moore would have described them as playing mouse. They're hiding. Who are the spokesmen for American business today? Name one quick—Where are today's Irving Shapiros, the Reggie Joneses, the Bud Warners? They stood up and spoke out." Wriston was recalling a short time ago in American business history when there were executive statesmen among the elite of American business leaders. They spoke out against abuses and solved problems such as the Arab oil boycott of the 1970s and the elimination of Regulation Q (the prohibition of the payment of interest on bank demand deposits). Wriston embodied the Drucker idea of management as a liberal art, in which executives internalize broader, agreed-upon societal values, communicate those values to their organizations, and embody those values in their daily behaviors.

Application of management as a liberal art holds the promise of providing a moral compass for executives. Drucker's body of work provides this moral compass, especially with regard to the treatment of human beings, management's most valuable resource. Management as a liberal art can restore human dignity in the workplace and can reverse the degradation of the human being that we are now witnessing in organizations across American institutions. Capitalism is not a flawless system; economic upheavals are part of the process. However, unless managers of organizations can prove that they understand that there is a difference between good and evil, that they are willing to deal with issues of morality and values, we cannot (and should not) expect the public to respect management as a profession or corporate America as a positive force.

Management as a liberal art offers some guidelines for preparing future executives to successfully carry out the high demands that will be placed upon them in the twenty-first century if freedom as we have known it is to survive. To accomplish this, executives must be educated both in the discipline of management itself (i.e., the body of knowledge that deals with the practice of management) and in the humanities and social sciences as well because, as Drucker notes, management "is deeply involved in spiritual concerns—the nature of man, good and evil."

The question remains: how do we deal with spiritual questions in a multicultural world? One of the complaints against the liberal arts is that historically they have been too focused on Western European values and traditions. Drucker was very conscious of this bias and advocated a shift in the focus of liberal arts training.[15] He was deeply involved in the post-World War II reconstruction of Japan and continued his involvement in Japanese business and government for the remainder of his life. He found in Confucian ethics fundamental guidelines for moral behavior that are appropriate for all stakeholders in an organization. And these guidelines are *modest* enough to achieve realistic levels of moral behavior given the nature of humans, good and evil. These guidelines are:

- *clear definitions of the fundamental relationships [among all stakeholders];*
- *universal and general rules of conduct—that is, rules that are binding on any one person or organization, according to its rules, function and relationships; And finally,*
- *an effective organization ethic, indeed an organization ethic that deserves to be seriously considered as ethics, will have to define right behavior as the behavior which optimizes each party's benefits and thus makes the relationships harmonious, constructive, and mutually beneficial.*[16]

These guidelines should be put into practice to accomplish the twin objectives of enhancing the growth and development of the person and the performance of the organization. Candid and timely feedback should be provided to assist the person to attain these objectives.

Clearly, Drucker's concept of management as a liberal art invokes the historical emphasis on the search for the "good" and "right" in life; it requires a definition of "right behavior." It also reflects the mutability of the liberal arts ideal; that Confucianism could be brought into the service of Greco-Roman and Christian tradition speaks volumes about Drucker's openness to different paths to the ideal.

Conclusion

Drucker left it to others to define the implications of management as a liberal art. Given the historical context of the origins of the liberal arts, as well as the role of liberal arts and professional education in America, Drucker's idea of management as a liberal art involves rethinking not just how we educate managers, but also how we approach management as a profession. By preparing students and managers in management as a liberal art, our society will expand the capacity of men and women to assume executive responsibility in a morally and socially constructive manner.

Peter Drucker was well known as an observer who tried to "see the future that has already happened." In a conversation with Bob Buford on August 10, 1996, he reflected on the condition of American civilization:

> *I'm going to make myself very unpopular in two weeks in Aspen at the seminar where I am the keynote speaker; by saying we have no economic problems. We have only social problems. But, we have those in spades. This morning when I woke up at three in the morning, you have no idea, I had to pray very hard to get over that despair, and I haven't gotten over it yet. Yes, I know, and yet the very fact that we are conscious of it is probably the only optimistic thing.*[17]

In *Landmarks of Tomorrow*, Drucker argues for humanity's need for spiritual values in order to shape culture. In Chapter 10, "The Human Situation Today," Drucker explores the question of where people fit in the postmodern world: "Man has achieved the knowledge to destroy himself physically, emotionally, psychologically, and morally." Specifically he refers to advances in knowledge from the behavioral sciences that through "operant conditioning"[18] can "turn man into a biological machine run by manipulation of fears and emotions, a being without beliefs, without values, without principles, without compassion, without pride, without humanity altogether."[19] Drucker's solution was a return to spiritual values in order to guide the use of the power created by new knowledge to serve the highest interests of the human being.

Drucker was strongly influenced by his own liberal arts education, which led him to see these moral and spiritual dimensions of management and society. But is there corroborating empirical and historical evidence for his views? We believe there is. Robert W. Fogel, economic historian and 1993 winner of the Nobel Prize in economics, believes the most pressing problem in the United States to be the acquisition and egalitarian distribution of *spiritual assets*, not material assets: "Although the consolidation of past gains cannot be ignored, the future of egalitarianism in America turns on the nation's ability to combine continued economic growth with an entirely new set of egalitarian reforms that address the urgent spiritual needs of our age, secular as well as sacred. Spiritual (or immaterial) inequity is now as great a problem as material inequity, perhaps even greater." In *The Soul of Capitalism: Opening Paths to a Moral Economy*, journalist William Greider argues that American capitalism can be modified to "conform more faithfully to society's broad values," essentially tying the engine of economic growth to the goals of the liberal arts. Sociologist Robert Wuthnow traces America's long history of attempting to reconcile religious values with economic growth, and points out that in today's society, "Our problems as a nation are spiritual as well as material." Drucker was not alone in his assessment of our need to consider moral and spiritual issues when operating in the world of management and business.

Ironically, a return to the ideals of the liberal arts may in fact make management once again valuable to the "real world." Fueled by corporate scandal and the behavior of out-of-touch executives who seem to have no moral compass, popular sentiment has turned against management as a profession; instead, corporate America is greeted with jeers and signs reading, "Bail out the people, not the banks." Perhaps the only hope of redemption for management as a true profession is to practice management as a liberal art: to ground it in an understanding of shared cultural values that are inculcated through education and modeled through executive behavior.

2

Drucker on Government, Business, and Civil Society: Roles, Relationships, Responsibilities

Ira A. Jackson

Henry Y. Hwang Dean of the Peter F. Drucker and Masatoshi Ito Graduate School of Management and Professor of Management at Claremont Graduate University

There is mounting evidence that government is big rather than strong; that it is fat and flabby rather than powerful; that it costs a great deal but does not achieve much . . . just at the time when we need a strong, healthy, and vigorous government.

We need government as the central institution in the society of organizations. We need an organ that expresses the common will and the common vision and enables each organization to make its own best contribution to society and citizen and yet to express common beliefs and common values.

The purpose of government, in other words, is to govern.

—Peter F. Drucker, *The Age of Discontinuity*

While Peter Drucker is rightly considered by many to be the "father of modern management" and the twentieth century's leading "business guru," approximately 60 percent of his writing and teaching focused on society, not on business per se. Drucker focused on organizations generally, not the private sector exclusively, and he focused not on how organizations and their people perform as stand-alone institutions, but rather on how they relate with one another across sectors. Drucker considered himself first and foremost a "social ecologist," observing the nature of man-made institutions in society the way a scientist might the nature and ecology of physical life on earth. The central organizing principle of society, Drucker firmly believed, needed to be personal, institutional, and collective responsibility—responsibility to be effective, responsibility to act ethically, responsibility to be respectful of others, and responsibility to the future.

Perhaps it is surprising, given his status as the "Einstein of business," that Drucker viewed government as the most important of the three indispensable sectors of society:

- **Public.** Government, he implored, needs to be strong and vigorous, now more than ever.
- **Private.** Business needs to be the engine of innovation, but it also must view its role as contributing benefits to society, not just to shareholders.
- **Philanthropic.** Nonprofits and civil society are the new glue that binds a functioning society with engagement and responsibility to the community.

With balance among these sectors and with each sector having a distinctive purpose, society can function, and we can become a responsible society, as well. Though this is difficult to achieve in practice, he viewed a "functioning society" as the only likely guarantee against tyranny and extremism, which he had experienced personally in his youth. He saw effective and responsible institutions in all sectors as the best hope for civilization to endure and for individuals, communities, and society to thrive.

This chapter attempts to capture Drucker's observations about the role of government; the relationship of the public, private, and philanthropic sectors; and the responsibility of all organizations to work in concert to create and sustain a responsible society. It concludes with some speculation about how Drucker's construct and perspective might inform some of the many challenges that we currently face, both nationally and globally.

The Need for Government to Steer, Not Row

The choices for the economy—as well as for all other sectors—are no longer either *complete governmental indifference or complete governmental control.*

—Peter F. Drucker, *The Age of Discontinuity*

The megastate that this century built is bankrupt, morally as well as financially. It has not delivered. But its successor cannot be "small government." There are far too many tasks, domestically and internationally. We need effective government—and that is what the voters in all developed countries are actually clamoring for.

—Peter F. Drucker, "*Really* Reinventing Government"

Drucker was an acute observer of politics, business, culture, technology, history, philosophy, sociology, and human nature. He approached management as a liberal art, and he was almost a Renaissance man: expansive, sweeping, holistic, interconnected, and thoughtful. Indeed, Drucker is best understood as a systems thinker. He devoted his life to reflecting upon ways to advance coherence, effectiveness, and purpose in a society of organizations. He had many original insights that today have been validated by their incorporation into our daily DNA. Much of his brilliance is now accepted simply as common sense. These are among Drucker's many insights and observations that continue to shape our understanding of how society, business, and organizations generally function:

- We live in a knowledge society.
- Employees are an asset, not a liability, and knowledge workers need to be respected and engaged, not directed or controlled.
- Management is about doing things right; leadership is all about doing the right thing.
- A healthy economy cannot survive in a sick society.
- The social sector is growing in importance.
- Managers need to manage and motivate themselves before they can manage and motivate others.
- Every business must continually innovate and market if it is to survive and succeed.
- It is important to "see what is visible and not yet seen" and to act upon the future that already exists.
- As Drucker's insight found, "the best way to predict the future is to create it."

These and scores of other seminal, original contributions reveal how much Drucker's ideas permeate both our vocabulary and our thinking.

Less well known are Drucker's thoughts about government. Here, too, we discover Drucker to be insightful, frequently original, prescient, and incredibly relevant.

What is widely known about Drucker and government is that his worldview was largely shaped by the rise of fascism and totalitarianism in his native Austria and in Germany, where he apprenticed. His first works were banned and burned by the Nazis. He fled Europe for America, where he wrote the first of his 39 books, *The End of Economic Man.* Churchill was said to have been so impressed with this book that he assigned it as required reading for his general staff. Drucker's focus on organizations, institutional effectiveness, personal ethics, and social responsibility all flow from the formative experience of witnessing the dysfunction of society and the collapse of its principal institutions. He was haunted by the resulting tyranny and by the ideology of isms—fascism, totalitarianism, communism. Drucker was hardly a utopian or a dreamer. He had experienced the worst of societal failure. He devoted a lifetime to combating the vulnerabilities that would allow for a recurrence of extremism as a consequence of ineffective managers, unethical leaders, and irresponsible citizens. His aim was a functioning or responsible society: balanced, fair, innovative, effective, sustainable, and just.

Later in life, and largely reflecting upon the contemporary American experience, Drucker wrote about "the sickness of government." He was typically incisive and unforgiving in observing in *The Age of Discontinuity* that while "government surely has never been more prominent than today" and is "certainly all-pervasive," there is "mounting evidence also that the citizen less and less believes in government and is increasingly disenchanted with it. Indeed, government is sick—and just at the time when we need a strong, healthy, and vigorous government." He noted that the growing "disenchantment with government cuts across national boundaries and ideological lines," and that "[w]e are rapidly moving to doubt and distrust of government and, in the case of the young, even to rebellion against it." "We no longer expect results from government." Indeed, Drucker found that "the greatest factor in the disenchantment with government is that government has not performed." In functions other than waging war and inflating the currency, government was seen as incompetent. Drucker's specific criticism was directed at the failures of the welfare state and the war on drugs, and he finally speculated in serious conversations that perhaps we should legalize drugs and take the profit and crime out of the drug trade. Modern government, he claimed, had become "ungovernable." Government has become expensive, "large and cumbersome," "a poor manager," a "government of forms," and concerned more about procedures than about results. Elsewhere, in *The New Realities*, Drucker observed that "[g]overnments find it hard to abandon an activity even if it has totally outlived its usefulness . . . [and] thus become committed to yesterday, to the obsolete, to the no longer productive." He was viewed as an early advocate of privatization and was skeptical that "reinventing government" would lead to the kind of basic restructuring and rethinking of government that he felt was needed.[1]

Drucker is best remembered for his focus on business, and many of his observations and prescriptions about the role of the public sector are less well known, remembered, or embraced. Much of his narrative on the multiple failures of the modern welfare state was expropriated by conservatives at a time when the pendulum had swung sharply toward deregulation and the embrace of markets. Ironically, these forgotten insights are among his most telling, timeless, and constructive for our current condition.

Today, when public distrust and cynicism are at an all-time high and confidence in the integrity of both business and government are at historic lows, Drucker reminds us simply and powerfully, in the chapter "The Sickness of Government" from *The Age of Discontinuity*, that the "purpose of government is to make fundamental decisions, and to make them effectively." Government of course has a necessary monopoly on the use of force, because its first obligation is to ensure the safety and security of its people. But the central purpose of government is to "focus the political energies of society. It is to dramatize issues. It is to present fundamental choices." Government is the instrument through which we ensure fairness and a level playing field.

Drucker returns us to the basics and first principles: we need government, and we need it to govern, but we shouldn't confuse governing with bureaucracy. Drucker didn't foresee or call for the "withering away of the state." On the contrary, he asserted that we need "a vigorous, a strong, and a very active government." It is not the size or the cost or the scope of services provided by the government that is most important; rather, it is the capacity of government to make major decisions. Drucker invoked vivid imagery to enliven this perspective, comparing governing to conducting. "The conductor himself does not play an instrument. His job is to know the capacity of each instrument and to evoke optimal performance from each. Instead of being the 'performer,' he has become the 'conductor.' Instead of 'doing,' he leads." We need, in essence, a government that steers, not rows, that "is strong because it confines itself to decision and direction and leaves the 'doing' to others."

As the "conductor" of society, government needs to decide the rules, ration the resources, and deploy the tasks where they best belong: delivered by business or nonprofits through competitive bidding, or held exclusively by government where it alone has the authority (presumably, in conducting wars, ensuring the peace, and collecting taxes). Rather than signaling a retreat for government, Drucker paints a portrait of a society that needs a stronger, more effective, more purposeful, and more deliberate government—but, hopefully, with less government, per se.

Putting It All Together

My takeaway from Drucker on government is that, almost predictably, he was right. Given his 1930s experience in Europe, he might have been expected to call for a weak state and to minimize the role of government. Certainly, his experience helped to inform his outrage and disgust at the excesses of the modern state: its inefficiencies, its bewildering bureaucracy, its growing size and cost, its inability to abandon functions that are no longer required, and the resulting cynicism of its citizens. He was equally wary of the charismatic leader, given the devastation caused by the three most evil but charismatic leaders of the twentieth century: Hitler, Mao, and Stalin. Largely as a result of their legacy, Drucker labeled this period the "lost century." But, as usual, Drucker surprises us with a firm set of convictions that assert that we need a strong and effective government as a precondition and prerequisite for growth, social justice, and sustainable progress. Good governance enables the other organizations in the private and nonprofit sectors to flourish effectively and to provide balance and ballast for society.

The government's role of ensuring equity and fairness has to be balanced with the strengths of business to provide efficiency and innovation and the benefits of civil society in creating community and offering legitimacy. In other words, government needs to govern, business needs to innovate, and civil society needs to flourish and be encouraged. In aligning itself this way, society sets a clear path toward its goals, channels its activities to those organizations that are best capable of achieving results, and gains the legitimacy that keeps it grounded in community and common purpose. Call it equity, efficiency, and legitimacy or public, private, and philanthropic, this is in essence what Drucker defined and described as a functioning society. At its best, society has democratic institutions that govern wisely and implement effectively and lightly; functioning and efficient markets that encourage risk taking, innovation, and entrepreneurship to meet customer needs and to satisfy the need for growth and progress; and nonprofit institutions at the local and community level that provide needed services through collective action and reciprocal obligations. Each sector needs to act according to its role in Drucker's social symphony: government ensuring safety, providing fairness, and basically conducting; business creating, innovating, abandoning, and achieving measurable results; and nonprofits engendering community and expressing shared interdependence through voluntary action and local initiative.

On top of that construct, Drucker applies his simple but demanding tests to organizations in every sector: What is your mission? Who is your customer? What does the customer value? What are the results? What is our plan? If you didn't exist, would we need to create you? Have you outlived your useful life? Are you managing effectively? Are you leading ethically? Are you acting responsibly?

It's Called Responsibility, Stupid!

Peter Drucker was asked in early 1999, "What do you consider to be your most important contribution?" His answer:

That I early on—almost sixty years ago—realized that management has become the constitutive organ and function of the *Society of Organizations; That* management *is not Business Management;—though it first attained attention in business—but the governing organ of* all institutions in Modern Society; *That I established the study of* management *as a discipline in its own right; and That I focused this discipline on People and Power; on Values, Structure, and Constitution;* and above all, *on responsibilities—that is, focused the Discipline of Management on* management *as a truly liberal art.*

—Peter F. Drucker with Joseph Maciariello,
Management, Revised Edition

During the 1992 presidential campaign, James Carville kept a plaque on his desk to remind himself, "It's the economy, stupid." If Drucker were with us today, perhaps he'd have suggested something similar: terse, to the point, and focused. It's likely that Peter would have warned about the subprime lending mess, the credit default swap fiasco, the overleveraging of the banks and hedge funds, and the unsustainability of our consumer debt. He would have seen clearly the shortsightedness of extreme deregulation and unbridled faith in the invisible hand in channeling the market to new heights of efficiency, and the consequence of the irrational exuberance, hubris, and greed that gripped our society and held us hostage to irresponsibility. As far back as 1980, Drucker wrote about the excesses of CEO compensation—at a time when the average CEO was earning 40 times what the average worker on the line received ("Pigs gorging at the trough are always a disgusting spectacle," he observed[2]). By the time the bubble burst in 2008, the ratio had widened to 400:1. Throughout his writings and teachings, Drucker consistently warned of the excesses of financial capitalism—our vulnerability to manipulation and creating financial instruments so sophisticated that only their designers fully comprehended the likely consequences of their implementation.

Drucker would have seen in the ideological sweep of the deregulation pendulum a dangerous abrogation of responsibility in exchange for blind faith in markets. He was concerned about rising inequality well before any Gini coefficient registered the growing disparity of income between rich and poor and the declining purchasing power of the middle class. Drucker had an uncanny knack for looking out the window to see and feel trends and realities that others were blind to or blinded by; he saw clearly the future that is already here. Drucker's theory and conviction that a functioning society needs balance, equilibrium, and recognition of the respective roles of each sector would have led him to see a dangerous disequilibrium in the excesses of consumerism, borrowing, and greed. His writings from previous decades suggest what he might have said about our current predicament and the way forward.

Perhaps I'm taking too much license, but I think Drucker would have favored the stimulus bill and certainly the investments in education, health care, energy sufficiency, and the environment. I'm less certain that he would have supported the bank bailout or the subsidies for GM (he first wrote of GM's problems some 40 years ago, and he felt that GM's decline was the result of poor, ineffective, and shortsighted management and predicted that restructuring was inevitable and needed). He would have favored new international institutions like the G-20 and the WTO, the increased reach of the IMF, the emergence of the UN's Global Compact, and other mechanisms for tackling global issues that are beyond the power of sovereign states to manage or control. It would be too hazardous to guess whether he would have favored all the actions of the Fed or the size of the likely deficits—I think not. Drucker would have thought that this was a perfect time to ask some fundamental questions about the role, responsibility, and capacity of government. He would have been insistent that the new authority vested in the government should be temporary and should have a fixed termination, especially with regard to running any previously private function. And he would have insisted on transparency and accountability, believing, as Frankfurter suggested, that "sunlight is the best disinfectant."

Looking Out the Window to See What Is Visible but Not Yet Seen Today

If Drucker were alive during this, the 100th year since his birth, what might he see, looking out his window here at the Drucker School or from his comfortable home here in Claremont, California? Let me simply offer a few observations that are *suggestive* of the value of seeing things through Drucker-like eyes—looking at current circumstances through the lens of Drucker's systems thinking and his focus on a functioning society that balances the sectors and places emphasis on effectiveness, ethics, and responsibility. These are only a small fraction of the many issues that would no doubt be preoccupying Peter, our preeminent social ecologist, if he were alive today. In the manner in which Drucker approached so many topics, I don't postulate answers. These issues elicit, instead, a set of urgent concerns and probing questions. Let me mention just a few.

First, at a time when government is growing in size and importance, we don't yet see a commensurate increase in the attractiveness of public-sector employment for what might be called the "best and the brightest." As Paul Volcker and others have observed, this is a "quiet crisis in public service."[3] Declining status, low compensation, and increased public scrutiny have all combined to make public service even less attractive precisely at a time when government needs the best talent available. This is the moment when society is most in need of a renewal of trust and competence in public service. The GAO goes so far as to put the human capital needs of our government on its "high risk" list of national vulnerabilities.[4] We ignore this strategic vulnerability at our peril.

Second, government is tackling many intractable problems that have strategic long-term importance, which is good. But government, or, rather, the political system that supports our government, hasn't yet tackled the need to simultaneously engage in "planned abandonment" by discarding those laws, programs, and costs that are no longer necessary or relevant to our times. Drucker would warn that we can't afford to do one without the other. He would surely join Pete Peterson and former GAO Administrator David Walker in supporting their jeremiad against the unfunded liabilities that we have left for future generations to confront (in the *New York Times*, Peterson, the senior chairman of the Blackstone Group and former U.S. secretary of commerce, has called this the "make-or-break point in American history,"[5] and that was before the market meltdown in late 2008). As the Peterson Foundation advances its cause of keeping "America strong and the American Dream alive by promoting responsibility and accountability today to create more opportunity tomorrow," it warns about a federal debt burden of $56.4 trillion—or "your share of $184,000."[6] Drucker would have applauded.

Third, Drucker would have agreed with the assessment made by the *Economist* that we are living at a perilous moment, as 40 percent of the world lives in "flawed democracies." These new democracies are on the knife edge between freedom and tyranny and can go either way: open or closed, pluralistic or statist.[7] We are, Drucker would have agreed, at a dangerous tipping point. Since the fall of the Berlin Wall, an unprecedented number of people (2,508,845,187, according to the *Economist* cover story) have joined the ranks of those living in quasi-democratic, quasi-market-oriented nations. Drucker would have asked: Will the center hold? Will prosperity be adequately shared? Will the institutions of an incipient democracy take hold and mature, along with the rule of law, a free press, and transparency and accountability in major public institutions? Or will an oligarchy develop, along with a growing divide between rich and poor? Will strong institutions of civil society be established and encouraged, or will the government crush dissent and restrict the freedoms of nongovernmental organizations (NGOs)? Drucker would be asking these and other questions, pushing us to provide more compelling answers and solutions, and warning us that the future hangs in the balance.

Fourth, Drucker would celebrate the rebirth of volunteerism and citizen initiative, just as de Tocqueville did nearly two centuries ago. There has been an explosion in the growth of nonprofit institutions in the United States and around the world (growing by 36 percent, from 1.08 to 1.48 million, from 1996 to 2006, according to the National Council of Nonprofit Associations, U.S. Census Bureau, and Bureau of Labor Statistics), which is a welcome and necessary trend. But he also would have asked: Are we doing enough to support and encourage the effective management of nonprofit organizations? Have we created effective capital markets to fund them and to help bring them to scale? While he was a tremendous advocate and booster of civil society, I think he would have had the courage to call into question the quality and effectiveness of nonprofit governance, and he would have been concerned about what the Association of

Certified Fraud Examiners claims is an annual loss of $40 billion to fraud in the nonprofit sector.

Fifth, Drucker might ask why we aren't yet capable of harnessing the productivity of the knowledge worker more effectively. Proudfoot Consulting finds that on average 34.3 percent of private-sector working time around the world is effectively wasted.[8] Three-quarters of this wasted time is a result of poor planning and management. What, we might fearfully ask, is the percentage of public-sector working time that is wasted? In a world in which global GDP is $50 trillion, can we really tolerate leaving as much as $15 trillion worth of productive value on the table? What mechanisms need to be put in place to capture this wasted value, just as we are putting in place technical solutions for capturing wasted energy? How can we better accelerate our understanding of how to manage and motivate workers in an economy that increasingly needs to be driven by the renewable energy of knowledge?

Sixth, businesses around the world are beginning to embrace and act upon Drucker's insight that "every social and global challenge of our day is a business opportunity in disguise." Examples include Ecomagination at GE, what Procter & Gamble calls "corporate social opportunity," and Wal-Mart's green supply chain. These and other businesses are seeing in the bottom of the pyramid opportunity for innovation, new market penetration, and the value of contributing to social progress and promoting economic opportunity while also advancing their own bottom line. Drucker would be thrilled by this new wave of companies that truly "get it"—not by giving more to philanthropy or making grand pronouncements about corporate social responsibility, but by internalizing a societal orientation into their corporate strategy and DNA—and are gaining competitive advantage by being at the cutting edge of creating what I call in *Profits with Principles* "value with values." There are now 3,000 members of the UN's Global Compact, which binds multinational corporations with governments and NGOs in an alliance committed to voluntarily advancing the UN's Universal Declaration of Human, Labor, and Environmental Rights. New products are being created and delivered in previously marginalized nations, and business is becoming a very visible force for good in many places, even as it is seen as a villain elsewhere.[9] I believe that if Peter were with us today, he'd say: amen, what took you so long, why aren't we yet seeing even more of this good stuff, and what can we do to provide incentives and accelerate this conception of the firm and this commitment of business to creative and sustainable social problem solving?

Seventh, we are obviously witnessing another shift, perhaps of tectonic proportions, in the balance of power, resources, and authority between government and business. No longer commanding from the towering heights (to use Daniel Yergin's vivid imagery), the private sector is in retreat, chastened, weakened, humbled, and occasionally even a supplicant. Government again commands the high ground and is back in the business of governing, Drucker might have said. He would also have cautioned that we seem to lurch from one extreme to the other, when what is really needed is balance, equilibrium, and common sense. He'd have been concerned, as we all should be, about the unprecedented powers of the state in the economy and about mounting deficits. But he would see in this transitional, perhaps transformational, moment the opportunity to evolve a new theory and practice of what he called a functioning or responsible society. This is precisely the time for creative abandonment of old, useless, and costly functions of government. This is the right moment to "reprivatize," to use Drucker's phrase, much of the existing work that government does, but that NGOs or businesses could and should do more effectively. I think he'd see the chance for a major realignment of sectors along the lines of convergence and collaboration—but also greater clarity about the respective strengths of organizations in the different sectors.

I also hope that Peter might have reconsidered some of his skepticism about reinventing government. Frankly, I think he was too harsh on the efforts of many to create or recreate government functions that deliver good "customer" service, to measure their effectiveness, and to engage in the kind of entrepreneurial innovation that is more typically found in cutting-edge private firms. My personal and professional experience as commissioner of revenue in the Commonwealth of Massachusetts 20 years ago is only one of many examples of the public sector being capable of mission focus. We captured our new mission in three simple words: "honest, fair, firm." We expressed an explicit customer orientation, with a guarantee of record fast refund returns and new color-coded tax forms that have been rewritten from bureaucratese back into English— so simple that even the commissioner could fill out his own tax return! We demonstrated effectiveness by increasing the rate of voluntary compliance through vigorous and visible enforcement, allowing the governor to cut taxes eleven times in five years. And we worked hard and apparently successfully to restore public trust in this most pedestrian and basic of governmental functions—by, among other things, staying open until midnight on April 15 to help taxpayers fill out their returns; offering a tax amnesty that brought in 56,000 former delinquents and evaders; showing on the tax forms themselves where the tax revenue comes from, who pays what, and where it goes; and convincing honest taxpayers that "tax evasion is not a victimless crime."[10] I mention my own experience only to suggest that it may well be more typical than exceptional, and that beneath the cynicism about the capacity of government to reinvent or effectively manage itself, there is a proven corps of governmental professionals who are creating a very different public sector from what Drucker had time to discover.

Finally, caveat emptor! Peter spent his last 35 years here in Claremont, writing and teaching from his home and in the classroom at his school. I am sure he would have been among the first to suggest that graduate schools of business may have been guilty of at least contributory negligence in terms of partial responsibility for the serious predicament that we now face as an economy and as a society. Too many of the titans of industry who were found so lacking in morality, competence, and ethics were the products of our citadels of capitalism and our leading MBA programs. Too much of the intellectual capital of the academy may have been devoted to documenting the marvels of the market, instead of analyzing the consequences of its externalities or the destruction of what economists call the commons. Drucker was, as usual, prescient and pointed on this score, writing in a letter to the *Economist* back in December 1994 of "Fagin's School of Pickpockets and Prostitutes," a not-so-veiled reference to the narrow vocational trend that he found alarming in prominent business schools and the attendant enthusiasm for the MBA as a credential for financial advancement as opposed to a path for business as an agent for social progress. As Rakesh Khurana and others have demonstrated, the marketization of business schools has led to the deprofessionalization of management education.[11] There is an urgent need for a market correction, so to speak. Happily, it is well under way. Humbly, I note, values have been part of the mainstream here at the Peter F. Drucker and Masatoshi Ito Graduate School of Management for all of our nearly 40 years. *BusinessWeek* reports that 56 percent of MBA students nationwide admit to cheating while earning their MBA.[12] Clearly, there is a societal correction necessary, one that goes well beyond what we do in the classroom, what we research, and what values we convey by the time our students arrive as budding capitalists.

The good news, I think Peter would have said, is the desire of this next generation to do good while doing well. Teach for America is as competitive in its entry requirements as Wharton. Another positive indicator is that the largest student activity at the Harvard Business

School isn't the venture capital or investment banking club, but the social entrepreneurship organization.

For our part, we at the Drucker School are trying to play a role in emphasizing Drucker's principal insight: that management is first and foremost a liberal art. We approach management with humility and values; with an appreciation for history, culture, and philosophy; and with an integrative approach that places equal emphasis on effectiveness, ethics, and responsibility.

3

Leading Knowledge Workers:
Beyond the Era of Command and Control

Craig L. Pearce

Knowledge has to be improved, challenged, and increased constantly, or it vanishes.

—Peter F. Drucker

Drucker identified the dawning of the age of knowledge work more than half a century ago. As was typical of him, he was peering over the horizon, seeing what was unseen, yet in retrospect has clearly come to be. In 1968, Drucker, in his prescient book *The Age of Discontinuity*, declared, "In the past twenty years the base of our economy has shifted from manual to knowledge work." Since that time, knowledge work has become an increasingly important component of the economy, and it has become an increasingly team-based task. The reason for this shift to team-based knowledge work is clear. It is ever more difficult for any individual to develop the expertise required for all aspects of the work that need to be achieved, no matter what the context, and this phenomenon is being driven ever deeper into and ever wider across organizations. With this emphasis on team-based knowledge work comes the imperative to question our traditional models of leadership.

Leadership has typically been regarded as the purview of the one person who is "in charge," while the rest are simply followers—what is termed *vertical* or *hierarchical* leadership. Having said that, recent research indicates that leadership can move to the person with the key knowledge, skills, and abilities for the tasks facing any particular group at any given moment—what is termed *shared* leadership. The research on this is very clear: it indicates that poor-performing groups tend to be dominated by an appointed leader, while high-performing groups display more dispersed leadership patterns,[1] that is, they share leadership. Obviously this does not mean that leadership from above is unnecessary. On the contrary, the role of the hierarchical leader is absolutely critical to the ongoing success of knowledge work.

What Is Knowledge Work?

Before we proceed much further, it is critical that we move forward with a common understanding of knowledge work. Knowledge work requires significant investment in, and voluntary contribution of, intellectual capital by skilled professionals: concomitantly, knowledge work is increasingly becoming a team-based task.[2] The increasing need for team-based knowledge work is a result of both top-down and bottom-up pressures. The organizationally based top-down pressures are a result of competition, both domestic and global, which has caused firms to seek more effective ways to compete.[3] As a result, firms are seeking ways of reducing costs and improving efficiency in order to remain competitive. Naturally this also entails the need for a more flexible workforce, a reduction in lead time, and the full engagement of organizationally resident knowledge, which can, at least partially, be achieved through the synergies of team-based knowledge work and shared leadership.

Conversely, the aggregated individually based bottom-up pressures that firms face have emerged from the dramatically changing nature of the workforce, be it domestic or global. Let us look, for example, at the fact that the workforce is increasingly more highly educated. As a result, the workforce has greater knowledge to offer its organizations. Today's employees also require more from work than a simple paycheck: they increasingly demand to make a meaningful impact,[4] which is increasingly achieved through team-based approaches to knowledge work,[5] which rely on shared leadership.

This shift toward team-based knowledge work creates the need to question our traditional models and approaches to leadership—do they need to be retooled and reshaped? It would appear that the answer is yes. To wit, while we typically think of leadership as a role, with one person projecting downward influence on followers, if we instead think of leadership as a process, is it possible for all members of knowledge worker teams to engage in the leadership process through shared leadership?[6] The research on this is quite clear—across a wide variety of organizational contexts ranging from the laboratory to the military, from face-to-face teams to virtual teams, from top management teams to entire organizations.[7] Simply put, shared leadership entails a simultaneous, ongoing, mutual influence process within a group that is characterized by the "serial emergence" of both official and unofficial leaders.

The Challenge of Leading Knowledge Workers

There is one fundamental challenge in leading knowledge workers: there is generally a knowledge gap between the nominal leader and the rest of the group, and sometimes this gap is rather extreme. This naturally calls into question our traditional notions of top-down, command-and-control leadership, established through historical paradigms and reinforced by the popular media—who used to search for the heroic leader to glorify and currently are looking for the narcissistic leader to vilify.

In addition to identifying the dawn of the knowledge economy, Drucker also foreshadowed the coincidental dawning of the age of shared leadership. He stated, "Most discussions of decision making assume that only senior executives make decisions or that only senior executives' decisions matter. This is a dangerous mistake." Clearly he envisioned a role for wider participation in the knowledge creation process, whether by design or through mere emergence. In retrospect, the superior course is obviously through purposeful engagement of the workforce, using such processes as shared leadership. Having said that, as Drucker would instruct, it is imperative that we look at the evidence, which we do in the following section.

Leadership in Historical Context

It was during the Industrial Revolution that the task of management began to be formally studied in a scientific manner. Management was formally recognized as a factor of production in 1803, when Jean Baptiste Say, a French economist, stated that entrepreneurs "must possess the art of superintendence and administration." Prior to Say, economists were primarily occupied with the other factors of production—land, labor, and capital. The Industrial Revolution initiated the concept that leadership might be an important component of economic endeavors. Nonetheless, the early recognition of leadership as an important component of industrial enterprise was myopic: the endorsed view of leadership was one of command and control, and it was not until much later that the world observed even a tiny glimpse of concepts related to the notion of shared leadership.

During the Industrial Revolution, the emphasis was on managerial control or oversight—in other words, the vertical model of leading. For example, in 1840, James Montgomery published a book that critically examined and compared the cotton manufacturing industries of the United States and Great Britain. He lauded the British organizations for their enhanced level of managerial expertise, and this expertise was largely focused on the establishment of tight control systems.

Throughout the nineteenth century, management thinking was primarily shaped by the needs of the emerging railroad industry. The advent of the railroads, the first large-scale American business, necessitated more systematic approaches in order to coordinate and control these expansive firms that were geographically dispersed, employed thousands of people, and required enormous capital investments. One important management thinker of this era was Daniel C. McCallum. In the mid-1800s, he developed six principles of management, one of which was unity of command.

By the turn of the twentieth century, and proceeding well into the twentieth century, thinking on management had crystallized into what was ultimately termed scientific management. The cornerstone of scientific management was that all work could be studied scientifically, and optimal procedures could be developed to ensure maximum productivity. Importantly, scientific management separated managerial from worker responsibilities. Managers were given the task of identifying precise work procedures, and workers were charged with following those protocols equally precisely. Scientific management clearly articulated a command-and-control perspective on the role of leaders in organizational life. Leaders were to oversee and direct those below them. Subordinates were to follow the dictates they were given unquestioningly. The notion that leaders and their subordinates might mutually influence one another was unthinkable.

Peter Drucker recalled a conversation that he had with a member of the National Labor Relations Board (NLRB) in the 1940s that powerfully illustrates the prevailing attitudes at the time. Drucker explained that, "When I said something about both management and workers having 'a common interest in the survival and prosperity of the company' my friend cut me short: 'Any company that asserts such a common interest,' he said, 'is prima facie in violation of the law and guilty of a grossly unfair labor practice.'" Thus, the common wisdom through the mid-twentieth century (and well beyond) has been very much one of command and control: leaders and followers in the modern industrial organization were to have separate roles and conflicting goals. Influence was to remain vertical and unidirectional—downward—which is diametrically opposed to the needs of the knowledge era in which we are today. Having said that, once they are established, paradigms linger, to say the least.

How to Lead Knowledge Work—It Is All in the Recipe

We need to move beyond the moribund concepts of the past if we are to take on the challenge of knowledge work in the twenty-first century, and sharing leadership is central to that challenge. Accordingly, it is critical to understand the mechanisms through which both vertical and shared leadership can leverage the knowledge, skills, and abilities of knowledge workers. The following sections detail specific leader behaviors through which both hierarchical leaders and the knowledge workers they lead can successfully help one another to mutually beneficial gains.

Decades of research on both leadership and knowledge work have identified a range of leadership strategies or behaviors that serve as the bases of knowledge creation in organizations, and when we shift to shared leadership, these behavioral strategies continue to be relevant, with one important difference: the agents and targets of influence are often peers. That said, research has clearly identified four important types of leadership behavior that can emanate from hierarchical leaders or be shared and distributed among knowledge workers: directive, transactional, transformational, and empowering.[8]

Directive Leadership

Directive leadership involves providing task-focused direction, as the term implies.[9] Directive leadership provides much-needed structure for inherently unstructured tasks.[10] Highly skilled knowledge workers, whether they are designated leaders or "followers," generally will find a receptive audience for well-meaning and constructive instruction and direction among less-experienced or less-knowledgeable members. Directive leadership is particularly important in newly formed teams. For instance, shared directive leadership might be expressed in conversation as peers explore knowledge boundaries with one another through a directive give-and-take about how to approach assignments, allocate roles, or resolve divergent points of view. Indeed, the CEO of Cisco has been purposely striving to broaden participation in decision making and direction giving in its leadership process. Reflecting on difficulties Cisco faced following the dot-bomb era, CEO John Chambers stated, "All decisions came to the top 10 people in the company, and we drove things back down from there." Now Cisco has a purposeful strategy of engaging shared leadership, with impressive results. According to Chambers, "The boards and councils [we created] have been able to innovate with tremendous speed. Fifteen minutes and one week to get a [business] plan that used to take six months!" By engaging the directive capabilities of those lower in the hierarchy, Cisco has been able to reap innovative benefits that elude its hierarchical competitors.

Transactional Leadership

Transactional leadership entails influence through the strategic supply of rewards—praise, recognition, compensation, or other valued outcomes—that are contingent on follower performance.[11] The source of such rewards has traditionally been the appointed, vertical leader; however, shared transactional leadership in the context of knowledge work can take the form of collegial praise for exemplary contributions. In addition, colleagues might also award valued assignments or recommend financial distributions based on individual- or team-level attainment of project milestones, quality targets, or other key performance metrics. For instance, one management team I have worked with in my consulting practice, which was in charge of an engine production facility, actively campaigned for and successfully changed its compensation system from an individually based bonus system to one that contained team-based bonuses. Naturally, the incorporation of team-based bonuses led to positive team outcomes: this organization recently won its State Senate Productivity Award (analogous to the Malcolm Baldrige Award at the national level).[12]

Transformational Leadership

While transactional leadership emphasizes rewards that are immediate value, transformational leadership adopts a more symbolic emphasis on commitment to a collective vision, emotional engagement, and fulfillment of higher-order needs such as the creation of meaningful professional impact or desires to engage in breakthrough achievements. One of the tasks of the hierarchical leader, at least initially, is that of clarifying the vision. On the other hand, knowledge workers can engage in shared transformational leadership through peer exhortation or by appealing to collegial desires to design groundbreaking products and services, launch exciting new ventures, outmaneuver the competition to capture the most market share in the industry, or simply make the world a better place to live in.

Shared transformational leadership is particularly critical in the knowledge worker context because this context depends on significant and, by their very nature, voluntary intellectual contributions of highly skilled professionals. A recent article in *Fortune* magazine, for example, declared the creation of a shared vision to be the most important leadership idea of the twentieth century.[13] This idea was resiliently echoed in a recent interview with Leslie E. Stocker, president of the Braille Institute of America. He claimed, "We all have a voice in creating our common mission . . . the key is to help others lead you, when they have the relevant knowledge."

Empowering Leadership

The last type of leadership we examine here, and perhaps the most important type to consider in the context of knowledge work, is empowering leadership, which emphasizes employee self-influence rather than top-down control. In many ways, empowering leadership epitomizes the idealized role of the designated leader in knowledge work. Following are excerpts from interviews of successful leaders of change management teams from my consulting practice.One team leader claimed, "My most important role is for building the team—getting them to interact without being directed," while another team leader stated, "You have to play cheerleader sometimes [and] you have to be careful not to be a dictator." One team leader, however, summed up his role in the knowledge creation process by stating: "I have told them [the team members] their goal is to replace me."

Like the other leadership strategies discussed earlier, empowering leadership can also be shared and projected laterally among peers. Examples of shared empowering leadership include peer encouragement and support of self-goal-setting, self-evaluation, self-reward, and self-development. Shared empowering leadership particularly emphasizes building self-influence skills that orchestrate performance while preserving autonomy. As a result, it may be particularly suited to knowledge workers, who so clearly desire autonomy on the job.[14]

Scientific Evidence on Shared Leadership

Drucker instructs us to base our conclusions on facts and logic. Accordingly, we need to examine the scientific evidence on shared leadership in knowledge work. Here the evidence is crystal clear. While few teams or organizations achieve a high level of shared leadership, the initial evidence indicates that shared leadership has a significantly greater impact on team and organizational effectiveness than the more traditional model of hierarchical leadership alone. This scientific evidence comes from a wide variety of contexts, including groups responsible for managing change in organizations (e.g., implementing new protocols, procedures, and work systems), virtual groups (geographically dispersed teams that primarily interact via communication technology) and, perhaps most importantly, top management teams. In every case, the groups that demonstrated higher levels of effectiveness were those that engaged in higher levels of shared leadership. Low-performing groups tend to be dominated by the leader, while high-performing groups actually have most of their leadership coming from group members. Thus, a relevant question is, "Why not just get rid of the hierarchical leaders in knowledge work and let the experts lead themselves?" Here again, let's look at the evidence. From our research, three of the four measures of hierarchical leadership are higher in high-performing groups. The only measure of hierarchical leadership that was lower in high-performing groups was the measure of how much the leader attempted to empower the rest of the group. We might speculate that the reason for this is that the group members simply didn't need to be empowered by the leader; they empowered each other.

Is Shared Leadership a Panacea?

Shared leadership is not a panacea for the plethora of problems that plague knowledge work. For example, if knowledge workers, and particularly key organizational leaders, resist the notion of shared leadership, its potential will be blunted. This raises an important question: What should be done with a technically sound and otherwise successful knowledge worker who rejects shared leadership out of hand? Here again we can look to Drucker for advice. Drucker stated, "The task of leadership is to create an alignment of strengths in ways that make weaknesses irrelevant." Thus, those who resist shared leadership should be placed in individual contributor roles where their talents can be nurtured and their contributions reaped. Having said that, overreliance on any one individual in the knowledge creation process introduces considerable risk to the organization: what happens if that person leaves the organization? Clearly this can undermine the robustness of the knowledge creation process.[15]

The Future of Leading Knowledge Work

In the late 1960s, Drucker stated, "We do not know how to manage the knowledge worker so that he wants to contribute and perform. But we do know that he must be managed quite differently." This chapter is an attempt to address the challenges that Drucker identified. Leadership is not just a role; it is an unfolding social process, and it is through this process—one that engages the total human spirit—that true knowledge work and true breakthroughs can be achieved. We are indeed in a new era, the era of knowledge work—one that Drucker so clearly identified over half a century ago.

Is the knowledge era the postvertical, hierarchical leadership era? Unambiguously no. It is not a matter of choosing between vertical leadership and shared leadership when it comes to knowledge work. On the contrary, the issues are (1) When is leadership most appropriately shared? (2) How does one develop shared leadership? (3) How does one facilitate smooth leadership transitions? By addressing these issues, we will move organizations toward a more appropriate model of leadership in the age of knowledge work. As Drucker so astutely observed, "Knowledge work [is] a team-based task."

4

Value(s)-Based Management: Corporate Social Responsibility Meets Value-Based Management

James S. Wallace

"It is not enough to do well; it must also do good." But in order to "do good," a business must first "do well."

—Peter F. Drucker, *Management: Tasks, Responsibilities, Practices*

For a firm to be successful in creating wealth, everyone who has a stake in the business must receive their share of the economic pie.

—John Martin, William Petty, and James Wallace, *Value-Based Management with Corporate Social Responsibility*

Ask an economist why firms exist, and you are likely to be told that it is far more efficient to perform complex tasks inside a firm than it would be for an individual to contract separately for the same task. Just imagine how difficult and costly it would be for an individual to purchase a cell phone if there were no firms producing such devices. You would need to contract with one engineer to design the circuits, another to write the software, still another to produce the case, and on and on.

Leaving the purely economic reasoning behind, we may also ask the question: what should be the goal of a firm? At this point, we are venturing into an area that is filled with far more emotion and far less hard evidence. In this chapter, I will attempt to explore this question through the lens of management as a liberal art, utilizing the writings of the father of modern management, Peter F. Drucker.

Answers to why firms exist run along a long continuum. At one end are the followers of the late economist Milton Friedman, who preached in his 1962 book, *Capitalism and Freedom*, that the firm should exist only to make money for its owner shareholders. Anything else, he felt, was wasting money:

> *Few trends could so thoroughly undermine the very foundation of our free society as the acceptance by corporate officials of a social responsibility other than to make as much money for their stockholders as possible.*

Not everyone shares this view of a corporate purpose. Some have argued that this value-based management (VBM) approach is simply greed.[1] Questions arise as to whether firms have an obligation to a multitude of stakeholders. Is making money important only so that the firm can do something nobler? Followers of the stakeholder theory of the firm will argue that the firm must consider and balance the needs of all its stakeholders. Stakeholders in this case include any group that is affected by the actions of the firm. This includes not only shareholders, but also employees, customers, vendors, the government, the community where the firm is located, and society at large. As Charles Handy has said,

> *The purpose of a business . . . is not to make a profit, full stop. It is to make a profit so that the business can do something more or better.*

That "something" becomes the real justification for the business. . . .
It is a moral issue. To mistake the means for the end is to be turned in
on oneself, which Saint Augustine called one of the greatest sins. . . .
It is salutary to ask about any organization, "If it did not exist, would
we invent it?" "Only if it could do something better or more useful
than anyone else" would have to be the answer, and profit would be
the means to that larger end.

A related question is just how the trend toward corporate social
responsibility (CSR) fits into the VBM model. Are they at odds with
each other, or are they perhaps interrelated? To answer these difficult
but very important questions, I will first explore the VBM model,
with its emphasis on the shareholder, and the CSR approach, with its
emphasis on multiple stakeholders. I argue that these two philosophies are really far more complementary than they are at odds with
each other. In fact, successful VBM companies are learning that practicing a strong CSR program, something that I call value(s)-based
management, can actually be a win-win situation. Rather than these
expenditures amounting to a zero sum, value is added. This can lead
to the "virtuous circle," where doing good leads to doing well, which
can provide the ability to do more good. As the opening quote by
Peter Drucker states: *"'It is not enough to do well; it must also do*
good.' But in order to 'do good,' a business must first 'do well.'"

Adam Smith, the Invisible Hand, and Value-Based Management

The idea that firms exist to make money traces its intellectual roots
back to 1776, when Adam Smith published his seminal work titled
The Wealth of Nations.

Every individual endeavors to employ his capital so that its pro-
duce may be of greatest value. He generally neither intends to pro-

mote the public interest, nor knows how much he is promoting it. He intends only his own security, only his own gain. And he is in this led by an invisible hand to promote an end, which has no part of his intention. By pursuing his own interest he frequently promotes that of society more effectually than when he really intends to promote it.

Adam Smith used the invisible hand metaphor to illustrate that individuals (or firms) seek wealth by following their own self-interest, and in so doing create wealth for the economy as a secondary effect. To understand how this is accomplished, consider that as long as consumers are free to choose what to buy and sellers are free to choose what to sell and how to produce it, the market will determine the products sold and the prices charged that add value for the entire society. This naturally follows from everyone following his own self-interest. The idea that profit maximization produces the best outcome for society in general can be shown with the following simple example, based on the work of Michael Jensen. A firm purchases resources in the form of materials, labor, and capital. These purchases are contracted from their owners through voluntary exchanges. The firm combines these inputs to produce goods and services that are sold to customers, again through voluntary exchanges. Since all exchanges are voluntary, one can conclude that the exchanges are made at a price where the buyer and seller each place a value on the exchanged item that is equal to the price paid. It then follows that value has been added to society by producing a profit, where the goods and services are sold at a higher price than the cost of producing them. The more profit the firm produces, the more value that is added to society.

An interpretation of Adam Smith's ideas was repeated a couple of hundred years later in *The Quest for Value* by G. Bennett Stewart III, a leader in value-based management consulting.

It is easy to forget why senior management's most important job must be to maximize its firm's current market value. If nothing else, a greater value rewards the shareholders who, after all, are the owners of the enterprise. But, and this really is much more important, society at large benefits too. A quest for value directs scarce resources to their most promising uses and most productive uses. The more effectively resources are deployed and managed, the more robust economic growth and the rate of improvement in our standard of living will be. Adam Smith's invisible hand is at work when investor's private gain turns into a public virtue. Although there are exceptions to this rule, most of the time there is a happy harmony between creating stock market value and enhancing the quality of life.

It is not uncommon to see corporate mission statements that endorse the invisible hand concept of creating shareholder value while improving society as a whole. For example, the 2008 annual report of the Briggs & Stratton Corporation states:

We will create superior value by developing mutually beneficial relationships with our customers, suppliers, employees and communities.... In pursuing this mission, we will provide power for people worldwide to develop their economies and improve the quality of their lives and, in so doing, add value to our shareholders' investments.

While some firms may still be promoting their dedication to value-based management, one unfortunate outcome following the infamous scandals such as Enron and WorldCom is the perception that somehow value-based management is synonymous with greed, and that this greed is synonymous with taking advantage of other stakeholders. This perception is probably the result of a misunderstanding of VBM. Adam Smith believed that when people are free to pursue their own interests, society will be better off than it would be under a system where what is "good" is determined externally. Others, however, argue a different perspective.

A Stakeholder Perspective

What has become known as stakeholder theory was first presented by Edward Freeman in his 1984 book *Strategic Management: A Stakeholder Perspective*. In contrast to Friedman's shareholder value theory, which posits that the corporation should be concerned only about the shareholder, stakeholder theory posits that corporations have multiple stakeholders, each of them important, and each with needs that must be balanced. Stakeholders include not only the shareholders, but also customers, employees, suppliers, the community, the government, the environment, and society in general.

Closely linked with stakeholder theory is the corporate social responsibility (CSR) movement. Like stakeholder theory, CSR also involves an organization's identifying its various stakeholder groups and then attempting to balance their respective needs within the organization's strategy. CSR advocates believe that there are strategic advantages in considering the needs and values of all stakeholder groups. This is in sharp contrast to devout followers of Friedman, who advocate doing for nonshareholder stakeholders only what is required by regulation and law.

Value(s)-Based Management: A Marriage of Value-Based Management and Stakeholder Theory

On first inspection, it may appear that there is little common ground between the views of Friedman and Freeman. Fortunately, this is not the case. Perhaps the greatest mind to address the issue of a firm's purpose was that of Peter F. Drucker. Drucker defined the purpose of a business in terms of the customer in his 1954 book *The Practice of Management*:

> *If we want to know what business is, we have to start with its purpose. And the purpose must lie outside the business itself. In fact, it must lie*

in society, since a business enterprise is an organ of society. There is
only one valid definition of business purpose: to create a customer.
The customer is the foundation of a business and keeps it in existence.
He alone gives employment. And it is to supply the customer that so-
ciety entrusts wealth-producing resources to the business enterprise.

Drucker also considered the concept of social responsibility in depth. His writings incorporated the views of both Friedman and Freeman; however, Drucker articulated it in a way that brought these divergent views together in his 2002 book *Managing in a Time of Great Change*:

A business that does not show a profit at least equal to its cost of cap-
ital is socially irresponsible; it wastes society's resources. Economic
profit performance is the base without which business cannot dis-
charge any other responsibilities, cannot be a good employer, a good
citizen, a good neighbor. But economic performance is not the only
responsibility of a business. . . . Every organization must assume re-
sponsibility for its impact on employees, the environment, customers,
and whomever and whatever it touches. That is social responsibility.
But we know that society will increasingly look to major organiza-
tions, for-profit and nonprofit alike, to tackle major social ills. And
that is where we had better be watchful, because good intentions are
not always socially responsible. It is irresponsible for an organization
to accept—let alone pursue—responsibilities that would impede its
capacity to perform its main task and mission or to act where it has
no competence.

While some may promote the idea of value(s)-based management, like that of corporate social responsibility, as a "responsibility" of the firm to do good or to give back to society, others promote the concept more on economic grounds. Rather than casting it as a corporate obligation, value(s)-based management provides a process for structuring win-win agreements between the different stakeholders in sharing (and creating) value.

Robert Jensen, a noted economist, asks:

> *Can corporate managers succeed by simply holding up value maximization as the goal and ignoring their stakeholders? The answer is an emphatic no. In order to maximize value, corporate managers must not only satisfy, but enlist the support of, all corporate stakeholders— customers, employees, managers, suppliers, local communities.*

In *Strategy and Society*, Michael Porter and Mark Kramer explain further:

> *If corporations were to analyze their prospects for social responsibility using the same framework that guides their core business choices, they would discover that CSR can be much more than a cost, a constraint, or a charitable deed—it can be a source of opportunity, innovation, and competitive advantage.*

Strategic reasons for engaging in a value-based approach to management include recruitment (potential recruits are increasingly making career choices based on social responsibility), risk management, and brand differentiation.

SCA Packaging, a Sweden-based diversified company employing more than 43,000 people in 43 countries, found that it needed to close three factories. When trying to decide how to proceed, the company "put ourselves in the shoes of our stakeholders, most notably our staff. The company explained the business case for the closures, but we also had to be open enough to be questioned and to provide counter arguments, and in some cases to be sufficiently flexible to agree to change." The company worked with its employees in an attempt to mitigate, as much as it could, any hardships. This included resettling employees at different plants, job search help, and severance payments. The company found that it achieved multiple benefits from acting in a responsible manner. These benefits included a lack of disruption in running the business during the closures, enhanced staff loyalty, and a burnished reputation as a responsible employer.

While it often requires decades or more to develop a superior reputation, an accident or scandal can destroy that reputation in days. Recent examples range from sexual molestation within the Catholic Church to steroid use in professional baseball. A proactive CSR program can help prevent such episodes from occurring and can mitigate damages if they do occur. High-profile CSR activities can help to divert attention from existing problems. Examples of such CSR activities include Merck's partnership with the Bill & Melinda Gates Foundation and the government of Botswana to fight AIDS, British American Tobacco's health initiatives, BP's alternative energy wind programs, and Wal-Mart's decisions to sell organic groceries and build eco-friendly stores.

Firms are constantly looking for ways to differentiate themselves from their competitors in an effort to capture the consumer's dollars. Examples of organizations that have successfully used CSR as a brand differentiator include Whole Foods Market, Ben & Jerry's, and The Body Shop.

C. W. Goodyear, CEO of BHP Billiton, a leading natural resources company, stated it the following way:

> *BHP Billiton realized a long time ago that working in partnership with communities is more than about being a good corporate citizen. It's a powerful competitive differentiator. It has the potential to establish us as the company of choice, giving us better access to markets, natural resources and the best and brightest employees. By doing so, we can maximize profits for our shareholders while also ensuring we do the right thing by those who are impacted by our business.*

Value(s)-Based Management—The Evidence

The statement, "In theory, theory and practice are the same. In practice, they are not" has been credited to both Albert Einstein and Yogi Berra. Regardless of who first made the statement, it remains true that what looks good on paper (theory) does not always hold in the real world (practice). Therefore, it is instructive to see whether the theory behind value-based management makes good business sense.

There has been no shortage of studies exploring many facets of value-based management. The majority of these studies attempt to answer the question of how operating in a socially responsible manner is linked to a firm's financial performance. Because of the inconsistency among these studies regarding data sets, time periods, and methodologies, it is very difficult to arrive at any definite conclusions. Fortunately, a team of researchers—Orlitzky, Schmidt, and Rynes, brought some clarity to this chaos by performing a comprehensive analysis of 52 studies that had investigated the relationship between corporate social performance and corporate financial performance. The researchers discovered commonalities within the prior research and concluded that corporate social responsibility is likely to pay off in improved financial performance. Specifically, they found that (1) corporate social responsibility and financial performance go hand in hand, (2) there is a so-called virtuous cycle between corporate social performance and financial performance: financially successful companies spend more on CSR outlays because they can afford to, but CSR also helps them to be more successful financially, and (3) corporate social responsibility improves financial performance because it helps the firm build a positive reputation with external stakeholders.

This research is consistent with a survey of 500 business executives conducted by Grant Thornton LLP in 2007. The three greatest benefits of these programs noted in the survey were (1) an improvement in public opinion, (2) an improvement in customer relations, and (3) an improvement in attracting and retaining talent.

A recently published study by this author and Barbara Lougee went further by looking at not only whether it makes sense for investors to invest in socially responsible firms but also whether it makes sense for firms to invest in socially responsible endeavors. While it is one thing to show that socially responsible investing (SRI) can make financial sense, this is not the same thing as showing that it makes business sense for firms to invest in CSR programs.

In order to test whether investing in socially responsible firms makes financial sense, we compared the returns on the Domini 400 index, one of the portfolios of firms developed to provide an index for socially conscious investing, with the returns on the S&P 500. We found a slight advantage for the Domini index from its inception in April 1990 through December 2006. The Domini 400 has yielded an annual rate of 12.09 percent over this period, compared to an annual rate of 11.45 percent for the benchmark S&P 500. This study was completed prior to the recent meltdown of the financial markets. At the time of this writing, through May 2009, the Domini 400 is still outperforming the S&P 500, but now by a slightly wider margin of 8.50 percent to 7.77 percent.

In order to test whether it makes business sense for firms to invest in CSR programs, we next looked at how various CSR behaviors related to the performance of an individual firm. Characteristics of the firm that were labeled as CSR strengths showed a very strong positive association with the firm's return on assets (ROA), whereas firm characteristics that were labeled as CSR concerns showed a very strong negative association with the firm's ROA. This same relationship was exhibited for both the Domini 400 and the S&P 500 firms. Overall, the evidence tells a consistent story: value-based management makes sense from a financial perspective.

Conclusion

In this chapter, I explore the fundamental question of corporate mission. Passionate opinions on this issue have ranged from "a firm exists only to make money" to "the firm should make money only so that it can do something more or better." In other words, some see earning a profit as the ultimate goal, arguably a pure value-based management approach, while another group considers profits as only a means to an end, with that end being something more "noble."

Rather than looking at this debate as a case of one side being right and one side being wrong, I take the approach of, "What did Peter Drucker have to say about this?" As it turns out, he had a great deal to say. (In fact, in Chapter 5 in this book, Cornelis A. de Kluyver discusses Peter Drucker's writings on the impact of corporate social responsibility on boards of directors.) Not surprisingly, through the lens of Peter Drucker, it appears that neither side is right, nor is either side wrong. An alternative view of this debate takes something from each side to stake out a place somewhere in the middle, an approach I label value(s)-based management.

Value-based management is about providing a cultural mindset for creating firm value. Value(s)-based management moves this mindset toward considering not just what to do (make money), but also how to do it (operate in a socially responsible manner). Long-run sustainable wealth creation can be achieved only by involving all the stakeholders of the firm.

Drucker summed this all up in his 2003 book *A Functioning Society*:

> *We no longer need to theorize about how to define performance and results in the large enterprise. We have successful examples. . . . They do not "balance" anything. They maximize. But they do not attempt to maximize shareholder value or the short-term interest of any one of the enterprise's "stakeholders." Rather, they maximize the wealth-producing capacity of the enterprise. It is this objective that integrates the*

short-term and long-term results and that ties the operational dimensions of business performance—market standing, innovation, productivity, and people and their development—with the financial needs and financial results. It is also this objective on which all the constituencies—whether shareholders, customers, or employees—depend for the satisfaction of their expectations and objectives.

Author's Note: This chapter is based, in part, on the book *Value-Based Management with Corporate Social Responsibility*, 2nd ed. (Oxford University Press, 2009), with John Martin, William Petty, and James Wallace.

5

Drucker on Corporate Governance

Cornelis A. de Kluyver

Whenever an institution malfunctions as consistently as boards of directors have in nearly every major fiasco of the last forty or fifty years, it is futile to blame men. It is the institution that malfunctions.

—Peter F. Drucker

The most remarkable aspect of this quote is not its forthrightness (which characterizes much of Drucker's writing), but its timing. He made it in 1976, when institutional investing in U.S. public companies had just gained momentum—well before the highly publicized takeovers and restructurings of the 1980s and the corporate scandals at Enron, WorldCom, Tyco, and others that occurred around the turn of the century, and certainly well before the financial crisis of 2008. It also suggests a question: has anything changed?

Boards: The Perennial Villain

Skepticism about the efficacy of boards of directors and the corporate governance function is not a recent phenomenon. When Drucker reached his conclusion, boards all over the world were also under attack and being pressured to change. In Europe, "codetermination" (including labor union representatives on the board) was the issue of the day. In the United States, the focus was on representation of minorities and the "public interest" in the boardroom, not only for public companies, but also for the boards of universities, hospitals, and professional societies.

Like Berle and Means, who, in their widely cited 1932 book *The Modern Corporation and Private Property,* had warned of the concentration of economic power brought about by the rise of the large corporation and the emergence of a powerful class of professional managers, insulated from the pressure not only of stockholders but of the larger public as well, Drucker worried about the growing rift between the values of top executives and those of their constituencies. And, as a lawyer, historian, and economist, he appreciated the inertia of legal systems and the gap that this was creating between corporation law and the challenges of creating transparency and accountability in an increasingly complex and global corporate environment:

> *The rules for boards in our corporation law—in this country as well as in Western Europe—were written in the middle of the nineteenth century. They assume a business which is small and regional, if not local. It has one or two products. It is owned by a very small number of individuals, either the people who started it or their descendants. In turn, their stake in the business is the major, if not the only, property of these people or their families. So they have a strong interest in its performance and success. In such a situation the board can be what the law expects it to be, i.e. knowledgeable and close to the affairs of the business. And it can give direction to management.*[1]

The 2002 U.S. Governance Reforms

Drucker rarely spoke and never wrote about the avalanche of structural and procedural reforms adopted in the aftermath of the corporate scandals at the turn of the century. Taking a Drucker-like perspective on this issue is therefore a speculative exercise. In particular, I refer to the Sarbanes-Oxley Act of 2002, which imposes significant new disclosure and corporate governance requirements for public companies, and also provides for substantially increased liability for public companies and their executives and directors under the federal securities laws; and subsequent rule changes by the New York Stock Exchange, the Nasdaq Stock Market, Inc., and the Securities and Exchange Commission aimed at strengthening transparency and accountability through more timely and accurate disclosure of information about corporate performance.

It is likely that Drucker would have approved of the greater scrutiny of the behavior of corporate boards by the government, regulatory authorities, stock exchanges, investors, ordinary citizens, and the press. He also might have been sympathetic to the rationale behind many of the recent reforms. Consider, for example, the rationale for increasing *director independence*: that shareholders, by virtue of their inability to monitor management behavior directly, rely on the board of directors to perform critical monitoring activities, and that the board's monitoring potential is reduced or perhaps eliminated when management itself effectively controls the actions of the board. Requiring a board and its major subcommittees to have a majority of independent directors therefore increases the quality of board oversight and lessens the possibility of damaging conflicts of interest. At the same time, it is also very likely that he would have had doubts about the efficacy of many of the new reforms and would have expressed concern about possible unintended consequences.

The Board's Role

Moreover, along with his skepticism and misgivings, Drucker would have reiterated his strong belief that large, complex institutions, whether private or public, need a "truly effective, truly independent outside" board:

> The need is not primarily rooted in the "public interest" or in the wish to make boards "democratic." The need is, above all, a need of the institution itself. It cannot function well in all of its complexity unless it has an effective board.

Specifically, he defined the board's role in terms of six essential duties, the first and most important of which was to ensure strong, competent management. He considered the removal of less than fully competent managers and ensuring orderly management succession essential to organizational effectiveness.

Second, he argued that complex organizations need an independent organ to ask the "hard" questions and make sure that management thought about them. What is our mission? What are valid "results" in our undertaking? Who are our stakeholders, and what can they legitimately expect from us? What are our plans for the future? What should we emphasize? What should we abandon? Are we innovating enough?

Acting as the organization's "conscience"—the keeper of its human and moral values—was the third essential function on Drucker's board responsibility list. To do this, he argued that directors should regularly meet with people other than top management, both within and outside the organization—an idea that did not endear him to many senior executives.

The fourth board function he identified defines the advisory role of the board. With greater complexity, he argued, comes the need for more counsel. An effective board—one that understands the institution, its opportunities, and its problems—could fill this gap.

Fifth, as another consequence of the growing complexity of the business environment, Drucker saw an effective board as the organization's "window to the outside world" or, as he once put it, its "channel of outside perception."

Finally, and also somewhat controversially, he viewed the board as having a responsibility to communicate what goes on "on the fourteenth floor" to the organization's various constituencies and the community at large through regular, open dialogue.[2]

Interestingly, today's conceptions of a board's responsibility are not that different. The frequently cited definition by the Business Roundtable, issued in 2005, for example, apart from its greater emphasis on shareholders, has many similar elements, as does the slightly broader perspective taken by governance scholars such as Milstein, Gregory, and Grapsas.[3]

The fact that such descriptions have changed little also points to a common weakness. Descriptions are useful for developing a basic understanding of a board's responsibilities: (1) to make decisions, (2) to monitor corporate activity, and (3) to advise management. However, they do not provide much guidance or insight into resolving a board's principal dilemma: deciding which posture is appropriate at what time. Indeed, while the law, corporate bylaws, and lists of responsibilities frame many of the key decisions that a board must make, such as appointing a CEO or approving the financials, they do not provide much guidance with respect to the board's most important decision: when *must* board oversight become active intervention? When, for example, should a board step in and remove the current CEO? When should it veto a major capital appropriation or strategic move?

What's more, the precise role of a board will vary depending on the nature of the company, its industry and competitive situation, and the presence or absence of special circumstances such as a hostile takeover bid or a corporate crisis, among other factors. The challenges faced by small private or closely held companies are not the same as those faced by larger public corporations. In addition to their traditional fiduciary role, directors in small companies are often key advisors in strategic planning, raising and allocating capital, human resources planning, and sometimes even performance appraisal. In larger public corporations, strategic oversight rather than planning, capital allocation and control more than the raising of capital, and management development and succession instead of a more broadly defined human resources role better describe the board's main domains of activity. Similarly, global corporations face different challenges from domestic ones, the issues in regulated industries are different from those in technology or service industries, and high-growth scenarios make different demands on boards from more mature situations.

Finally, in times of turbulence or rapid change in an industry, boards are often called upon to play a more active, strategic role than in calmer times. Special events or opportunities such as takeovers, mergers, and acquisitions fall into this category. Company crises can take many different forms: defective products, hostile takeovers, executive misconduct, natural disasters that threaten operations, and many more. But, as boards know very well, they all have one thing in common: crises threaten the stock price and sometimes the continued existence of the company. And, as many directors have learned, there are few situations in which a board's fiduciary duty is more clearly on view as in times of crisis.

Management versus Governance

In the aftermath of the recent governance debacles, the issue of what differentiates management from governance has received a lot of attention. Many scholars and practitioners, for example, counseled boards to become more involved. Rubber-stamping decisions, populating boards with friends of the CEO, and convening board meetings on the golf course are out, they said; engagement, transparency, independence, knowing the company inside and out, and adding value are in. This all sounds good. There is a real danger, however, that the rise in shareholder activism, the new regulatory environment, and related social factors are pushing boards toward micro-management and meddling.

This issue is troubling, and there is clear evidence that the important differences that separate *governance* from *management*—which are critical to effective governance—are still not sufficiently well understood. And, regrettably, faced with the need to be more involved, the most obvious opportunity (and danger) is that boards will expand their involvement into—or, more accurately, intrude into—management's territory.

The key issue is how and to whom boards add value. Specifically, and in this respect I beg to differ with the venerable Peter Drucker, the potential of directors to add value is all too often framed in terms of their ability to add value to management by giving advice on issues such as strategy, choice of markets, and other factors affecting corporate success. While this may be valuable, *it obscures the primary role of the board—to govern, the purpose of which is to add value to shareholders and other stakeholders.*

A greater arm's-length relationship between management and the board therefore is both desirable and unavoidable. Recent governance reforms focused on creating greater independence and minimizing managerial excess while enhancing executive accountability have already created greater tension in the relationship between management and the board. Sarbanes-Oxley, for example, effectively asks boards to substitute verification for trust. Section 404 of the act requires management at all levels to "sign off" on key financial statements.

This is not necessarily bad, because trust and verification are not necessarily incompatible. In fact, we need both. But we should also realize that effective governance is about striking a reasonable accommodation between verification and trust, not about elevating one above the other. The history of human nature shows that adversarial relationships can create their own pathologies of miscommunication and mismanaged expectations with respect to risk and reward.

This is what makes defining the trade-offs that shape effective governance so difficult. Is better governance defined primarily by the active prevention of abuse? Or is it defined by the active promotion of risk taking and profitability? The quick and easy answer is that it should mean all of those things. However, as recurrent crises in corporate governance around the world have shown, it is hard to do even one of those things consistently well. What is more, a board that is trying to do all of these things well is not merely an active board; it is a board that is actively running the company. This is not overseeing management or holding management accountable—it *is* management. So the corporate governance reform agenda risks becoming an initiative that effectively dissolves most of the critical, traditional distinctions between the chief executive and the board.

Director Independence versus Board Independence

The recent reform movement's almost exclusive focus on director independence also merits reexamination. The proposition that boards should "act independently of management, through a thoughtful and diligent decision-making process" has been a major focus of corporate governance reform in recent years.[4] In the United States, the Sarbanes-Oxley Act of 2002, as well as the revised NYSE and Nasdaq listing rules as affirmed by the SEC, are premised on a belief that director independence is essential to effective corporate governance. In the United Kingdom, the Cadbury Commission's report of 1990 (the Code of Best Practice) included a recommendation that there be at least three nonexecutive directors on the board. Reflecting this broad consensus, today about 10 out of the average 12 directors of a major U.S. public company board are nonexecutives; in the United Kingdom, the corresponding number is a little less than half.

The idea of an independent board is intuitively appealing. Specifically, director independence, defined as the absence of any conflicts of interest through personal or professional ties with the corporation or its management, suggests objectivity and a capacity to be impartial and decisive, and therefore a stronger fiduciary ability. At times, a board needs to discuss issues that involve some or all of the company's senior executives; this is difficult to do when senior executives are on the board. The independence requirement also stops destructive practices such as "rewarding" former CEOs for their accomplishments by giving them a role on the board. Having the former CEO on the board almost always limits the ability of the new CEO to develop his own relationship with the board and put his imprint on the organization. There is also limited evidence that outsider-dominated boards are more proactive in firing underperforming CEOs, less willing to go along with outsized compensation proposals, and less willing to vote for poison pills.

Director independence should not be viewed as a proxy for good governance, however. At times, not having more insiders on the board can actually reduce a board's effectiveness as an oversight body or as counsel to the CEO. Independent, nonexecutive directors can never be as knowledgeable about a company's business as directors who are executives or senior managers. CEOs say that some of their most valuable directors are those with experience in the same industry, contrary to the current independence tests. The higher the proportion of outside directors, therefore, the more difficult it is to foster high-quality, deep board deliberations. Moreover, it is less likely that a CEO can mislead a board, intentionally or otherwise, when some of the directors are insiders who also have intimate knowledge of the company.[5] Boards that are mostly made up of independent directors must therefore, at a minimum, create regular opportunities for the board members to interact with senior executives other than the CEO. The more complex a company's business is, the more important such communications are. The bottom line is that effective corporate governance depends not on the independence of some particular subset of directors, but on *the independent behavior of the board as a whole*. The focus should be on fostering *board independence* as a *behavioral* norm, a psychological quality, rather than on quasi-legal definitions of director independence. Drucker would probably have agreed with the conclusion that director independence contributes to but is no guarantee of better governance.

The New Focus: Board Leadership

Board leadership was not making headlines when Drucker wrote his essay. Today, few issues in corporate governance are as contentious as the question of whether the roles of chairman and CEO should be separated or combined. In the United Kingdom, about 95 percent of all FTSE 350 companies adhere to the principle that different people should hold each of these roles. In the United States, by contrast, most companies still combine them, although the idea of splitting the two roles is gaining momentum. In the last few years, Boeing, Dell, the Walt Disney Company, MCI, Oracle, and Tenet Healthcare all have done so, and a new study finds that roughly one-third of U.S. companies have adopted such a split-leadership structure, up from a historical level of about one-fifth. This issue surfaced again recently when Kenneth D. Lewis, the beleaguered head of Bank of America, was stripped of his chairman's title. This action was taken at a contentious annual general meeting at which frustrated investors held him accountable for a series of missteps that made it necessary for the bank to accept two successive government bailouts. While the board expressed its unanimous support for Mr. Lewis's remaining as CEO, its decision to remove him as chairman reflected the bank's directors' recognition that he had lost the confidence of a large number of shareholders.

Arguments for splitting the two roles, which are emanating chiefly from the United Kingdom and other countries that overwhelmingly embrace the idea of separate roles (particularly Germany, the Netherlands, South Africa, Australia, and, to a lesser extent, Canada), fall into four categories.

The first is that the separation of the chairman and CEO positions is a key component of board independence because of the fundamental differences and potential conflicts between these roles. The CEO runs the company (the argument goes), and the chairman runs the board, one of whose responsibilities it is to monitor the CEO. If the chairman and the CEO are one and the same, it is hard for the board to criticize the CEO or to express independent opinions. A separate chairman who is responsible for setting the board's agenda is more likely to probe and encourage debate at board meetings. Therefore, separating the two roles is essentially a check on the CEO's power.

A second argument is that a nonexecutive chairman can serve as a valuable sounding board, mentor, and advocate to the CEO. Proponents of this view note that CEOs today face enough challenges without having to run the board as well and that a relationship with the chairman based on mutual trust and regular contact is good for the CEO, shareholders, and the company. For this to happen, however, it is essential that the two roles be clearly defined from the outset to avoid territorial disputes or misunderstandings.

A third reason for supporting the two-role model is that a nonexecutive chairman is ideally placed to assess the CEO's performance, taking into account the views of fellow board members. Advocates maintain that the presence of a separate, independent chairman can help maintain a longer-term perspective and reduce the risk that the CEO will focus too much on shorter-term goals, especially when there are powerful incentives and rewards for doing so. They add that he is also in a good position to play a helpful role in succession planning. And when a CEO departs, voluntarily or otherwise, the chairman's continued presence in charge of the board can reduce the level of trauma in the business and the investor community.

A fourth and final argument concerns the time needed to do both jobs and do them well. It can be argued that as companies grow more complex, a strong board is more vital than ever to the health of the company, and this requires a skilled chairman who is not distracted by the daily pull of the business and can devote the required time and energy. This may take one or more days per week and involve such tasks as maintaining contact with directors between meetings, organizing board evaluations, listening to shareholder concerns, acting as an ambassador for the company, and acting as a liaison with regulators, thereby allowing the CEO to concentrate on running the business.

Although these arguments are increasingly resonating with U.S. directors and shareholders, many CEOs are resisting the change. Why, they ask, should corporate wrongdoing at a small number of S&P 500 companies be a compelling reason for changing a system that has worked well for so long? Moral and ethical failures are part of the human condition, they note, and no amount of rules or regulations can guarantee the honesty of a leader. Some allow that a temporary split in roles may be desirable or even necessary at times—when a company is experiencing a crisis, for example, or when a new CEO who lacks governance and boardroom experience is appointed. But they maintain that such instances are infrequent and temporary and do not justify sweeping change. Overall, they argue, the combined model has served the U.S. economy well, and splitting the roles might set up two power centers, which would impair decision making.

Critics of the split-role model also point out that finding the right chairman is difficult and that what works in the United Kingdom does not necessarily work in the United States. Executives in the United Kingdom tend to retire earlier and tend to view the nonexecutive chairman role (often a six-year commitment) as the pinnacle of a business career. This is not the case in the United States, where the normal retirement age is higher.

To allay concerns that combined leadership compromises a board's independence, opponents of separation have proposed the idea of a "lead director": a nonexecutive who acts as a link between the chairman-CEO and the outside directors, consults with the chairman-CEO on the agenda of board meetings, and performs other independence-enhancing functions. Some 30 percent of the largest U.S. companies have taken this approach. Its defenders claim that, combined with other measures—such as requiring a majority of independent directors and holding board meetings without the presence of management—this alternative obviates the need for a separate chairman.

On balance, the arguments for separating the roles of chairman and CEO are persuasive because separation gives boards a structural basis for acting independently. And reducing the power of the CEO in the process may not be bad: compared with other leading Western economies, the United States concentrates corporate authority in a single person to an unusual extent. Furthermore, rather than creating confusion about accountability, the separation of roles makes it clear that the board's principal function is to govern—that is, to oversee the company's management and hence to protect the shareholders' interests—while the CEO's is to manage the company well.

Separating the two roles, of course, is no guarantee of board effectiveness. A structurally independent board will not necessarily exercise that independence: in some companies with a separate chairman and CEO, the board has failed miserably in carrying out its oversight functions. What is more, a chairman without a strong commitment to the job can stand in the way of board effectiveness. The separation of roles must therefore be complemented by the right boardroom culture and by a sound process for selecting the chairman. The challenge of finding the right nonexecutive chairman, who not only must have the experience, personality, and leadership skills to mesh with the current board and management but also must show that the board is not a rubber stamp for the CEO, should not be underestimated. The ideal candidate must have enough time to devote to the job, strong interpersonal skills, a working knowledge of the industry, and a willingness to play a behind-the-scenes role. The best candidate is often an independent director who has served on the board for several years.

Should Directors Engage with Stakeholders?

Although wildly unpopular with and opposed by many CEOs and other senior executives, Drucker's recommendation that directors should engage regularly with people other than top executives and maintain an ongoing dialogue with the organization's major constituencies and the community at large is, if anything, more relevant today. The rise of the "corporate social responsibility" (CSR) movement is leading boards of directors into new governance territory occupied by stakeholders other than shareholders. While pressure on corporate *executives* to pay greater attention to stakeholder concerns and make corporate social responsibility an integral part of corporate strategy has been mounting since the early 1990s, such pressure is only now beginning to filter through to the board.

Specifically, the emergence of CSR as a more prominent item on a board's agenda reflects a shift in popular opinion about the role of business in society and the convergence of environmental forces, such as:

- **Globalization.** There are now estimated to be more than 60,000 multinational corporations in the world. Perceptions about the growing reach and influence of global companies have drawn attention to the impact of business on society. This has led to heightened demands that corporations take responsibility for the social, environmental, and economic effects of their actions. It has also spawned more aggressive demands for corporations to not just set their sights on limiting harm, but actively seek to *improve* social, economic, and environmental circumstances.

- **Loss of trust.** High-profile cases of corporate financial misdeeds (Enron, WorldCom, and others) and of social and environmental irresponsibility (e.g., Shell's alleged complicity in political repression in Nigeria, Exxon's oil spill in Prince William Sound in Alaska, Nike's and other apparel makers' links with "sweatshop" labor in developing countries, and questions about Nestlé's practices in marketing baby formula in the developing world) have contributed to a broad-based decline in trust in corporations and corporate leaders. The public's growing reluctance to give corporations the benefit of the doubt has led to intensified scrutiny of corporate impact on society, the economy, and the environment, and a greater readiness to assume—rightly or wrongly—immoral corporate intent.

- **Civil society activism.** The growing activity and sophistication of "civil society" organizations, many of which are oriented toward social and environmental causes, have generated pressure on corporations to take CSR seriously. Well-known international nongovernmental organizations (NGOs) such as Oxfam, Amnesty International, Greenpeace, the Rainforest Action Network, and the Fair Labor Association have influenced corporate decision making in areas such as access to essential medicines, labor standards, environmental protection, and human rights. The advent of the Internet has increased the capacity of these organizations—along with a plethora of national and local civic associations—to monitor corporate behavior and mobilize public opinion.

- **Institutional investor interest in CSR.** The growth in "socially responsible investing" has created institutional demand for equity in corporations that demonstrate a commitment to CSR. Recent growth in assets directed toward socially responsible investing has outpaced growth in all professionally managed investment assets in the United States, even though the mainstream financial community has been slow to incorporate nonfinancial factors into its analyses of corporate value.

These trends indicate that there is both a growing perception that corporations must be more accountable to society for their actions and a growing willingness and capacity within society to impose accountability on corporations—what Drucker long wrote about and called for is finally coming to pass. This greater accountability has profound implications for the future of corporate governance. It suggests that before long, boards will have to deal with a growing pressure to give stakeholders a role in corporate governance; disclose more and better information about their management of social, environmental, and economic issues; cope with increased regulatory compulsion related to elements of corporate activity that are currently regarded as voluntary forms of social responsibility; and respond to a growing interest by the mainstream financial community in the link between shareholder value and nonfinancial corporate performance. The discussion about corporate accountability to stakeholders, while often couched in the vocabulary of CSR, is therefore really a discussion about the changing definition of corporate governance, which is why it should receive a greater priority on the board's agenda.

In response, a growing number of boards are creating committees to better communicate with and stay abreast of the concerns of external stakeholders. Names for such committees include the *Corporate Social Responsibility*, *Stakeholder Relations*, *External Affairs*, or *Public Responsibilities Committee*. The board of General Electric, for example, has created a Public Responsibilities Committee to review and oversee the company's positions on corporate social responsibility and public issues of significance that affect investors and other GE key stakeholders. Also, with the blessing of their boards, companies are increasingly joining forces—with competitors, human rights and environmental activists (often formerly considered enemies), socially responsible investors, academics, and government organizations—to address social issues. At the 2007 World Economic Forum gathering, for example, two such coalitions were announced to address the issue of global online freedom of expression, particularly in repressive regimes. One, facilitated by Business for Social Responsibility (BSR), consists of companies that are facing intense criticism over their complicity with suppressing online free speech in China. This coalition includes such big names as Google, Microsoft, and Yahoo!. The other gathered together socially responsible investing firms and human rights advocates such as Amnesty International, Human Rights Watch, and Reporters without Borders.

Conclusion

So what would Peter Drucker, one of corporate America's most important critics, say about the state of corporate governance today? Undoubtedly, he would remind us that the efficacy of any reform should be measured in terms of results. By that standard, there have been some encouraging signs, but real progress has been modest.

He would also be concerned about "unintended side effects." Specifically, preliminary evidence is emerging that some boards have become even more defensive than before in the face of increased exposure to shareholder and legal action. And although there is no critical shortage of qualified directors at this time, it is not unreasonable to ask whether the new regulatory environment has made it harder to attract the right talent to serve on boards. It is therefore time to ask some penetrating questions: Has the regulatory pendulum swung too far? Do more highly regulated boards produce greater value for shareholders? For other stakeholders? For society? And could the additional regulatory burdens reduce business productivity and creativity, or even board assertiveness, especially in smaller firms?

His greatest concern, however, would be about the pervasive influence of greed and its erosive impact on capitalism and corporate culture. Drucker had long been disturbed and discouraged by boards' long-standing inability to rein in executive pay. In a 1984 essay, he persuasively argued that CEO pay had rocketed out of control and implored boards to hold CEO compensation to no more than 20 times that of the average worker. What particularly enraged him was the tendency of corporate managers to reap massive earnings while firing thousands of their workers. "This is morally and socially unforgivable," wrote Drucker, "and we will pay a heavy price for it." Maybe that time has come.

Author's Note: Substantial portions of this article are based on the author's recent book, *A Primer on Corporate Governance* (New York: Business Expert Press, 2009).

6

Corporate Purpose

Richard R. Ellsworth

There is only one valid definition of business purpose: to create a customer.

—Peter F. Drucker, *The Practice of Management*

The "Drucker difference" springs from and is grounded in a strong philosophy of management. This philosophy forms a foundational set of beliefs about the purpose of corporations, about human aspiration and behavior, and about the responsibilities of leaders to produce results. Peter Drucker's work is guided by a clear, coherent, and cohesive philosophy of management—a philosophy that has withstood the test of time. Central to his beliefs is a clear, unequivocal understanding of the purpose of businesses—a purpose that focuses the organization on serving the Good, or as Drucker puts it, "serving the commonweal." More than half a century ago, in his classic work, *The Practice of Management*, he declared,

> *A business's purpose must lie outside of the business itself. In fact it must lie in society since business enterprise is an organ of society. There is only one valid definition of business purpose: to create a customer. It is the customer who determines what a business is.*

His philosophy of purpose is even more relevant in today's world of knowledge-based competition and global markets. Yet, if you were to ask U.S. or U.K. executives what they believe the purpose of their company is, most would answer, "to make a profit" or, more precisely, "to maximize shareholder wealth." This outdated ideology has a stranglehold on the competitive performance of most corporations.

This chapter extends Peter Drucker's work by exploring the critical role that a customer-focused purpose has in satisfying valid societal needs, fostering more effective organizational performance, and giving work greater meaning.

What Is Corporate Purpose?

Corporate purpose sits at the confluence of strategy and values and answers the most fundamental question of corporate life: "Why does the company exist?" The answer to this question will affect the organization's strategy, determine the nature of its goals and objectives, influence its decisions, shape its way of managing, determine the degree of harmony or conflict among its goals and values, and affect the intrinsic motivation that employees receive from their work and consequently their commitment, initiative, and creativity.

At one level, the answer to this central question is easy. Corporations the world over are creations of their societies, designed to serve people's needs. The moral justification of corporate ends and the corporation's legitimacy to act rest on its benefits to society. Fundamentally, corporations exist to satisfy human needs by providing useful goods and services and meaningful, fulfilling work—and to do so while adding to society's wealth.

At the next level, the answer becomes more controversial and is burdened with greater ideological baggage. What specific purpose best serves these social ends? When the interests of the corporation's major constituents conflict, which interest should dominate? Management must ultimately decide whether the firm's highest priority is to satisfy customer needs, provide for the employees' welfare, maximize shareholder wealth, serve the national or community interest, or some other end. Peter Drucker is clear: the customer is the business's raison d'être.

Why a Customer-Focused Purpose Is Superior

The leaders of great companies that are capable of exceptional and sustained achievement—longtime industry-leading companies like Johnson & Johnson, Hewlett-Packard, Wal-Mart, and Procter & Gamble—have long known that providing value to customers (not the maximization of shareholder wealth) is fundamentally why their organizations exist, and that this purpose is key to their outstanding performance. In the intensely competitive, knowledge-based global markets of the future, this will be even more true.

A customer-focused purpose is superior to alternative formulations of purpose because it satisfies each of the following criteria more effectively:

- Provide the greatest focus on achieving competitive advantage.
- Create greater harmony among purpose, strategy, goals, and shared values.
- Raise employees' moral aspirations by focusing their work on meaningful human ends.
- Motivate managers to create the optimal level of total value—not just value for one particular constituent.
- Heighten intrinsic motivation, subordinating narrow self-interest to corporate ends.
- Enhance the firm's ability to create knowledge and, as Drucker admonishes us, to "make knowledge productive."
- Enable employees to see how their work is related to the firm's ultimate end.

- Sustain its meaning and relevance across cultural and national boundaries.
- Increase the legitimacy of the corporation's actions in society.

A customer-focused purpose not only satisfies each of these criteria but also can be readily aligned with the strategic needs of the competitive marketplace, the employees' welfare, and long-term shareholder wealth creation. The choice of this raison d'être and its embodiment in action significantly affect the outcome of critical, character-defining corporate decisions that shape strategies, commit resources, build core competencies, stimulate people's dedication to their work, and increase organizational cohesiveness. An ultimate corporate purpose of maximizing shareholder wealth does none of these things as well as a customer focus does them.

Balancing Stakeholders' Interests
Is a Vacuous Purpose

Some managers purport to resolve the problem of priorities by stating: "Our purpose is to balance the interests of all stakeholders." But the problem cannot be wished away by such a facile and vague proclamation. This solution is simply not practical. The interests of shareholders, customers, and employees often conflict. In fact, some of the most perplexing and critical decisions that senior managers face involve conflicts among the main constituents' interests. Someone has to resolve these conflicts.

A purpose that calls for the balancing of all constituents' interests provides no cohesive organizational focus. The definition of the ultimate purpose of each particular action is left up to the individual decision makers. Since there is no objective way of measuring the conflicting claims, managers must apply their own sense of the appropriate balance among the vying interests. A powerful strategy requires coherence and consistency—both internally among its parts and externally with the marketplace. A call to balance interests provides neither coherence nor consistency.

If corporate leaders do not clearly define and consistently reinforce a set of priorities, middle managers will do so. And the way they will do so will often be driven by self-interest, which flourishes in the absence of clear priorities and under the pressure of reward systems that are usually dominated by measures of short-term financial performance. The result often is decisions that are designed to meet budget targets and further individual managers' self-interests rather than to serve customer needs.

Why Not an Employee-Focused Purpose?

Similarly, a purpose that makes serving employees the ultimate priority has three major disadvantages. First, the purpose threatens to create an excessively internal focus that diverts attention and resources from the intense competitive discipline of the marketplace. There is no compelling force that ensures that an employee-focused purpose does not degenerate into self-serving complacency. Measures of success become annual increases in compensation, status, and other employee benefits. The organization can become quite content with its internal performance, even when competitors are drubbing it in the marketplace. Being satisfied with 5 percent growth when the market is growing at 8 percent is a formula for competitive extinction.

Second, the purpose potentially encourages politicization of the organization as individuals and subgroups compete among themselves for a larger share of the corporate pie.

Third—and this is a subtle, counterintuitive, yet critically important distinction—placing paramount emphasis on the employees' interests does not best serve those interests. Appealing to the employees' narrow self-interest, rather than to their service to others, deprives them of the full measure of satisfaction that comes from work that is clearly dedicated to ends greater than oneself—ends that benefit the lives of *others* and infuse work with greater significance, meaning, and intrinsic value.

Why Not a Shareholder-Focused Purpose?

The roots of the dominant Anglo-American economic ideology of shareholder wealth maximization can be found in two central beliefs. The first is that society as a whole benefits most when corporations' primary purpose is the maximization of the shareholders' wealth. Seeking the greatest return, capital flows to its highest and best uses as determined by the "vote" of the free markets. This efficient allocation of financial capital is assumed to produce the greatest amount of wealth for society; greater wealth is believed to equate to greater happiness and therefore to greater societal well-being. This line of reasoning raises serious questions. In an age when knowledge has surpassed capital as the dominant source of competitive advantage (and therefore of wealth creation), is this primary focus on capital allocation valid? Should we be focused on the productivity of human capital instead? Is wealth truly the determinant of human happiness? Most studies have found that above the poverty line, there is little relationship between wealth and happiness. This seems to be true across national and cultural boundaries.

The second belief is that since the shareholders are the owners of the corporation, the only legitimate corporate purpose is to create wealth for them. This view emanates from deeply ingrained beliefs about property rights, ideas that originated with the thoughts of philosophers Thomas Hobbes and John Locke in the seventeenth century. The way in which historical thought regarding property rights is currently applied to share ownership ignores the individual responsibility upon which the moral justification for property rights is predicated. Ideas developed in a largely agrarian world, where management and owners were one, are applied today under very different circumstances. As Drucker himself pointed out in *Reckoning with the Pension Fund Revolution*, the separation of management from ownership and the subsequent institutionalization of that ownership through pension funds, mutual funds, and other financial intermediaries have dissolved the remnants of the individual shareholder's responsibility in exercising her rights. The resulting imbalance of rights without responsibilities generates a serious tension in society. Thinking in America regarding how this tension should be resolved is still evolving.

There is consensus that shareholders "own" the right to the corporation's residual cash flow—the cash remaining after employees, suppliers, lenders, government entities, and other claimants have been satisfied. They also have the right to buy, sell, or give away their common stock. But do they "own" the right to have corporations managed primarily to satisfy their financial wants and needs? It would seem not. Three primary factors limit the shareholders' rights: first, the shareholders' inability (and, in many cases, their unwillingness) to fulfill the responsibilities commensurate with their ownership rights; second, the practical limits on their control over corporate actions; and third, the reality that both competitive advantage and value creation are derived primarily from the employees' (not the shareholders') ability to create knowledge and make it productive. Consequently, it falls to corporate leaders and boards of directors to ensure that the purpose, mission, strategy, and actions of the organization are directed toward aspirational ends and that operations in pursuit of these ends are executed ethically and in society's best interests.

Defining corporate purpose in terms of shareholder wealth maximization has proved to be quite analytically seductive. The return to shareholders in the form of dividends and stock-price appreciation is readily measurable and highly visible, and can be internalized by management in such seemingly objective metrics as return on investment, profit margins, and capital turnover. Consequently, total return to shareholders—particularly through the stock price—is seized upon by the business press as a convenient, real-time measure of corporate and CEO performance.

The arguments for a purpose of maximizing shareholder wealth contain several other serious flaws of logic. First, and this might be their biggest flaw, they ignore the impact of a purpose based on shareholder value on the members of the organization—on their commitment, motivation, and decisions. More on this later.

Shareholder Wealth Maximization Measures a Company's Wealth-Producing Capacity Too Narrowly   The wealth-producing capacities of the modern corporation are truly awesome and something to be treasured. But a single measure that narrowly circumscribes corporate contributions is inadequate to capture the multiplicity of ways in which a corporation generates value for society. Shareholders' wealth is a relatively small portion of the total value created by corporations. If society's interests are to be best served, a much broader view of the corporation's contribution is necessary—one that includes both wealth and value. Corporations can directly improve the material well-being of their customers, employees, investors, suppliers, distributors, and communities; and indirectly, they benefit society through tax payments. Also, customers are often able to purchase products at prices far below the product's value to them (for example, the value of laptops and lifesaving drugs). The value created is not all material. By offering employees work that serves worthwhile ends in an enriching environment, corporations can enable individuals to achieve a greater sense of personal dignity, self-worth, and meaning for their lives. One might ask, in terms of human benefit, is the quality of individual lives influenced more by growth in their net worth through investment income on common stocks than by the sum of the other benefits produced by corporate activity, including useful products, income, and the psychological and social benefits that individuals receive from working?

Wealth Capture Is Not Wealth Creation There is a danger that focusing on shareholder wealth will be transformed into a focus on "wealth capture" rather than "wealth creation." Most advocates of a shareholder-focused purpose agree that beyond a certain point, customer satisfaction and employee welfare potentially conflict with creating the maximum value for shareholders. Consequently, shareholder wealth measures encourage the development of strategies to capture wealth from customers, employees, governments, and suppliers for the benefit of shareholders. Strategies that produce the maximum increase in shareholder wealth are considered good, even if the wealth of these other constituents has been diminished by an amount greater than the increase in the shareholders' wealth. Clearly, society as a whole does not benefit from such a strategy.

Current Shareholder Value Does Not Equate to Future Competitiveness A firm's long-term ability to create value for society is dependent on its competitiveness—its ability in a fair and open market to provide customers with products and services that have greater perceived value (in terms of functionality and quality) than those of competitors at a lower cost, while making the necessary investments to ensure its future ability to do so. Declining competitiveness eventually leads to declining wealth production, and vice versa. Therefore, measures of wealth-producing capacity need to capture both the firm's competitive trajectory and its economic efficiency in using the human and financial resources at its disposal. Financial measures such as ROI, net present value, and economic value added are insufficient to capture the essence of sustained wealth creation.

Competitiveness and the maximization of current shareholder wealth are not synonymous. Although competitiveness and shareholders' returns tend to converge in the long term, it is a fallacy to believe that future competitiveness can be equated with achieving a high discounted rate of return on capital today. Often the opposite is true.

The pursuit of high returns can curtail investment and thus undermine competitiveness. The fact is that it may be necessary to sacrifice some economic value today to ensure tomorrow's competitiveness. Even in the long term competitiveness and returns can meet at either a high or a low level. This raises a critical question for corporate performance. In crafting the company's strategy, will focusing on the customer or on the shareholder—on the product market or on the capital market—be more likely to cause a higher-level convergence of competitiveness and shareholder wealth in the long term? A drive to maximize shareholder wealth potentially constrains expenditures on people, plant, and research and development, creating a cycle in which eroding competitiveness causes returns to decline, which motivates managers to try to bolster returns by further reductions in investment, leading to a further decline in competitiveness. Returns and competitiveness converge, but in an ever-downward spiral. The result is the destruction of a firm's value-producing capacity.

Managers of Financial Institutions Are at a Disadvantage in Making Resource Allocation Decisions Implicit in the ideology of shareholder value maximization is the belief that employees of capital-market institutions generally make better resource allocation decisions than do managers of industrial enterprises. Granted, investment bankers and professional fund managers see a wide array of investment alternatives and may be able to distance themselves from the more parochial company-specific concerns of corporate managers. However, they have serious limitations that prevent them from making optimal resource allocation decisions. Primary among these barriers are insufficient access to information, motivations that are not aligned with value-maximizing decisions, a lack of commitment to the long-term health of individual firms, and little control over the decisions of the corporate managers who ultimately invest the funds provided by the capital markets.

Shareholders Are Not a Monolithic Body Too often, discussions regarding shareholder wealth maximization are conducted at a theoretical level, ignoring the realities of the shareholders' widely varying motivations. The investments of all shareholders are motivated by the desire to increase their own or their clients' net worth. But shareholders are a diverse group made up of individuals (a group that ranges from the proverbial "widows and orphans" to short-term speculators); traders; institutional money managers at pension funds, mutual funds, and insurance companies; and a range of active investors. These shareholders have diverse objectives, and their time horizons vary greatly—from literally minutes to a decade or more. Warren Buffett's preferred holding period is "forever." Some shareholders are deeply concerned that "their" companies conduct themselves in a socially responsible manner. Active investors, such as Buffett, act like true owners and take responsibility for the performance of "their" companies. For others, a stock purchase is purely a financial transaction, and they feel no sense of responsibility for the firm's behavior. These people own "a stock," not a company, and they view their market transactions as "trades," not investments. Most individual investors do not even vote their proxies. This diversity among shareholders raises a fundamental question confronting managers who are seeking to maximize their firm's shareholders' wealth, "For which shareholders?" The answer determines the desired strategic action.

To counter corrosive capital-market pressures for short-term financial performance at the expense of longer-term competitive advantage, some forward-looking corporate leaders have actively pursued campaigns to increase the amount of their company's stock that is in the hands of committed long-term investors who have a true ownership mentality. Coca-Cola and Nike have been among the pioneers in such efforts. In Coca-Cola's case, one result of the campaign has been a significant investment by Buffett's Berkshire Hathaway.

What Is the Role of Profits?

Nothing that has just been said should be construed as meaning that customer-focused competitors do not aggressively seek to make a profit—they do. Profits are critical to a firm's ability to provide benefits to society and are a measure of its effectiveness and efficiency in doing so. Profits provide a discipline for management's decisions, act as a guide to value creation, and are an important criterion in selecting which customers to serve. The critical issues are the *level* of profitability that companies seek, whether profits are viewed as *ends* in themselves or as a *means* to achieving other ends (and therefore must be adequate to achieve these ends, rather than being maximized), and how managers trade off profitability against other strategic concerns that directly affect competitiveness.

When the corporation's purpose is the maximization of shareholder wealth, the level and growth of profits are the internal measures of this end. The importance of profits is accentuated because they are measurable with some precision, provide seemingly objective measures of performance, and are to a degree under the direct control of management. Measurability, objectivity, and control are of critical importance to formal management systems. The results of decisions can be measured in terms of a common denominator: the profits and returns on investment that they generate.

When the corporation's purpose is serving customer needs, profits become a means. They are an important source of funds to finance actions that serve the organization's ultimate purpose and fuel its growth. For U.S. nonfinancial corporations in aggregate, 90 percent of their total sources of funds between 1995 and 2008 was their own cash flow. Profits are also measures of the firm's success in achieving its purpose. They reflect the value that customers place on the company's goods or services. They also measure the organization's efficiency in using its resources in the pursuit of its aims. They are the result of—and an effective measure of—people's ingenuity in increasing the company's productivity and innovativeness. When a company is providing greater perceived value to its customers in a more efficient manner than its competitors, it will be rewarded with greater operating profitability. However, to increase customer satisfaction, the company may choose to expend these "profits" on price reductions; additional research and development; entry into new markets; greater customer service; or enhanced product quality, performance, and features—actions that reduce accounting profits, but can increase competitiveness and value creation. Profits also provide insurance against mistakes, and this allows leaders throughout the organization to take more risks, thus enabling greater innovation and longer-term thinking. In addition, high levels of profitability shield the company from adverse capital-market pressures.

When profits become a means to achieving valued ends, their role in the organization is transformed. The pursuit of profits is no longer seen as a frustrating constraint on creativity and individual initiative, restricting a manager's freedom to do what he thinks is right. Instead, profits come to be valued by virtue of their connection to worthy ends. This transformation affects morale, decisions, and the effectiveness of measurement and control systems.

Hewlett-Packard has long held this view of profits. HP's first stated objective is "To achieve *sufficient* profit to finance our company growth and to provide the resources we need to achieve our other corporate objectives. In our economic system, the profit we generate from our operations is the ultimate source of the funds we need to prosper and grow" [emphasis added]. Profits are a means to more important ends. They provide the necessary financial resources that, as David Packard said, "make all of the proper ends and aims possible."[1]

Similarly, Johnson & Johnson's credo places customers' interests first and shareholders' last among four priorities. It states, "Our final responsibility is to our stockholders. Business must make a *sound* profit. We must experiment with new ideas. Research must be carried on, innovative programs developed and mistakes paid for. New equipment must be purchased, new facilities provided and new products launched. Reserves must be created to provide for adverse times. When we operate according to these principles, the stockholders should realize a *fair* return" [emphasis added].

Likewise, Peter Drucker sees profits as a means—often a limiting factor—not an end. But in *Management: Tasks, Responsibilities, Practices*, he goes further, warning of the danger of misunderstanding the role of profits:

> *A business cannot be defined or explained in terms of profit. Asked what a business is, the typical businessman is likely to answer, "An organization to make a profit." The typical economist is likely to give the same answer. This answer is not only false, it is irrelevant. . . . The concept of profit maximization is, in fact, meaningless. . . .*
>
> *In fact, the concept is worse than irrelevant: it does harm. It is a major cause for the misunderstanding of the nature of profit in our society and for the deep-seated hostility to profit which are among the most dangerous diseases of an industrial society. And it is in large part responsible for the prevailing belief that there is an inherent contradiction between profit and a company's ability to make a social contribution. Actually, a company can make a social contribution only if it is highly profitable. . . .*
>
> *[P]rofitability is not the purpose of but a limiting factor on business enterprise and business activity. Profit is not the explanation, cause, or rationale of business behavior and business decisions, but the test of their validity.*

Purpose and the Making of Meaning

Work, particularly when it is dedicated to the service of worthwhile purposes, has long been recognized as being critical to crafting a meaningful life. A customer-focused purpose has three profoundly important, but often unrecognized, roles in the process of making work a source of meaning. First, it infuses the ends of work with intrinsic value. People who "love their job" have been shown to be devoted to the intrinsic value of the ends of work rather than the nature of the tasks per se. This devotion, in turn, helps people transcend the boundary between the self and the other. As individuals experience a sense of being united with a cause that they value and with the colleagues with whom they work to serve the cause, the boundaries of the self are enlarged to encompass the relationships with these ends and people. As the self expands, it also becomes more permeable—people become more open to new realities, aspirations, and ideas.

Second, purpose enhances self-actualization. The connection to valued ends and openness to new ideas and experimentation result in more rapid development of the self—in skills and knowledge as well as in the complexity of one's consciousness. The individual becomes simultaneously more *integrated* with her outside world and more *differentiated* as a unique, highly capable human being. Abraham Maslow (a person who both influenced and was influenced by Peter Drucker) captures the essence of the human drive to self-actualize, saying, "What a man *can* be, he *must* be." Maslow, Viktor Frankl, and others have concluded that self-actualization can be realized only as a by-product of self-transcendence—of being devoted to a cause or ideal larger than oneself. In *The Farther Reaches of Human Nature*, Maslow summarized the findings of his 30 years of research on self-actualization and self-transcendence:

> *Self-actualizing people are, without one single exception, involved in a cause outside their own skin, in something outside of themselves. They are devoted, working at something, something that is very precious to them—some calling or vocation in the old sense, the priestly sense. . . .*
>
> *The tasks to which [self-actualizing individuals] are dedicated seem to be interpretable as embodiments or incarnations of intrinsic values*

(rather than as a means to ends outside the work itself, and rather than as functionally autonomous). The tasks are loved (and introjected[2]) BECAUSE they embody these values. . . . [U]ltimately it is the values that are loved rather than the job as such.

Third, employees' personal identification with the customer-focused purpose, greater self-transcendence, and the resulting self-actualization have significant beneficial consequences for a company's performance. Such a climate generates the intrinsic motivation, commitment, individual initiative, and openness to new ideas that are the wellsprings of the creation of competitively critical knowledge. Increased commitment brings with it lower turnover, more stable relationships, and the subordination of narrow self-interest to the common interest. The firm's knowledge is less likely to walk out the door, and knowledge-creating networks remain intact. People are more aware of those to whom they can go to receive useful insight and knowledge applicable to solving a particular problem. As the boundaries surrounding the self become more permeable, the barriers between people fall, and trust is enhanced. Consequently, individuals are more open to the ideas of others, exchange ideas more freely, and are more willing to take the initiative (and the related risk) in pursuing new ideas. Clearly, a company with a committed, creative, ever-improving workforce that is capable of rapidly generating valuable knowledge has an advantage over a company with cynical, indifferent—even alienated—employees. Commitment increases, work becomes more focused, greater collaboration and cohesion are fostered among the organization's members, actions throughout the organization are more consistent with the corporate ends, people work harder and more thoughtfully, and people naturally take more responsibility for their own development. This purpose-driven self-actualization unleashes latent human potential and engages more of the full person.

Purpose and Strategy

Corporate purpose is the central unifying concept of strategy—the core guiding principle to which all aspects of a company's strategy should relate. It provides the reason why the company's strategy is important and brings significance to the corporate mission and direction to critical decisions. Corporate purpose shapes the content of strategy, the process by which strategy is formulated, the goals that flow from the strategy, and the decisions through which strategy becomes reality. As Vijay Sathe explores in depth in Chapter 7, strategy exists to achieve the purpose of the corporation.

A company's purpose also affects its vision. Vision is not something that is separate from purpose, mission, strategy, and shared values. It is the quality that is ingrained in each of these that defines a desired future state resulting from the fulfillment of the purpose and the strategy to get there. If the purpose itself is not inspirational, the envisioned future certainly cannot be. The vision cannot rise above the quality of the ultimate ends it is designed to achieve. The power of the vision rests in its ability to define a future that connects individuals within the organization with the service of noble ends beyond themselves. The vision provides people with a clear sense of not only why the company exists, but why its existence is important. The purpose defines the cause. The mission gives it depth and richness. Strategy gives it life.

But not just any purpose will do. The greatest power to infuse vision with value and a meaningful cause is provided by a customer-focused purpose.

Purpose and Strategic Orientation

A corporation's purpose orients its strategy and its dominant operating goals either internally to the organization or externally to the capital markets or product markets.

Regardless of its corporate purpose, a company's stated strategy is by its very nature aimed at a product market. Manifestly, a sound strategy requires an external focus on the competitive realities of the marketplace—on customers, competitors, and the firm's own core competencies. Because a customer-oriented purpose reinforces strategy by focusing on the product market, it produces the closest alignment of purpose, strategy, and operational goals.

For companies with a purpose of shareholder wealth maximization, however, the product-market strategy is potentially in conflict with its capital-market-oriented purpose. This high-level conflict is reflected throughout the organization in functional policies, subunit strategies, and the dominance of specific financial goals. While the firm is espousing a capital-market purpose, the daily decisions that execute the strategy must deal with specific product-market realities. Yet, the purpose demands that the goals that guide daily decisions be oriented to the needs of the capital markets and most particularly of the shareholders. The purpose and its related financial goals establish one set of priorities, and the strategy establishes another. The ultimate reference points that provide policy with meaning are ambiguous, causing confusion. The result is organizational schizophrenia, with the purpose and goals saying one thing and the strategy saying another. Consequently, operating decisions often lack coherence with strategy or are inconsistent at times with the competitive needs of the product markets. In either case, the organization begins to lose the close, harmonious contact with its competitive market environment that it needs.

Purpose and the Way of Managing

Ultimately, purpose must be transformed into action. As purpose is internalized in the company's management systems and informal processes, its influence on decisions affecting strategy and shared values, and thus on competitive performance, increases. By providing a strong central value that is capable of guiding thought and action, a customer-focused purpose fosters internal consistency, enables greater decentralization of decision making, and facilitates greater self-control.

For purpose to have significance, it must be infused into the way managers manage—into the way the company's strategy is formulated, and into the formal management systems (for example, performance measurement, compensation, control, and resource allocation systems) and organizational structures. It must also permeate the informal assumptions, beliefs, and values that form the company's culture. When this occurs, corporate purpose influences the deployment of people and capital, the investment returns deemed acceptable for these commitments, the time horizon incorporated into managers' decisions, and the measures used to judge performance. In each of these decisions, a customer-focused purpose can be a powerful counterbalance to short-term financial pressures.

Purpose and the Strategy Formulation Process

The strategy formulation process can differ significantly depending on the content of the corporate purpose. When the purpose is shareholder-focused, strategy is often shaped to conform to top-down financial goals such as return on investment and earnings growth. Measures of competitiveness (such as market share, efficiency, speed of new product development, and product functionality and quality) are significant only as means for producing the required returns. As a result, financial targets drive the decisions that form the *real* strategy.

In contrast, a customer-focused purpose directs the organization's attention to changing customer needs, competitors' actions, and the company's long-term competitiveness. Consequently, there is no inherent conflict between purpose-derived corporate goals and business-unit strategies. Both are product market–driven. When managers must make difficult decisions, the central issue guiding their deliberations is whether the action will enable the firm to serve customers better and more efficiently than its competitors can over time. Financial considerations are an important part of the discussion, but, unlike the situation in shareholder-focused companies, they do not drive it.

Reflecting Purpose in Operational Goals

The specific goals that guide decisions throughout an organization have their genesis in the corporate purpose. In essence, goals internalize the preferences of the markets that the company has chosen to serve. A principal task of management is to embed the corporate purpose into a set of ever more precise and specific goals and performance measures that act as targets of aspiration as well as measures of achievement. Eventually, these strategies and related goals must, as Peter Drucker says, "degenerate into work."

The purposes of increasing shareholder wealth and serving customers' needs are manifested in fundamentally different priorities among goals. One set of goals reflects the capital market; the other, the product market. One set emphasizes financial returns; the other, market share, customer satisfaction, and innovation. For the long-term health of the company, financial goals should be the results—not the drivers—of product-market strategies. They should act as guideposts for measuring progress in achieving the desired competitive results and in generating the necessary internal funds to finance the chosen strategy.

Unfortunately, however, when budgets, performance measures, and resource allocation decisions continually reinforce the message that the shareholders' interests are paramount, the employees' inclination to be responsive to customer needs is undermined. Financial objectives are blunt instruments, providing little strategic direction. Budgets do not discriminate among the multitude of line items based on their importance. Each item is a candidate for cutting in order to "make the budget." The budget becomes an embodiment of the disharmony of purposes between the individual and the company.

But this need not be the case. A remarkable change in mindset occurs when the profit pressures represented by the budget are internalized as vital *means* for serving the customer and as measures of the firm's success in doing so. When this occurs, the budget becomes a tool for achieving valued ends. It is no longer seen as an unwanted financial constraint on a manager's activities imposed from above. Of course, the tension between profit and customer interests remains, but two important transformations take place.

First, profits are regarded not as ends in themselves, but as a necessary source of funds for investing in the future and as a valid measure of current performance in serving customers.

Second, managers at all organizational levels assume greater ownership of the responsibility for resolving the tension between current profits and the interests of the customers and between the short term and the long term. During the year, actual performance relative to the budget may present difficult choices—for example, whether to "make the budget" by cutting costs or to overrun the budget in order to maintain a given level of service or product development expenditures. The trade-off is made based on what will best serve present *and future* customers.

Managerial Influence through Shared Values Grounded in Purpose

Corporate purpose is *the* core end value of the organization. The values, beliefs, and assumptions embedded in corporate purpose are the bedrock of the corporate value system. They shape corporate character. The values that cluster around alternative conceptions of purpose have a decidedly different quality, and consequently generate cultures with disparate strength and character. The company can be viewed either as a moneymaking machine or as a vehicle for satisfying human needs. By definition, if the central end value is not shared—if employees do not believe in its intrinsic worth—then this foundation and the resulting corporate culture are weakened, and corporate values lose much of their power to influence and direct actions.

Managing Change with Purpose

When a firm focuses on its sustained ability to provide greater value to customers than competitors do, the organization becomes more sensitive to anticipating customer needs, competitors' moves, and the evolution of the firm's valued core competencies. A major responsibility of leadership is to make people aware of the contradictions *among* their values (for example, the priority among constituents reflected in the organization's purpose) and *between* reality (the organization's current performance and the market dynamics) and their values (as embodied in the organization's purpose-driven vision), and then to recognize and accept the need for change to overcome the undesirable contradictions. Change may not be comfortable, but it is seen as necessary. In fact, change can even be valued when it is seen as a means of better serving the customer—the firm's most valued and highest end.

The Responsibilities of Leadership

At the heart of effective corporate leadership is the responsibility to define, promote, and defend a meaningful, overarching purpose for corporate activity—one that ennobles those who serve it, stimulates individual commitment, and brings unity to cooperative action. This responsibility is at once strategic and moral. It has its origin in two fundamental duties of management. The first is grounded in duties to customers, employees, shareholders, and communities—the leader's responsibility for corporate performance. The company's contribution to each of these constituents can be measured by its ability to create value (recall the distinction made earlier between creating value and maximizing shareholder wealth). Value creation is determined solely by the contributions of the firm's people and their ingenuity in using the resources at their disposal. People who find meaning and opportunities for personal growth and achievement through their work perform at higher levels, with more commitment, intensity, cohesion, and creativity; and thus they enhance corporate performance, to the benefit of all major constituents.

The second responsibility of management is to ensure that employees are treated with respect and dignity, not as tools to corporate ends. In the pragmatic reality of daily competitive life, this is possible only if there is a harmony of individual and corporate purposes related to work. When the corporate end is one that the individual finds to be of personal value and worthy of service, then actions to achieve this end become, in essence, actions to encourage the achievement of personal aims. From the employees' viewpoint, the company becomes an instrument for realizing some of their highest aspirations through their work. Only when the corporation truly becomes a path to meaning, fulfillment, and achievement of *common* purpose for the people who work there is it possible to treat people as ends in themselves.

Guided by a constructive, widely shared purpose, the corporation can be a positive moral force. If they are led well, corporations can become a source of valued products that enrich lives, opportunities through work that yield individual self-realization and bring increased meaning to life, and economic performance that increases society's wealth. If they are led poorly, they will be a source of increasing personal alienation and frustration—oppressive to the human spirit and its highest aspirations and corrosive to value creation. The choice of corporate purpose defines the difference.

Author's Note: This chapter is based on Richard Ellsworth's book *Leading with Purpose* (Stanford, Calif.: Stanford University Press, 2002).

7

Strategy for What Purpose?

Vijay Sathe

The profit motive and its offspring, maximization of profits, are just as irrelevant to the function of a business, the purpose of a business and the job of managing a business. In fact, the concept is worse than irrelevant. It does harm. It is a major cause for the misunderstanding of the nature of profit in our society and for the deep-seated hostility to profit which are among the most dangerous diseases of an industrial society.

—Peter F. Drucker, *The Practice of Management*

In far too many companies, the answer to the "what" question about vision is "To be #1." But #1 in what? . . . And even if the "what" is clear, why should employees and the other stakeholders care?

—Vijay Sathe, *Manage Your Career*

Strategy integrates the various functional perspectives of a business and takes a holistic view of what the firm is trying to achieve and how it can perform better. It is at the heart of what managers do, and everyone in the organization must understand and align with the strategy if the enterprise is to serve its customers better than its competitors do, thus gaining competitive advantage.

But most thinking about strategy fails to ask a fundamental question: strategy for what purpose? Strategy as taught and practiced in most places focuses on industry analysis and competitive advantage but ignores this fundamental question because the answer is taken for granted—the purpose of the enterprise is to increase shareholder value.

There are two problems with this line of reasoning. First, how can strategic thinking be applied to nonprofits, volunteer organizations, and government agencies that do not have shareholders? Second, how can strategic thinking be applied in companies and countries that do not pray at the altar of shareholder value or that are beginning to question its primacy? Even in the United States, long a bastion of shareholder value maximization, this dogma is coming unglued. As the *Financial Times* recently reported on March 16, 2009:

> *A palace revolution in the realm of business is toppling the dictatorship of shareholder value maximization as the sole guiding principle for corporate action. As so often with regicide, many of the knives are in the hands of the old regime's own henchmen. Jack Welch, the former General Electric chief executive who ushered in the reign of shareholder value maximization a quarter-century ago, told the* Financial Times *last week that "shareholder value is the dumbest idea in the world."*[1]

Welch had told the *FT* on March 13, 2009: "Shareholder value is a result, not a strategy. . . . Your main constituencies are your employees, your customers and your products."[2]

But the fundamental question remains unanswered. Shareholder value is a result, yes, but on the path to what purpose? Drucker was the first to provide a clear answer more than 50 years ago in *The Practice of Management*: "There is only one valid definition of business purpose: *to create a customer.*"

In Chapter 6 of this book, Richard Ellsworth expands on Drucker's seminal work and provides additional rationales for why the primary purpose of every enterprise must be to create and serve a customer. As he points out, the so-called balanced approach—which assumes that the interests of the various stakeholders need to be traded off, with one stakeholder's interests receiving priority at one time and another's at another time, depending on which wheel needs the most grease—provides no directional guidance for the enterprise. It is equivalent to driving a car with greased wheels but without any steering mechanism!

Starting with the primacy of purpose, this chapter will build on Drucker's original insights and also incorporate contemporary strategic thinking to present a simple framework for understanding, analyzing, and executing strategy in any enterprise. The resulting POSE framework can be used to ask and answer four central questions:

1. **Purpose.** What purpose is the strategy supposed to achieve, why, and how?
2. **Objectives.** Are there clear objectives to assess progress in the achievement of that purpose?
3. **Strategy.** What is the strategy, and is it appropriate for achieving the objectives?
4. **Execution.** How well is the strategy being implemented?

All four parts of the POSE framework must be internally consistent and must reinforce one another if the purpose of the enterprise is to be successfully achieved. I will now describe each part of the framework (summarized in Figure 7-1 for ready reference) and show how it can be used to *assess* and *diagnose* the success or failure of strategy.

Purpose

Every enterprise needs to ask three simple questions about its purpose:

PURPOSE
What Purpose Is the Strategy Supposed to Achieve, Why, and How?

Mission	*What* is the purpose of the enterprise?
Vision and Values	*Why* is the purpose worth achieving?
O, S, and E	*How* will the purpose be achieved (via objectives, strategy, and execution)?
Stakeholders	For whose benefit does the enterprise exist?
	To what extent are the expectations of all the stakeholders being met?
	What is the priority among the stakeholders? Which stakeholder is number one?

OBJECTIVES
Are There Clear Objectives to Measure the Achievement of Purpose?

Financial	Return on investment? Shareholder value? Value for other stakeholders?
Nonfinancial	Quantitative and qualitative? (e.g., employee turnover? customer retention?)

STRATEGY
What Is the Strategy, and Is It Appropriate Given the Objectives?

Drucker	What business are we in? Who is the customer? [*Business definition*]
	What does the customer consider value? [*Value proposition*]
Porter	*Industry attractiveness*: BTE, buyers, suppliers, substitutes, complements, rivals
	Competitive strength (versus rivals) [*Generic strategic position*]
	(1) Low economic cost position (*not* to be confused with low selling price!)?
	(2) Customer-perceived differentiation (customer WTP higher price)?
	(3) Blue ocean (low cost + differentiation)?
Resources	People? Brands? Money? Connections? Locations? Monopolies?
Capabilities	Quality? Innovation? Functional competence? Core competence? Activity system?
	[Do these resources and capabilities offer *competitive advantages* that support the company's value proposition per Drucker and its strategic position per Porter?]

EXECUTION
How Well Is the Strategy Being Executed?

Skills and Fit	Are the people properly selected, educated, and trained? (skills vs. challenge)
Policies	Do the policies motivate appropriate behavior? (alignment? motivation?)
Responsibility	Are the people responsible for performing activities or achieving results?
Accountability	Are the people held accountable? What are the consequences for nonperformance?

All four parts of this framework (purpose, objectives, strategy, and execution) must be internally consistent and reinforce one another to achieve success.

One or more of these elements may be embodied in the culture of the organization, i.e., may be among its important shared assumptions (cultural roots).

FIGURE 7-1 "POSE" Framework for *Assessing* and *Diagnosing* the Success or Failure of Strategy

1. *What* is the purpose of this enterprise? We will refer to this as its *mission*.
2. *Why* does the enterprise exist? Why is it important to employees and other stakeholders? We will refer to this as its *vision and values*.
3. *How* will the purpose be achieved? For any enterprise, the appropriateness of its *objectives*, *strategy*, and *execution*, and whether these are all aligned with its mission, vision, and values, will determine how successful the enterprise is in achieving its purpose.

The *how* question is obviously vital, but a focus on the *how* without the *why* puts the cart before the horse. The horse is not going to go very far or very fast.

Ask most people *why* their company exists, and you get a blank look. After a moment's reflection, most people, if they are honest, will say, "We exist to make money for shareholders." But as we've seen, Peter Drucker warned more than 50 years ago that profit is not an objective. Profit is necessary, but the purpose of the business enterprise is to create and serve a customer.

Drucker's wisdom and foresight unfortunately fell on deaf ears among the advocates of shareholder value, those who have led their enterprises with only the shareholder in mind, and this mindset fostered Enronitis and also contributed to the financial meltdown of 2008. There is public anger today, just as Drucker predicted in his famous quote at the beginning of this chapter, because of the widespread belief that business leaders are interested only in protecting their shareholders and lining their own pockets with fat paychecks and big bonuses, even as they beg for taxpayer dollars.

A recent award-winning documentary, *The Corporation*, captures this public perception very well by depicting capitalism's most important institution as a psychopath: "Like all psychopaths, the firm is singularly self-interested: its purpose is to create wealth for share-holders. And, like all psychopaths, the firm is irresponsible, because it puts others at risk to satisfy its profit-maximization goal, harming employees and customers and damaging the environment."[3]

An example of a company that does *not* fit this stereotype at all is Edward Jones, which was lucky enough to benefit directly from Peter Drucker's advice over many years. The company's *mission* is to offer sound financial advice to the serious long-term individual investor. Its *vision* is that this is a worthy undertaking because individual investors, particularly those without fat wallets, are not well served elsewhere. What these investors need is sound advice to secure their financial futures, and the employees of the firm providing this service can find this work to be meaningful and intrinsically rewarding. The *values* of the firm are to put the client first and to treat everyone—clients, employees, and suppliers—with integrity and respect.

Edward Jones is the highest-performing company in an industry that was dominated by giants such as Merrill Lynch prior to the recent financial implosion because it served its clients better than anyone else; maximizing shareholder value is not the company's purpose. And by the way, in pursuit of the company's purpose, the financial advisors (FAs) and other employees derive a special sense of satisfaction from changing their clients' financial lives for the better. That is one reason why the company is routinely in the top ranks of "Fortune's 100 Best Companies to Work For" and other similar surveys of customer and employee satisfaction. As the *Wall Street Journal* reported, "In the midst of the worst stock market since the 1930s, Edward Jones has been growing the old-fashioned way. . . . Whereas other securities firms are shrinking, its 12,000-broker force has added 998 brokers this year. It plans to add another 5,000 by 2012."[4] Thus, customer-focused Edward Jones continues to prosper and grow as its shareholder-focused rivals falter and fail.

I will return to the example of Edward Jones throughout this chapter to illustrate how the POSE framework can be used to both *assess* and *diagnose* a firm's strategy.

Traps

Leaders can fall into one or more traps that prevent the development of a clear and compelling answer to the what and the why questions concerning the purpose of their enterprise. Some examples of these traps are

1. **Believing that strategic decisions can come only from the top.** Strategic decisions can also come from lower levels—not all wisdom is in the CEO's cranium. Intel's realization that it was a microprocessor company, not a memory chip company, came from the actions of its middle managers. Honda's strategic shift to lightweight motorbikes for everyone resulted from actions of its U.S. managers, not Mr. Honda.

2. **Going to an executive retreat and coming down with the answer.** As has happened at many other companies, the top managers of ESL, a subsidiary of TRW, went to an "executive retreat" and came down with the answer, just as Moses came down from the mountaintop with the Ten Commandments! Unfortunately, unlike the words Moses brought down, the words of these top managers were neither clear nor compelling for the intended audience.

3. **Becoming obsessed with numbers.** Far too many leaders assume that a stretch target is their mission. For example, the strategy of the ESL top managers was to reach $1 billion in sales within five years. The mission was clear enough, but the why question remained unanswered. As a key lower-level manager observed, "It is like a book you read where you understand every sentence on every page, but when someone asks you what the book

is about, you have to say, 'I don't really know' because you can't see the big picture."

4. **Letting your need for growth drive your thinking.** As Clayton Christensen points out in *The Innovator's Dilemma*, top executives at Apple Computer in the early 1990s believed that the Newton, the firm's pioneering personal digital assistant, had failed because "only" 140,000 units were sold in the first two years after its introduction, whereas much higher sales had been expected. In contrast, Apple II, the company's pioneering personal computer, sold 43,000 units in its first two years after introduction, but this was heralded as a great success! Why? Because a few million dollars of sales was seen as a great result when Apple was a start-up company and had no sales to speak of, whereas Newton had to become a billion-dollar business to be of any interest to the top executives of a $7 billion Apple Computer.

The lesson for leaders who want to avoid this trap is this: *the market does not care about your growth needs!* So it makes little sense to judge the success of a pioneering product based on a company's growth needs. Newton's "failure" to achieve its vision led to Palm Pilot's "success," and Palm Pilot *did* eventually become a billion-dollar success story.

Stakeholders

If the what (mission) and the why (vision and values) questions cannot be readily answered, they may be deciphered by asking the following three questions:

1. **For whose benefit does the enterprise exist?** These are the key stakeholders. It is important to distinguish stakeholders from parasites—those who seek to extract some benefit from the en-

terprise without making any contribution to it. An example would be a frivolous lawsuit designed to harass an enterprise into settling a case without merit out of court.

2. **To what extent are the expectations of each stakeholder being met?** This provides an assessment of how successful the enterprise is. An enterprise that surpasses the expectations of *all* its key stakeholders is successful, and the amount by which their expectations are exceeded is an indication of its level of success. Conversely, an enterprise that does not meet the expectations of *all* its key stakeholders is unsuccessful, and the number of stakeholders whose expectations are not met, and by how much, is an indication of how unsuccessful the enterprise is.

3. **What is the priority among stakeholders?** Which stakeholder is the "north star," the number one stakeholder? When the interests of stakeholders come into conflict, the one whose interests prevail is the primary, north-star stakeholder. The unquestioned assumption that the shareholder is the north-star stakeholder in for-profit enterprises is now being challenged not only by scholars (see Richard Ellsworth's chapter in this book), but also by increasing numbers of practitioners, even in America, which is the bastion of shareholder capitalism. Informal surveys that I have conducted with managers around the world, for example, indicate that those from Asian cultures point to customers as the north-star stakeholder, those from France point to employees, and Scandinavians view society as the north-star stakeholder.

In addition to providing an assessment of the success or failure of an enterprise's strategy, the thinking and discussion needed to answer these questions typically provide important clues, if not direct answers, to the what question (mission) and the why question (vision and values) concerning purpose. In the case of Edward Jones, for example, the answers to the three questions just given are as follows:

1. The key stakeholders of Edward Jones are (a) its clients, the individual investors, (b) its financial advisors (FAs) and other staff members, (c) the suppliers of the financial products it offers to its clients, and (d) the firm's partners, who are the owners.

2. Edward Jones surpasses the expectations of all the key stakeholders. It is number one relative to its competitors in client and FA satisfaction surveys conducted by J. D. Powers and *Registered Rep*, its suppliers covet the firm's patient investors and its wide distribution reach, and the partners—whose firm earns the highest return on equity in the industry—plow capital back into the firm and have no intention of selling the firm or taking it public. Thus, we can *assess* the strategy of Edward Jones as being highly successful.

3. When the interests of the stakeholders of Edward Jones come into conflict, the interests of its clients always prevail. Most tellingly, the firm advises clients to buy and hold high-quality stocks and mutual funds for the long term; the resulting low turnover in its clients' portfolios generates lower trading commissions for the FAs and lower profit for the partners. By not yielding to the temptation of manufacturing and selling its own financial products to make more money for itself, Edward Jones sidesteps any conflict of interest and advises clients to choose the suppliers that best fit their needs. Clearly the clients, the individual investors, are the firm's north-star stakeholder.

So far, we have been able to assess the strategy of Edward Jones as being highly successful and determined that its fundamental purpose is to serve its clients, the individual investors, who are the firm's north-star stakeholder. We now need to diagnose *why* Edward Jones's strategy has been so successful in achieving its purpose. The short answer is that the firm has developed what Drucker calls a "theory of the business" that works extremely well, as he points out in a *Harvard Business Review* article:

> *A theory of the business has three parts. First, there are assumptions about the environment of the organization. . . . Second, there are assumptions about the specific mission of the organization. . . . Third, there are assumptions about the core competencies needed to accomplish the organization's mission. . . . It usually takes years of hard work, thinking, and experimenting to reach a clear, consistent, and valid theory of the business. Yet to be successful, every organization must work one out. . . . In fact, what underlies the current malaise of so many large and successful organizations worldwide is that their theory of the business no longer works.*

The POSE framework builds on Drucker's theory of the business and also incorporates contemporary strategic thinking on industry analysis and competitive advantage (see Figure 7-1). Having covered "P," let us now turn to "O."

Objectives

As Drucker emphasizes in *Management: Tasks, Responsibilities, Practices*, "The basic definition of the business and its purpose and mission have to be translated into objectives. Otherwise they remain insight, good intentions, and brilliant epigrams which never become achievement. . . . Objectives are not abstractions. They are the . . . standards against which performance is to be measured."

Objectives may be qualitative or quantitative, financial or nonfinancial, but they must be *meaningful milestones* on the path to the achievement of purpose.[5] Although most enterprises have plenty of financial and even nonfinancial targets, these often do not pass the test of being *meaningful milestones*. Why? Because most enterprises cannot answer the question "strategy for what purpose?" Without a clearly understood purpose, there is no way to talk about meaning-ful milestones on the path to that purpose.

A key objective for Edward Jones is *healthy growth* in the number of its financial advisors—*healthy* in the sense that the new FAs, who are carefully selected and intensively trained, must become produc-tive quickly, and *growth* because the firm views the opportunity to serve its number one north-star stakeholder, the serious long-term individual investor, to be far greater than its market share currently is. Specifically, Edward Jones aims to get to 20,000 FAs by 2017.

Strategy

Drucker's three famous questions provide clarity regarding the busi-ness and its customers in light of the purpose of the enterprise: What business are we in? Who is the customer? What does the customer consider value? Because all enterprises, whether for-profit, nonprofit, volunteer, or government, have "customers" that they serve, Drucker's approach can be applied to any organization, unlike the sole goal of maximizing shareholder value.

Once Drucker's three central questions have been answered, di-rect competitors can be identified—these are other players that are attempting to serve the same customers with the same value propo-sition. Contemporary strategic thinking can then be applied to de-termine the relative attractiveness of the industry and the firm's competitive advantage vis-à-vis its rivals, so there is no need to say more here except to note that the specific trade-offs that the enter-prise makes will determine whether the strategy is aligned with the purpose or not.

The specific trade-offs that Edward Jones made ensured that its strategy was always pointed to its north-star stakeholder, the indi-vidual investor. As John Bachmann, who was managing partner of Edward Jones from 1980 to 2004, wrote:

As Professor Porter points out in Competitive Strategy, *one defines trade-offs not in terms of what one chooses to do but what one chooses not to do. . . . I will identify and briefly examine some of the trade-offs Edward Jones made. None made us unique. None suggests moral superiority. However, each makes us a little more different and, together, they make us very different. So different, in fact, that few if any competitors would even want to emulate us. . . . That led us to a decision not to serve large institutions. All our competitors were doing so and we had nothing special to offer. We also chose not to serve those who trade frequently. . . . We chose not to manufacture our own products.*[6]

Thus, appropriate trade-offs are what give the firm a distinctive focus, alignment with its north-star stakeholder, and competitive advantage.

Execution

There is an old and very silly debate about which is more important, strategy or execution? The simple answer is both. Without a sound strategy, the firm will flounder. But what good is a sound strategy without effective execution? There are four key elements to effective execution: having people with the right skills that fit the job and the organization, motivating and aligning them with the purpose of the enterprise using the right policies, giving people responsibility for results, and holding them accountable for results.

Skills and Fit

An enterprise needs to carefully select people with the necessary skills who fit the job and the organization, and then invest in continuous education and training to facilitate their growth. With the proper skills and fit, it is possible that people will come to view their work not just as a job or as a career, but as a calling.

Edward Jones selects its financial advisors carefully from thousands of prospects each year and invests heavily in their education, training, and mentoring. Most new FAs join the firm viewing it as a job. Those FAs who learn to do the job well and progress in the organization may come to see it as a rewarding career that can sustain them and their families. Later, typically five to ten years after they begin, some of the FAs begin to hear from their clients about how the financial advice they gave had changed their clients' lives for the better, perhaps by enabling them to send their kids or grandkids to school or by allowing them to retire with dignity. For these FAs, what was once a job and then a career becomes a calling to change people's financial lives for the better. These FAs no longer work to make money; they work to serve others, and money becomes a by-product of a meaningful work life. For example, more than 1,000 Edward Jones FAs have voluntarily participated in the firm's "Goodknight plan," in which a seasoned FA gives up some of his compensation by handing over smaller accounts to a new FA in order to better serve the larger accounts, resulting in better service for both smaller and larger customers.

Policies

Do the policies of the enterprise motivate the appropriate behavior by promoting what Peter Drucker calls "self-control"—a situation in which people understand what needs to be done and why, and feel emotional ownership of it and accountability for getting it done? To achieve self-control, people must be given responsibility for delivering results, not for performing activities spelled out in a job description. And they must be held accountable for results.

Edward Jones encourages its associates to exercise self-control via its system of "responsibility-based management" (RBM). In consultation with the person to whom she is responsible (the word *boss* is taboo in the firm because it connotes authority rather than responsibility), each associate develops a list of four or five key responsibilities for which she is accountable, with the understanding that she has the freedom to determine how best to accomplish these results.

Responsibility and Accountability for Results, Not for Activities

It is easy to fall into the activity trap. For a salesperson, for example, results are not the number of sales calls made per week but the number of sales dollars generated. When it is difficult to quantify results, the danger of falling into the activity trap is greater, and this is an even larger problem when attempting to measure and improve the productivity of knowledge work. For developing other people, for example, it is easy to count the number of days of training provided for them, but did they develop new knowledge or skills as a result? Even a rough qualitative assessment of the latter is more meaningful than a precise quantitative measurement of the former.

What happens when people are held accountable for performing activities rather than for delivering results? Naturally, their focus then shifts to performing these activities rather than taking ownership of finding new and better ways to deliver the best results. Edward Jones's RBM system strives to ensure that people are held responsible and accountable for results, not for activities. For example, the firm does *not* use job descriptions, since these tend to focus on activities rather than on results. The "Goodknight plan" that the FA Jim Goodknight created was not part of his job description. He came up with the idea in the quest for better results.

Conclusion

The POSE framework is based on Drucker's seminal work and also incorporates contemporary thinking on strategy. It explicitly asks, "Strategy for what purpose?" and provides a method for answering this question that is at the heart of strategy.

As illustrated throughout this chapter with the example of Edward Jones, POSE is both an assessment tool and a diagnostic tool. It can be used to assess how well an enterprise is performing relative to its purpose and objectives. It can also be used to diagnose how an enterprise can do better. One common malady is purpose drift, that is, the strategy remains unchanged, but the purpose has drifted. Another is strategy drift, that is, the purpose remains the same, but the strategy has drifted. POSE can help to diagnose such problems and ensure that P, O, S, and E are internally consistent and aligned in order to achieve success.

8

The Twenty-First Century: The Century of the Social Sector

Sarah Smith Orr

It is in the social sector that we find the greatest innovation, the greatest results in meeting human needs and what we will do as a sector will determine the health, the quality and the performance of the twenty-first-century society.[1]

—Peter F. Drucker

Peter F. Drucker, who was both pragmatic and prescient about the turmoil and the challenges facing society in both the United States and globally in the late twentieth and early twenty-first centuries, offered this observation in various forms in his interactions with social-sector leaders as the twenty-first century began. He observed further that neither the government sector nor the business sector would "save"[2] society. Drucker was unwavering in this belief. He foresaw the upheavals in the business sector, and he was very clear about what government could and could not do. He believed that the critical components of a healthy civil society are embedded in the work and performance of the social sector. Indeed, he felt that the "one thing that stands between us and social catastrophe"[3] was the nonprofit/social sector.

Drucker and the Social Sector

During the last 30 years of his work and his life, Drucker became increasingly focused upon the work of the social sector. Beginning in the early 1970s, Drucker—along with John Gardner,[4] an active and distinguished leader in educational, philanthropic, and political life—served as an esteemed voice speaking about the social sector as the indispensable sector of society.

Seeking another's perspective on Drucker's role in and influence upon the social sector, I spoke with Frances Hesselbein, the founding president of the Peter F. Drucker Foundation for Nonprofit Management (the Drucker Foundation), and someone for whom Drucker had great respect.[5] Drucker and Gardner, according to Hesselbein, "gave leaders in the nonprofit sector the courage to be equal partners with business and government," and because of their influence, people began to listen.[6] Drucker's extensive work in this sector began to motivate other thought leaders to focus on nonprofit managers and leaders.

In August 1989, the *Harvard Business Review (HBR)* published an article written by Drucker, "What Business Can Learn from Nonprofits." Hesselbein had a chuckle in her voice as she described the general reaction to the article—people thought, "There must be a typographical error; he can't really mean nonprofits."[7] In the article, Drucker described the two areas of practice that he thought business gave only lip service to: mission and strategy, and the effectiveness of the board. While he conceded that not all nonprofits are doing well, he felt that in the crucial areas of motivation and productivity of volunteer knowledge workers, nonprofit management leaders are "truly pioneers, working out the policies and practices that business will have to learn tomorrow."

During the late 1980s and the early 1990s, Drucker began to immerse himself in the study and support of the nonprofit sector, primarily through consulting relationships and through the Drucker

Foundation. His quest, through the foundation that bore his name, was to improve the performance of nonprofit organizations. Drucker asserted that "good intentions are no longer enough," declaring that "results will be essential as expectations for the sector to perform will heighten."[8] This admonition was supported by the publication of a self-assessment tool for nonprofit organizations and leaders entitled *The Five Most Important Questions You Will Ever Ask about Your Nonprofit Organization.*[9] This tool provides a guide for volunteer board members and executives of nonprofit organizations to use to assess why they are in business, how they are performing, and what they need to do to improve the performance of their organization. It asks five essential questions: *What is our mission? Who is our customer? What does the customer value? What are our results?* and, *What is our plan?*

The second question is the most challenging one for nonprofit leaders because *customer* feels like a business term, not a term, activity, or focus for a social-sector organization. But Drucker challenged nonprofit leaders who resisted looking at their organizations as entities that served customers:

> *You cannot arrive at the right definition of results without significant input from your customers. . . . In a nonprofit organization . . . the focus must be on what individuals and groups value—on satisfying their needs, wants, and aspirations.*[10]

The Drucker self-assessment tool places emphasis on planning as an ongoing process. The focus on planning and results requires that an organization assess what it should do and also what it should not do, including what it should abandon—programs or activities that no longer contribute meaningful results.

In my work consulting with nonprofit organizations during the past two decades, I have seen and continue to see the application of the concepts promoted by the Drucker Foundation (now the Leader to Leader Institute) self-assessment tool within the growing number of social change initiatives in the United States. These concepts have become indispensable for nonprofit leaders who are seeking a high level of effectiveness in leading social change.

Because Drucker saw the social sector as the collective change agent of society, he challenged nonprofit leaders to see themselves "life-sized" and to see the mission of their organizations and the work they do as the means to "forge new bonds of community, a new commitment to active citizenship, to social responsibility, to values"[11]—the qualities of civil society that many, including Drucker, saw as decaying and dissolving during the last few decades of the twentieth century. Thus Drucker's conclusion was that it will be the social sector that will save our pluralistic society.

The Social Sector Defined

Drucker firmly maintained that the use of the term *nonprofit* to describe the sector is a misnomer because "nonprofit" is a financial and tax descriptor. It describes what an organization in the sector doesn't do, rather than what it does do. Instead, the terminology promoted by Drucker, which accurately describes the work of these institutions as a whole, is "the social sector."

In the United States, the nonprofit/social sector includes a highly diverse group of organizations, and it is in fact this very diversity that characterizes this sector.[12] The sector supports and advances a variety of religious, social, and economic endeavors. These organizations receive tax-exempt status and in return are expected to engage in charitable activities, which, in turn, benefit individuals, households, and communities. One way to gauge the potential impact of this sector is to consider its size, including the number of organizations that fall within it.

In 1996, the IRS identified a total of 654,186 groups in the United States that belonged to the social sector. Between 1996 and 2008, the number of social-sector organizations increased 81 percent to a total of 1,186,915. From 2007 to 2008, this sector experienced one of the highest percentage increases in recent years, rising by 5.2 percent, or 58,548 organizations. And that doesn't tell the whole story; not all nonprofits are included because certain organizations, such as churches, need not apply for tax exemption.[13] Further evidence of the size and impact of the sector is contained in the IRS publication *Statistics of Income Bulletin*, Winter 2008: "The aggregate book value of assets, as reported by charitable organizations that filed IRS information returns for Tax Year 2004, was $2.5 trillion, a real increase of 222 percent over the total reported for Tax Year 1985."

The same bulletin reported that expenditures by the same organizations, for the same period, increased by 182 percent, "a real annual rate of growth of nearly 6 percent," compared with that of the GDP, which grew at a real annual rate of 3 percent for the same period.[14]

Drucker was astounded by the number of social-sector organizations and their impact as he considered the growth in the sector's productivity, the scope of its work, and its contribution to American society[15]—his prescient view of the impact of the sector became a reality.

General acceptance of the label "social sector" has been incremental and, since the mid-1990s, its use has expanded to describe not only the sector, but also actions within the sector—specifically, the innovative and entrepreneurial social initiatives undertaken through traditional nonprofit organizations as well as the more independent initiatives that reach beyond the traditional definitions of organizations and sectors.

Leading Social Change: Innovation and Entrepreneurship through the Social Sector

In his classic work *Innovation and Entrepreneurship*, Drucker describes innovation as an entrepreneurial strategy. "The product or service it carries may well have been around a long time . . . but the strategy converts . . . [an] old, established product or service into something new." Those who use innovation as an entrepreneurial strategy in the social sector are frequently called *social entrepreneurs*, a relatively new concept.

> *Social entrepreneurs act as the change agents for society, seizing opportunities others miss and improving systems, inventing new approaches, and creating solutions to change society for the better. While a business entrepreneur might create entirely new industries, a social entrepreneur comes up with new solutions to social problems and then implements them on a large scale.*[16]

However, creative and enterprising people who have led innovative, entrepreneurial initiatives that benefit individuals and society have been around a long time.

Consider Andrew Carnegie's gift of millions of dollars to libraries. He believed that those who accumulated wealth had a moral obligation to give it back to society. From his perspective, however, "charity" dealt only with symptoms and not with the problem. He chose, instead, to establish institutions that created opportunities for "anyone with the right character to be successful and rich"—hence his establishment of more than two thousand Carnegie Libraries in Europe, the United States, and the English-speaking world in the late nineteenth and early twentieth centuries.[17]

Consider, too, Jane Addams, social worker and reformist, who founded Hull House in Chicago in 1889. Hull House offered a new model, a welfare center for the neighborhood poor, that was replicated across the country. Over the past century, there have been numerous mission-focused individuals, like Addams and Carnegie, leading social change.

As stated earlier, however, in more recent years, these change leaders have been described as social entrepreneurs, a term often credited to Bill Drayton, CEO and founder of Ashoka.[18] How have social entrepreneurs changed the nonprofit sector of old to the social sector of today? Ashoka's description of the social entrepreneur is

> *One who develops a strategic service vision, a competitive strategy, a strategy for building networks and partnerships, leads, retains, and rewards people, manages entrepreneurially, treats donors as investors, works with communities, develops viable earned income strategies, considers the scale of the project and strategies for success, and is able to manage organizational change.*[19]

If the conceptual work of social entrepreneurs, either through an organizational structure or independently, is not new, the question arises: What is different? Why would Drucker look to the social sector as the source of the greatest innovation, the greatest results in meeting human needs? Examining the work of two social entrepreneurs, the mission of their ventures, their organizational models, and the impact of their work reveals a context for Drucker's viewpoint as found in the chapter's opening quotation.

The following two social entrepreneurs are passionate, innovative, energetic change leaders who have designed new ways to respond not only to social problems, but also to opportunities to transform those problems. They have created new markets, new ways of doing business, new ways of creating relationships across traditionally restrictive boundaries, new financial resource models, and new types of partnerships, all resulting in the creation of sustainable social change. These are nontraditional entrepreneurs, the likes of which are flourishing around the world.

TransFair USA

Transforming lives and markets are measurable impacts (or results) that are evident in the work of TransFair USA. Upon graduating from college, Paul Rice, the founder, president, and CEO of TransFair, bought a one-way ticket to Nicaragua and spent 11 years working on economic development projects in remote farming communities. This experience led him to conclude that international aid, as a model for addressing poverty and social injustice, was not a sustainable and empowering change model. Instead, market-based approaches were more effective. After running a fair trade coffee cooperative in Nicaragua, Paul moved back to the United States, got an MBA, and launched TransFair in 1998, a nonprofit, mission-driven organization that certifies and promotes fair trade products in the United States. It audits and licenses U.S. companies to display the Fair Trade Certified[20] label on their products if they meet strict international, social, and environmental standards.

At a February 27, 2009, conference sponsored by the Kravis Leadership Institute[21] and cosponsored by the Peter F. Drucker/Masatoshi Ito Graduate School of Management and the Drucker Institute, Rice described TransFair's model as one that uses the market and partnerships between farmers and companies to address poverty and to lift farming communities out of poverty. He defined fair trade as a means of connecting farmers directly with the global market, bypassing the intermediary, so that farmers get a much better price for their harvest. This, in turn, allows farmers to put food on their tables, keep their kids in school, and invest in sustaining the land. Fair trade helps farmers build their communities without depending on government or international aid. Instead, market linkage and an empowered involvement are core strategies for community development—using the market as a source of opportunity rather than as a problem.

Why did Rice choose to launch this entrepreneurial initiative through a nonprofit model? It was due to his passion for social justice—a passion from his childhood—and his sense that this was an organizational model that the social justice movement would accept. Did that decision help or hinder his initiative? On the plus side, Rice explained that as his plan to launch TransFair USA evolved, he found that he was able to establish more credibility with the industry (the coffee industry initially) because its nonprofit status reinforced the message to farmers and industry that mission rather than financial gain was driving TransFair's certification service. On the minus side, at least initially, TransFair's mission and its nontraditional nonprofit business model created more challenges for him in raising capital to increase the scale of the venture because it was perceived as being too much like a business—it didn't feel or look like a "charity." In fact, it took him two years to raise the first $200,000.

If Peter Drucker had been in the audience at the conference at which Rice spoke, he would have found clarity in TransFair's mission, which relates to the first of the five important questions that Drucker would have asked about TransFair. Next, Drucker would have appreciated TransFair's customer focus—not only on Trans-Fair's primary customer, the farmer, but also on other customer groups. Rice described an early need to understand the primary market for coffee, the American consumer, and that customer group's value proposition; he learned that fair trade, from a consumer's perspective, was not only about charity for farmers who don't have high incomes, but, equally important, about access to high-quality products. TransFair, then, was launched based on the alignment between the interests of the farmers and what the marketplace values. Just as important for TransFair, it was promoting a connection between the coffee industry (another customer) and the core values of the customers of the coffee industry. As an example, Rice described an early marketing initiative of fair trade coffee through college campuses both as a "wake-up call" for the coffee industry to understand what a current and future consumer group considered value and as a great example of the power of social change driven through market forces (student consumers).

The example Rice gave was TransFair's initiative to encourage college students to call upon campus food-service departments to use Fair Trade Certified coffee. The food-service department of one large university declined to do so until students protested, then the department relented and contacted Starbucks, its provider. The department discovered that Starbucks didn't yet offer fair trade coffee through college campus food-service departments. As a result, the university canceled the contract with Starbucks and gave it to another company that immediately converted the account to fair trade.

Starbucks got the message—and shortly thereafter decided to make fair trade coffee available to all its college campus food-service customers nationwide. Currently, TransFair works with leading brands such as Starbucks, Sara Lee, Green Mountain, and Dunkin' Donuts. Major retailers, such as Whole Foods Market, Wal-Mart, Target, and Costco, are partners as well.

What have been TransFair USA's results, the fourth in Drucker's five questions?

> In the past ten years, TransFair has leveraged limited resources to certify over 334 million pounds of coffee for the U. S. market. This translates to an additional $140 million flowing back to rural farming communities, over and above what they would have earned by selling their harvests to local middlemen. This extra income enabled farming families to achieve a better standard of living, as well as invest in community development projects such as schools, healthcare clinics and potable water projects.[22]

In addition, TransFair is no longer just about coffee. There are other Fair Trade Certified products: tea, cocoa, fresh fruit, rice, sugar, wine, spices (vanilla), and flowers. Retail sales of Fair Trade Certified products in the United States exceeded $1.2 billion in 2008, while global sales of these products were almost $4 billion. Fair trade premium payments helped communities build infrastructure, support education, deliver affordable health care, protect the environment, and meet other community needs.

As a response to Drucker's fifth question, "What's our plan?" Rice sees fair trade as a global mainstream market and movement, one of the most important and vital sustainability trends in the world today. Eventually, TransFair USA seeks to extend the fair trade model to industrial as well as agricultural products, and to goods produced in the United States as well. In the end, its aim is to channel more of the opportunities and benefits of globalization to all the underprivileged farming and working families who today are being left behind.[23]

YWCA of Greater Los Angeles

The YWCA of Greater Los Angeles (YWCA/GLA) was established in the late 1880s as an organization for women who needed a safe-haven residence in an urban setting as they launched their careers. Its mission today is built upon these early roots—the empowerment of women and the elimination of racism. Yes, it has its community centers, swimming pools, exercise programs, and residences, but the difference now is in the YWCA/GLA's vision for what it must become to serve the needs of the community—a highly focused, results-oriented, mission-driven organization.

Faye Washington, CEO and chief social entrepreneur, described her journey of transforming the YWCA of Greater Los Angeles at a February 2009 conference. She defined the YWCA/GLA as an organization with a rich history, but with built-in obstacles that prevented it from thinking outside the box.[24] Washington asserted that it was a matter of survival that drove the transformation of the YWCA/GLA.[25] As she took the helm as CEO, she found that safe housing for a key segment of the population that the organization served—at-risk 16- to 22-year-olds who participate in the YWCA's federally funded job corps program—was lacking. Having recently retired from a long and successful career in the public sector, Washington had knowledge of the federal grant process, so she went to the federal government for assistance in creating a safe housing program. While there was interest, no timeline was provided for that assistance, so she countered with a different proposal: "Why doesn't the YWCA/GLA build a new facility, and you, the federal government, lease it back?" She knew that if the YWCA/GLA built the building, it could ensure safe housing arrangements for at-risk youth, but, equally important, it could create a sustainable funding stream flowing to the organization that could help underwrite other important programs. After government leaders accepted the proposal, the old building housing the program was sold and the YWCA purchased a parcel of land, over an acre in size, in downtown Los Angeles.

By early 2009 the building project had a cost of $60 million, an amount that was *fully funded*. How was that accomplished? The resource model that Faye Washington and her board partners designed involved funds from traditional private donations, foundations, and negotiated "deals" with other developers in the area: buying and selling affordable housing credits, selling air space, and the acquisition of a new-market tax credit. As Washington describes the organization's work, "Every financial instrument was brought to bear on the project." With a fully funded project, Faye Washington was able to negotiate a $4 million per year lease for the building with the federal government—funds that are now used as resources for the development of other programs.

The success of this project unleashed the YWCA/GLA's ability to think differently about what it can do as a nonprofit/social-sector organization. Through its planning process, there was a decision to position the YWCA/GLA in certain communities, establishing "empowerment centers." Through a partnership established with Supervisor Gloria Molina and the Los Angeles Board of Supervisors, the YWCA/GLA purchased a city block in East Los Angeles for $1, where a new $9 million facility is now under construction. The center concept includes an "Empowerment Council" composed of grassroots community members. The East Los Angeles community fully embraced the concept, took over the responsibility for raising funds, and assumed full ownership of the results. Through its partnership with the YWCA/GLA, the community will have a community center, a day-care center, online college classes, and workforce development programs—all free to the public. Washington sees this model as highly effective and one that will be used for the empowerment of other communities within the greater Los Angeles area—and one that exemplifies Drucker's vision for the social sector, "forging new bonds of community, a new commitment to active citizenship."[26]

Like Paul Rice of TransFair USA, Faye Washington is passionate about the mission of her organization and has tenaciously held onto the mission throughout organizational planning and negotiations with various business partners. By returning to the founding roots of the YWCA movement, she helped her board of directors stay true to this mission while engaging in new models of leadership, collaboration, resource development, community building, and program implementation. The leadership of the YWCA/GLA understands its customers and what they value; it has developed the ability to seek and secure a wide variety of resources, to know who fits with what, to engage and leverage various constituent groups, and just as important, to identify the programs that customers consider to have value and abandon those that are no longer relevant. According to Washington, "It's all a balancing act; you have to have determination and a commitment to your mission."[27]

Creating the Tomorrow of the Social Sector

In the April 1996 issue of *Drucker Foundation News*, Drucker wrote, "Innovation is risky, it's difficult, it's hard work." He continued with an admonition that to survive in a rapidly changing society, a social-sector organization will have to innovate, especially in raising revenues. Further, he stated his dislike for the word *problem*, preferring instead to talk of opportunities, "for every problem is an opportunity for us."[28] He affirmed his view that the old ways of doing business in the sector no longer suffice. "We are moving from charity to the social sector . . . an enormous opportunity and an enormous challenge."[29]

Drucker considered social entrepreneurship to be as important as economic entrepreneurship: "more important, perhaps. . . . [T]he social entrepreneur changes the performance capacity of society."[30] His view was that as a country, we were on the verge of enormous innovation through the social sector.

Nearly a decade and a half later, we have experienced what Drucker foresaw: enormous opportunity, enormous challenge, and the changed performance capacity of society through the work of social entrepreneurs, as the previous two examples illustrate. We are seeing new and complex economic structures and funding opportunities emerge in the social sector.

The Edward M. Kennedy Serve America Act was approved by both houses of Congress and signed into law by President Obama in April 2009. This landmark bill will greatly enlarge national- and community-service programs, including the expansion of AmeriCorps; the promotion of community- and public-service activities; and direct aid to nonprofit groups. Included in the aid to nonprofit groups is the creation of a "Social Innovation Funds" pilot program to provide money for social entrepreneurs and nonprofit groups that are developing innovative and effective solutions to national and local challenges.[31] Government, as Drucker often professed, is not the answer, but it can be a viable partner; he felt that it could be an important area of entrepreneurship and innovation.[32]

The whole notion of using market approaches—hybrid approaches that combine nonprofit with for-profit approaches from both the traditional nonprofit model and a corporate social responsibility model, cross-sector partnerships and allies, new legal structures such as the L3C legal structure,[33] and nontraditional approaches alongside of traditional approaches for generating capital—is now seen as an acceptable way to respond to social needs.

Drucker's championing of the social sector has brought new thought leaders to the sector. Jim Collins (*Good to Great and the Social Sectors: A Monograph to Accompany Good to Great*, 2005) became a self-described "passionate student" of the social sector. Collins made this statement as he concluded his author's note:

> *I've come to see that it is simply not good enough to focus solely on having a great business sector. If we only have great companies, we will merely have a prosperous society, not a great one.*[34]

Collins gained a new understanding of the complexities of the social-sector organization as he explored the application of the *Good to Great* principles to social-sector organizations. He found, for example, that there are wide variations in the social-sector economic structures (funding sources), an area identified by Drucker as a primary focus of innovation for social-sector organizations if they are to thrive in the twenty-first century. Collins's study and his heightened appreciation of the social-sector organization are best framed in the following statement:

> *The inherent complexity requires deeper, more penetrating insight and rigorous clarity than in your average business entity. You begin with passion, then you refine passion with a rigorous assessment of what you can best contribute to the communities you touch.*[35]

Rice and Washington, the social entrepreneurs featured in this chapter, demonstrated penetrating insight and rigorous clarity combined with passion, and also demonstrated how they employed variations in economic structure and diverse social structures to achieve greater social impact. Innovative and entrepreneurial efforts such as theirs will provide the means for us, as a society, to address our most challenging social and environmental problems by reformulating them as opportunities. The evolution of social entrepreneurship is a phenomenon that has a context and is a source of credibility. It is creating a plethora of options for addressing great societal opportunities (problems) through sustainable social change. Leaders who may or may not define themselves as social entrepreneurs, who embody and act with passionate determination, who have the ability to build networks of resources, and who employ innovation with the skillfulness of an entrepreneur will indeed make the twenty-first century the century of the social sector that Drucker foresaw.

9

Economic Environment, Innovation, and Industry Dynamics

Hideki Yamawaki

The problem that is usually . . . visualized is how capitalism adminis-ters existing structures, whereas the relevant problem is how it creates and destroys them.

—Joseph A. Schumpeter
Capitalism, Socialism, and Democracy

The most important work of the executives is to identify the changes that have already happened. The important challenge in society, eco-nomics, politics, is to exploit the changes that have already occurred and to use them as opportunities.

—Peter F. Drucker, *The Age of Discontinuity*

In ancient civilizations, whether Egypt, Greece, Rome, or China, any ruler's wish list would probably include the supernatural power to predict the future. In modern corporations, managers also wish for the ability to see into the future. I can almost hear what they are wishing: "I wish I could predict the future. Then I could see fu-ture market and societal needs, start investing now in future technology, and leave the competition in the dust when the future arrives." Unfortunately, most of us are not equipped with such a supernatural ability to predict the future. In *Managing for Results*, Peter Drucker even warned us that we will get into trouble if we try to predict the future. Instead, he suggested the more modest goal of trying to identify the future that has already happened. Leaving aside predicting the future, we still face the challenge of identifying the future that has already happened. We may then ask, how can we go about trying to find the changes that have already happened? Is there any framework available to guide us in our efforts to find the future?

One way to address this question is to look at the environment surrounding us. Although we understand the importance of the business environment in which a firm operates, we often refer to macro-economic indicators as the key source of information for assessing the state of the environment facing a firm. This approach is quite adequate if the question is how current fluctuations in the economy affect the business in the short run. On the other hand, if we want to ask about the changes that have occurred in the industry, the economic structure, and the society, we may want to resort to an alternative, more structural approach.

This chapter proposes three aspects of an organization's environment that must be analyzed to help us answer these questions.

Industrial Environment

No matter what industry you are in, the environment that affects your managerial decisions most directly is the specific industrial environment. There are two broadly defined sets of elements that make up the industrial environment: basic conditions and market structure. An industry's basic conditions are those that define the basic demand and supply conditions. The list of basic conditions on the demand side includes consumer preferences, purchasing patterns and methods, the existence of substitutes, the cyclical character of demand, and the marketing attributes of the product being sold. The list of significant basic conditions on the supply (or production) side includes the nature of the technology that underlies the production process; technological characteristics of the product sold; the scope for customization and standardization; the extent to which various activities such as product development, procurement, and production are coordinated; and the conditions associated with sourcing raw materials and intermediate inputs.

Identifying the economically significant basic conditions that are prevalent in an industry at a particular point in time is essential for a manager. These basic conditions fundamentally determine the economic features of a market (Figure 9-1). For example, consumer preferences, purchasing patterns and methods, and the scope of marketing attributes of the product being sold determine the price elasticity of demand, the extent to which product differentiation is an important element in the industry, and the scope of advertising and marketing that are present in competition. The characteristics of the relevant technology determine cost conditions, such as the importance of economies of scale.

The scope for product differentiation and the presence of economies of scale are also important sources for creating barriers to entry and determining the potential number of competitors in the industry. A variety of conditions associated with the location and ownership of raw materials and intermediate inputs and the characteristics of suppliers certainly determine cost conditions within the industry, the height of the barriers to entry for new firms, and the concentration of suppliers. The extent to which product design, procurement, and production are structured should determine opportunities for vertical integration and sources of operating efficiency and flexibility.

To summarize, important features of market structure, including the number of buyers and sellers, the height of the barriers to entry

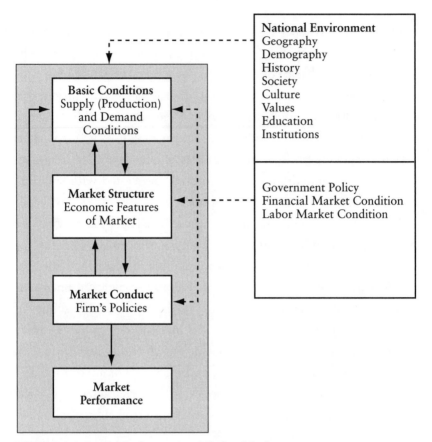

FIGURE 9-1 Industrial Environment and National Environment

for new firms, the extent of product differentiation, cost structures and the importance of sunk costs, and barriers to exit, are thus most likely to be dependent on basic conditions.

The notion that the industrial environment or the structure of the industry influences the conduct of sellers and buyers in the industry, which, in turn, determines the performance of the industry, was developed by Edward S. Mason at Harvard in the late 1930s and has been elaborated by many others, such as Joe S. Bain, Richard E. Caves, and F. M. Scherer. A firm's decisions on changing prices and outputs, product design and quality, R&D expenditures, marketing and sales-related expenditures, and investments in physical capacity are all influenced by the structure of the market.

This approach is a very general way to organize the key economic factors that affect your business and industry. In *Competitive Strategy*, Michael E. Porter reinterpreted and redesigned this approach for business executives. This approach, captured in his five-force industry analysis framework, has proved to be very useful.

But how does this approach to organizing the key environmental factors help us to find the future that has already happened? The traditional industry analysis conducted for a particular point in time is static in its nature and may not necessarily give us any clue to what is happening in the industry. On the other hand, if we take a series of snapshots of the industry environment over a certain period of time, we are able to recognize a pattern that suggests that some changes have occurred in the industry. Think of the PC industry in the United States in the early 2000s and compare it with the same industry in the late 1980s. As is well known, the difference in basic conditions and market structure between the two periods was dramatic. The change in market structure was induced because the key elements of basic conditions, such as consumer preferences and knowledge of personal computers, changed significantly, and all the key elements of basic conditions on the supply side—technological conditions in particular—also changed during this period. If we examine the basic conditions of the industry in the late 1990s through the early 2000s, we can easily observe the larger role played by the industries using the products and services of the computer industry in driving demand for the computer industry. Complementary products such as digital imaging and printing, music, multimedia, the Internet, e-mail, and smart phones all contributed to expanding the scope of the computer industry. The emerging new technologies in the related industries altered the basic conditions of the computer industry, while the emerging new generations of consumers who appreciated such new innovations and devices also changed the basic premise upon which the computer industry had operated for many years. Identifying the economically significant elements of basic conditions and market structure and recognizing the emerging pattern of changes in those elements and their trends are the starting points for the quest to determine the future that has already occurred.

The idea that we must recognize the changes that have taken place in the industry's basic conditions and market structure, however, runs counter to one's economic intuition. Business managers in an industry are used to considering market structures as being determined by some kind of natural force and believe them to last forever. No wonder the original premise of the structure-conduct-performance model was that market structure is to a large extent exogenous and solid. However, as more and more industries are exposed to fast-paced rivalry in technological innovations, this old premise of market structure being exogenous no longer holds. On the contrary, strategic decisions on R&D and innovation, and investments in tangible and intangible assets, are shaping industrial and market structures. In this classical Schumpeterian world, the firm's market conduct and interfirm rivalry are the major forces for changing the industry's basic conditions and market structure over time. As Schumpeter mentions in *Capitalism, Socialism, and Democracy*, the two prime movers are the inventor, who pioneers the change, and the entrepreneur, who develops it. In Figure 9-1, the arrows running from market conduct to basic conditions and market structure indicate the market forces that alter basic conditions and market structures. What this indicates to managers is that they need to recognize not only the discontinuous changes that have occurred in consumer preferences and behavior and the nature of technology, but also what forces are driving these changes.

A significant force for change is innovation, which occurs in multiple areas: design, product, process, or business model. Innovation, in turn, is induced by three broadly defined drivers: demand conditions, input (factor) conditions, and competition (Figure 9-2). Thus,

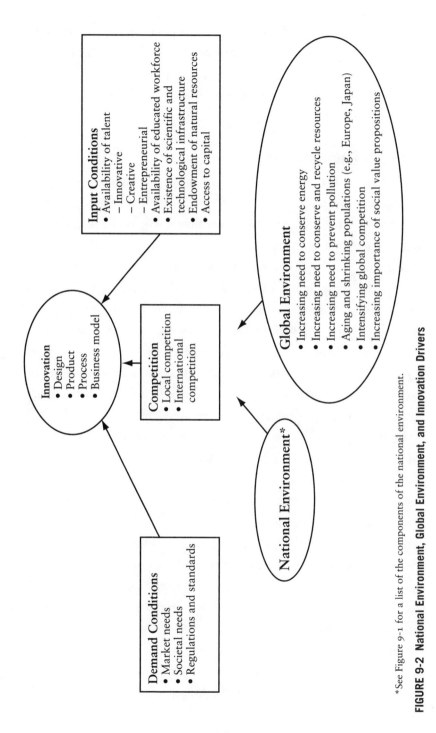

Input Conditions
- Availability of talent
  - Innovative
  - Creative
  - Entrepreneurial
- Availability of educated workforce
- Existence of scientific and technological infrastructure
- Endowment of natural resources
- Access to capital

Innovation
- Design
- Product
- Process
- Business model

Competition
- Local competition
- International competition

Demand Conditions
- Market needs
- Societal needs
- Regulations and standards

Global Environment
- Increasing need to conserve energy
- Increasing need to conserve and recycle resources
- Increasing need to prevent pollution
- Aging and shrinking populations (e.g., Europe, Japan)
- Intensifying global competition
- Increasing importance of social value propositions

National Environment*

*See Figure 9-1 for a list of the components of the national environment.

FIGURE 9-2 National Environment, Global Environment, and Innovation Drivers

the industry's basic conditions and market structure are altered by innovation, which, in turn, is driven by the elements of basic conditions and market structure. It is therefore important to identify those drivers of innovation and the factors that affect them.

National Environment

Peter Drucker first visited Japan in 1959 to give a seminar for Japanese managers at Hakone, a mountain resort. He later wrote that the main reason he accepted this invitation was that it would be a great opportunity to see Japanese paintings, not that he was interested in meeting Japanese managers.[1] Whatever the reason for his initial visit, he became a keen observer of Japanese management, the economy, the socioeconomic aspects of Japan, Japanese arts, and the country in general. Japanese managers, in turn, loved his books and writings and read more of his books on a per capita basis than managers in any other country in the world. Why did the Japanese read Peter Drucker so much? I guess an answer to this question lies in the way in which Drucker drew the managerial implications of the changing business environment. His deep understanding of Japanese history, economy, social aspects, and political system, and of course Japanese arts, was the framework that he referred to when he drew managerial lessons for changing environment (see Chapter 1 for a detailed discussion of management as a liberal art).

Given the existing institutions and environment, what would happen if a societal, political, or economic factor changed? What would you do if that were to happen? Drucker drew many of his lessons in terms of the country's context and its national environment. Many management consultants went to Japan, but none of them were more successful than Drucker—the notable exception being W. Edwards Deming. This presumably is because the consultants offered recommendations without taking the context into account, and their suggestions were often irrelevant in the Japanese setting.

What does this tell us? First, we must recognize the difference in the national environment that exists within a country and among countries. This is important because the national environment affects basic conditions and industrial and market structures, and is an important element in shaping corporate organization and business practices for the firms that located in the country (see Figure 9-1). To make this point, it is sufficient to point out that the representative models of Japanese, German, and U.S. corporations are distinctive when they are compared with one another. These corporate models are different because the underlying economic, social, cultural, institutional, and historical elements of the national environment differ among these countries. Second, and more relevant to the topic of this chapter, the key elements of a national environment—demography, society, culture, and values—also change and create discontinuities in the economy and in society. We must recognize these changes in national environments as well. Third, the elements of the national environment will affect both the demand and input conditions as they become drivers of innovation (see Figure 9-2). Market and societal needs for innovation are determined by the stage of economic development, the degree of consumer sophistication, demography, and the goals of government and its institutions, among other factors. The availability of creative, innovative, and entrepreneurial talent; the existence of a well-educated workforce; the existence of scientific and technological infrastructure; and access to capital to finance R&D projects and promising new business ventures are all dependent to a certain degree on national environment.

Think about Japan in the late 1950s and early 1960s. If you worked for one of the Japanese automobile companies, what options did you have in order to compete with the U.S. and European automakers? The first thing that managers had to recognize was that Japan in those days faced a multitude of constraints, both domestic and international. Given the limited geographic space and the limited supply of skilled workers after World War II, managers had to address the question of how to increase productivity, lower production cost, and improve quality without damaging labor relations. There was a growing, potentially huge demand for a wide range of vehicles in both domestic and international markets. (West) German automakers had to address the same question during this period. However, they lived and worked in a context and national environment different from those in Japan. For Japanese firms, thinking about using low-wage immigrant workers was a nonstarter, given Japan's traditional public sentiment and policy toward immigrant workers. And, indeed, Japanese firms, particularly Toyota, came up with the concept of lean production.

German firms, on the other hand, leaned toward relying on immigrant workers from the neighboring lower-wage countries.[2] If we use the terminology of Figure 9-2, the Japanese and German automakers faced similar situations in terms of demand conditions. In this competitive situation, Japanese firms felt that it was more urgent to catch up with the U.S. and European automakers. The input conditions faced by Japanese and German automakers differed markedly. As Drucker noted in *Innovation and Entrepreneurship*, for Japanese firms, the constraints they faced in their national environment drove their processes of innovation. Here need was the source of innovation.

One can then speculate that the type of innovation that one country tends to pursue is different from another country's path of innovation because their national environments, basic conditions, and market structures are different. A casual comparison between the national and economic constraints faced by the corporations in China and Japan leads us to conclude, without much doubt, that their corporate models and business practices have developed and are evolving differently, and that incentives for innovation and innovative solutions will not be the same. Again, what is important for us is to recognize that one country's national environment differs from another country's national environment and that their evolutionary and change patterns are quite distinctive. Accordingly, the differences in the types of innovation, their patterns, and the speed of innovation and diffusion that emerge among different countries reflect these underlying national factors.

As I suggested earlier, it is important to determine the changes that have occurred in basic conditions and market structure, and also to recognize the changes that have occurred in the key elements of the national environment. The changes in the economy and society will shape a country's industry structure and corporate organization in the future. These changes will create opportunities and incentives for innovation.

Global Environment

It is not an exaggeration to say that the global environment is currently the most often discussed of the three environments introduced in this chapter. It is widely recognized that the following four trends in the global environment should be integrated into a company's product offerings, value system, and strategy in general:

- Intensifying global competition
- Increasing importance of environmental constraints
- Increasing importance of social value propositions
- Demographic changes

Instead of describing each of these new trends, I would like to use the remainder of this chapter to illustrate how these trends affect the other two environments. Figure 9-2 presents three conditions as drivers of innovation: demand conditions, input (factor) conditions, and competition. These drivers are composed of a number of factors, which are, in turn, determined by the elements of market structure and national environment described in the previous section. For example, the availability of innovative and entrepreneurial talent, which Schumpeter considers to be the prime mover of the economic frontier, is the key element of the input conditions, and this, in turn, is determined by a number of nation-specific socioeconomic factors. The needs of market and society are important elements in the demand conditions. It is increasingly important to recognize the needs of society, as they are often not adequately served by the market because they are often caused by market failures. Finally, competition among corporate innovators and among individual innovators promotes innovation.

How are these classic national environments influenced by the newly emerging trends in the global environment? Figure 9-2 superimposes the new trends listed previously on the national environment. The increasing need to conserve energy and recycle resources and the increasing need to prevent and reduce pollution have become significant constraints and are beginning to affect the input conditions. They will increase the need for more "green" innovations and thus change the demand conditions. Intensifying competition in global markets is raising the level of rivalry in terms of scope and intensity for local as well as international competitors. Demographic changes in the next decades, particularly the aging and shrinking of populations in a number of industrialized countries, including Germany, Italy, Spain, Japan, South Korea, and China, will have a significant impact on demand and input conditions. They will change the needs of consumers, both individually and collectively. Aging and shrinking populations will influence corporate policies on human resources and significantly change the labor-market conditions. These are indeed the changes that have already happened.

In the previous section, I referred to the development of lean production by the Japanese automakers as an example of the effect of national environment on innovation. The recent experience of Japanese corporations is a useful example of the effect of the changing global environment on innovation because it is in sharp contrast to the previous example. Many changes have occurred in the national and global environments that have surrounded Japanese corporations since the mid-1990s. Among them are the emergence of strong global competition, particularly from China, and the increasing importance of an aging and shrinking population. Japanese corporations are faced with the challenge of addressing the issues associated with their once-successful business model and the relative paucity of entrepreneurs (corporate and individual) and innovators in the country. Many of Japan's manufacturing companies, which were started by remarkable entrepreneurs and emerged strongly after World War II, are now reaching the stage of slow growth as they age and as their primary industries mature. Where is the new generation of innovators and entrepreneurs in Japan? The notion of Schumpeterian competition is now more relevant. The importance of innovation and entrepreneurs is higher than ever, given the need to address these challenges. The business model under which many Japanese firms operated successfully in the past now needs to be revitalized and revamped. The question for managers in Japan and elsewhere now becomes: as the national and global environments have changed, what should you do? Here, the need for managerial ability to understand and recognize the changing environments and address the relevant questions on how to manage the future that has happened is much stronger than ever.

Conclusions

In this chapter, I have introduced three layers of environment—industrial, national, and global—that a manager needs to recognize and understand. Industrial environments are not created by natural forces, but are endogenous in the sense that they are transformed by innovative forces and by the entry of new firms. Innovations in product, process, or business model are essentially created by the inventor and designed by the entrepreneur, who is nurtured by a variety of nation-specific socioeconomic conditions. These entrepreneurs take advantage of technological opportunities and respond to the emerging new trends in the global environment. Again, it is important to recognize these national and global conditions and their new trends as they present to us the future that has happened.

Predicting the future can only get you in trouble. The task is to manage what is there and to work to create what could and should be.

—Peter F. Drucker, *Managing for Results*

10

A Pox on Charisma: Why Connective Leadership and Character Count

Jean Lipman-Blumen

Indeed, charisma becomes the undoing of leaders. It makes them inflexible, convinced of their own infallibility, unable to change.

—Peter F. Drucker, *The Essential Drucker*

Max Weber undoubtedly never envisioned the explosion that his definition of *charisma*—a "gift of grace"—would ignite.[1] From academia to the media, Weber's description of charisma kindled a firestorm of fascination with the

> quality of an individual personality by virtue of which he is set apart from ordinary men and treated as endowed with supernatural, super-human, or at least specifically exceptional powers or qualities.[2]

According to Weber, observers were "compelled" to regard with "awe" leaders who emanated this innate "mana." But not Peter Drucker.

A quick Google search for "charisma" produces 11,100,000 hits, while "charismatic" yields 7,850,000 more citations. Amazon.com reports that there are 7,956 books on "charismatic leadership" and another 58,698 with "charisma" in the title. More than a few "how to" books blatantly claim to teach the "desperately seeking" reader the secrets of developing charisma (despite Weber's insistence on its rare, inborn character). The number of times the media have used the term *charismatic* (mostly loosely and incorrectly) in reference to leaders, celebrities, and heroes is beyond enumeration.

Peter Drucker, a contrarian to his marrow, would have considered most, if not all, of these charisma junkies "dead wrong" (to use one of his favorite phrases). The media and wooly-headed academics may have been enthralled by charisma. But not Peter Drucker.

Drucker's discomfort with charisma stemmed largely from his observations of European Fascist leaders in the early twentieth century. Eventually, Drucker tempered his rejection somewhat, allowing that "good charisma" had its place, particularly as he saw it used in megachurches.[3] Nonetheless, Drucker remained acutely aware of the rampant misuse of charisma. He worried about how detrimental it could be to charismatic leaders themselves, as well as to their organizations and constituents. This apprehension prompted Drucker to suggest serious controls to protect those very leaders and the organizations they led from charismatic "fallout."

Not only was Peter Drucker skeptical about charisma, but for years he denied the very concept of leadership. In fact, for most of the several decades that my colleagues at the Drucker/Ito Graduate School of Management and I knew him, Peter repeatedly insisted that he "didn't believe in leadership." Many of us interpreted that claim, however, as a Druckeresque indulgence in hyperbole. After all, we understood that Peter's lifelong passion was to free the field of "management" from the long shadow of "leadership" and endow it with what he considered its rightful seriousness and respect. And he did just that with immense insight and eloquence.

Nonetheless, in the last decade of his life, Peter Drucker began— perhaps somewhat ruefully—to acknowledge books on leadership. Even then, however, he remained lukewarm to charisma and focused, instead, on the foundational issues of character, performance, results, and responsibility.

When Drucker did write about leadership, he was succinct. He focused on several related themes. First, he conceptualized leadership as work, responsibility, and trust earned through the demonstration of integrity. Second, in a relatively short list, he outlined a set of behaviors that he felt encapsulated the *sine qua non* of leadership. He emphasized a leader's

- Performance, that is, achieving the goals or mission of the group
- Exemplary behavior that followers could emulate
- Selection, support, and pride in qualified people
- Capacity to make a difference and to do so partly by transforming the personalities of followers
- Tolerance of diversity

Then, coming full circle, Drucker demanded

- Performance, standards, and values from *followers*

Nowhere in this list do we see Drucker bowing at the altar of charisma. Yet, within this catalog of leadership essentials, I detect some important characteristic ingredients of what I describe as "connective leadership."

Charisma versus Character and Performance

As the epigraph at the outset of this chapter suggests, Drucker viewed charisma quite skeptically. In my mind's eye, I can almost imagine Peter muttering, "A pox on charisma!" although I never actually witnessed him doing so. Nonetheless, Drucker regarded charisma as a force that was quite likely to undermine leaders who were endowed with this awesome gift. Charisma, he believed, could bloat leaders with such inflated self-regard that they would lose their footing and stumble over their own rigidity and hyperconfidence.

Character, Drucker wrote, requires strength, integrity, and authenticity. For Drucker, character, the bedrock of management, was perfused with decency, morality, ethics, and a respect for the law.[4] In fact, he often decried the lack of ethics in business.[5]

Drucker measured a leader's performance by results. Yet results do not grow in a vacuum. They are constrained by circumstances. Performance depends upon the unique demands created by the historical moment.

And this is where "connective leadership," an emerging form of leadership, imbued with ethics, integrity, authenticity, and accountability (all components of character), enters the scene.[6] Before we turn to a more detailed discussion of connective leadership and its special characteristics, however, let me first sketch the background of the Connective Era, which has only recently come into view.

The End of the Geopolitical Era; the Emergence of the Connective Era

Over long periods of time, certain modes of leadership develop in response to existing historical circumstances. Currently, we are witness to the ebbing of one historical era as another comes into full flow. We are, in fact, poised on the cusp of a new historical era, the Connective Era, in which everyone and everything are connected. In the Connective Era, "six degrees of separation" now seriously understates the tightness of our worldwide interdependence. One thing is clear: if leaders continue to use outmoded leadership strategies, they are destined to fail. Only a new leadership paradigm, one that addresses the challenges of the new historical moment, will promise leaders the success they desperately need in these new and perilous times that I call the "Connective Era."

The Connective Era began to emerge toward the end of the twentieth century as the Geopolitical Era, defined largely by geographic boundaries and political ideologies, gradually waned. In the Geopolitical Era, authoritarian leaders created and commandeered long-standing alliances, like the New Deal, the Warsaw Pact, and the original North Atlantic Treaty Organization (NATO), designed to act in unison to implement mutually beneficial policies. [In practice, of course, these policies usually favored the strongest member(s).] By the end of the cold war, the obsolete "command-and-control" leadership paradigm, as well as the institutions of the Geopolitical Era, had essentially lost both their vigor and their relevance.

Simultaneously, a hazy awareness of our complex global interconnectedness began to emerge. As the Connective Era gradually took hold, authoritarianism lost ground to more collaborative, consultative, and connective modes of leadership. Thus, by 2008, the U.S. presidential candidates who called for change were tapping into an important burgeoning reality. That historic transformation of the political landscape brought a fresh political sensibility, not only to the United States, but to countries around the world. The new-style American president immediately demonstrated his determination to reconnect the United States to its global neighbors. Moreover, President Obama's election symbolized the country's growing awareness of the significance of diversity and interdependence (two key aspects of the Connective Era, as we shall see). In fact, Barack Obama, the United States' first African-American president, represented these forces in his very persona and history.

Forging new leadership styles and institutions, the Connective Era gradually swept away all but the empty husks of the rigid, long-term geopolitical coalitions. In their place, the Connective Era began to shape short-term, shifting coalitions, focused on narrower, more specific topics in limited, periodic meetings, such as economic and environmental "summits." These short-term coalitions, with expandable membership, zeroed in on clearly defined issues within the United States and abroad. Other expandable international policy groups have also appeared. For example, the G-6, a group of finance ministers from industrialized nations, easily morphed into the G-7 when Canada joined the coalition. The G-8 brought together representatives from eight industrialized nations.

A curious coincidence of timing in the first week of April 2009 underscored the shift from the Geopolitical Era to the Connective Era: the G-20, representing the "foremost economic countries in the world," met in London, while simultaneously a NATO summit, held in Strasbourg-Kehl, celebrated that organization's sixtieth anniversary. Pundits nostalgically toasted NATO, with its new, former-Soviet-bloc members, as an anachronistic forum bereft of power and purpose. Simultaneously, they hailed the G-20 as the "most important global financial meeting in more than 60 years."[7] How much more clearly could the change be underscored?

Challenges of the Connective Era: Diversity and Interdependence

As the economist John Kenneth Galbraith once suggested, in every era, effective leaders must confront the major tensions of their times. That is no less true today. In the Connective Era, however, leaders face a special, more difficult challenge—the need to connect and integrate two equally important, but intrinsically *contradictory*, tensions: diversity and interdependence. Those societal tensions are fundamental to the human condition; they echo the enduring tensions between self and other. For leaders, they represent the immense challenge of two major forces pulling in opposite directions.

Diversity reflects the uniqueness of each group—gender, ethnic, religious, racial, social, occupational, organizational, and national—and its claim to independence. It requires us to acknowledge our singular identities with a sophisticated understanding of and respect for our *dissimilarities* to others. Beginning with male/female differences, we witness diversity and distinctions wherever we look. At the global level, we observe an ongoing fragmentation and proliferation of distinct nations seeking independence. Ethnic, cultural, religious, and demographic diversity continues to abound. At the organizational level, too, we see increasing diversity, from large, multinational corporations to more limited joint ventures, partnerships, networks, and temporary alliances, as well as nonprofit groups and governmental bureaucracies.

Diversity also characterizes the workforce, both at home and abroad, with more females and other previously underrepresented groups increasingly joining the fray. And, of course, every human being (with the arguable exception of identical twins) represents the ultimate unit of diversity, with unique and special gifts, as well as diverse needs and aspirations. Within each of these groups, myriad distinctive subgroups call for independence, divergent agendas, and the right to live according to their own (not others') lights.

Faced with growing diversity, some leaders (particularly those who are still mired in the Geopolitical Era) continue to engage in a Politics of Differences.[8] Leaders who are locked into a Politics of Differences exploit the disparities among various groups, recruiting their own supporters as stalwarts in the seemingly "inevitable" conflicts with "outsiders," in the ongoing tension between self and other.

Interdependence, on the other hand, demands recognition of the complex and multiple interconnections that bind together all the diverse individuals, groups, organizations, and nations, willy-nilly, in this globalized political/economic/environmental world. We need only log on to the far-flung Internet to see firsthand how it serves as an appropriate metaphor for the Connective Era. NetCraft reported in November 2008 that there were upwards of 182 million known Web sites and still counting.[9] More stunning, perhaps, is the number of worldwide Internet users: as of March 31, 2009, 1,596,270,108 of the world's 6,710,029,070 total inhabitants use the Internet.[10] That's some set of connections!

In this globalized milieu, if we are to achieve any modicum of peace, prosperity, and success, we have no recourse but to respect those connections, work together, and share and renew the limited resources of the planet. Thus, interdependence calls for collaboration, mutual respect, at least partially overlapping agendas, and empathy for people who are quite different from ourselves. In a context framed by interdependence, leaders need to engage in a Politics of Commonalities,[11] seeking out mutualities and governing from whatever common ground they can detect and gradually increase.

Integrating Diversity and Interdependence

Clearly, diversity and interdependence are centrifugal forces, spiraling in opposite directions. That is the indisputable character of the Connective Era, and no amount of ostrichlike denial will diminish it. Thus, we need leaders who can cope with, and perchance tame, these complex, conflicting forces. The Connective Era calls for leaders who can integrate diversity and interdependence. It requires leaders who can balance the needs of self and other to achieve constructive and productive outcomes for all the diverse groups that must inevitably coexist on a limited planet.

Within these overarching tensions of the Connective Era, leaders face many challenging questions. Two examples will suffice:

- How can leaders remain true to their own constituents while connecting their vision to the visions of seemingly contradictory, competitive groups with which they and their supporters must necessarily live and work cheek by jowl?

- How can leaders effectively address complex issues—from international economic meltdowns, to free trade, to pandemics, to global warming, to nuclear proliferation—without compromising their most fundamental values if those values conflict with those of other groups?

To maintain their commitment to their followers, their mission, and their values, leaders who are faced with the clamor of diverse groups promoting opposing agendas may be tempted to rely solely on "tried-and-true" charisma. Peter Drucker knew better than that!

A more reliable strategy, however, might be to draw from the wellsprings of connective leadership. This model of leadership acknowledges the occasional, strategic usefulness of principled, nonnarcissistic charisma. Connective leadership, however, reaches far beyond that limited traditional leadership strategy to a much broader repertoire of leadership behaviors that we shall describe later as "achieving styles." Connective leadership is deeply rooted in character—that is, integrity, strength, trust, authenticity, and accountability: all the fundamentals about which Peter Drucker cared so passionately.

Authenticity and Accountability: Hallmarks of Connective Leadership

Authenticity and accountability are two major imperatives of connective leadership. Without them, the connective leader's complex behavior—and we shall soon see just how complex that behavior can be—can easily arouse suspicion and confusion.

Authenticity carries special meaning within the context of connective leadership. It refers to the leader's consistent dedication not to his personal goals, but to those of the group, organization, or society. Drawing upon their fundamental integrity and ethical foundation, connective leaders understand that demonstrating their unwavering commitment to the group's mission will sustain their followers' trust in the *person* of the leader, even when the leader's *behavior* seems contradictory or confusing.

Authenticity is particularly crucial for connective leaders, who draw upon a more intricate mosaic of behaviors than their geopolitical predecessors used. It is an array of behavioral strategies that organizational psychologist Harold J. Leavitt[12] and I have called "achieving styles."[13] Without the reassurance of their unquestionable authenticity, connective leaders' broad behavioral repertoire may make these new leaders appear more chameleon than champion to the casual observer. When the leader's authenticity is palpable, followers are more willing to give that individual the benefit of the doubt, particularly in the face of the confusing behavioral shifts that connective leaders are able and wont to make.

Accountability, the second imperative of connective leadership, "means accepting the obligation to explain, the willingness to be held accountable to a widening jury of stakeholders."[14] Accountability goes beyond transparency. Accountability not only opens to scrutiny the leader's decisions and the rationales prompting them, but also subjects the leader's actions to critiques from many quarters. As if this were not sufficient, accountability bespeaks the leader's firm commitment to learn from her mistakes.

Denatured Machiavellianism: Ethical Instrumentalism

While authenticity and accountability are critical, so, too, is another aspect of connective leadership: *denatured Machiavellianism*. When we hear the adjective "Machiavellian," most ethical individuals experience a distinct unease. We immediately recall the dictionary definition that describes Machiavelli's advice to the ruler in his renowned treatise, *The Prince*, where

Political expediency is placed above morality and . . . craft and deceit
[are used] to maintain the authority and carry out the policies of a ruler.[15]

Machiavelli describes manipulating and using individuals covertly
to accomplish the ruler's ends as well as to keep and enhance the
ruler's power at any cost. Not surprisingly, most ethical leaders are
repelled by such covert, ego-driven manipulation.

If, on the other hand, we were able to distill Machiavelli's wisdom, purge it of deceit and covert manipulation, and turn such behavior into ethical, overt instrumentalism to be exercised only on
behalf of the entire community, we'd have something useful and hon-
orable, to boot. I call such instrumental strategies—that is, the open
and ethical use of self and others in pursuit of moral purposes for
the benefit of the whole group—"denatured Machiavellianism."

This moral, sophisticated, altruistic willingness to use—even sacrifice—oneself to achieve an important group goal was something
that Gandhi understood and used very effectively and honorably.
When leaders explicitly recruit others to join them as instruments to
achieve valued group goals, they can jump-start their supporters'
flagging motivation.

Connective leaders are very skilled at denatured Machiavellianism. They are quite adept at using these political strategies for the
common good. They understand and openly utilize the "interconnections among persons, institutions, and processes everywhere."[16]

Connective leaders part company with the Machiavelli of *The
Prince* in other important ways that add to their effectiveness.[17] Such
connective actions include:

- *Joining their vision to the dreams of others; connecting and combining, rather than dividing and conquering*
- *Striving to overcome mutual problems to attract diverse constituents (instead of using common enemies to corral frightened followers behind their leader)*

- *Creating a sense of community, where many diverse groups can hold valued membership*
- *Bringing together committed leaders and constituents for common purposes*
- *Encouraging active constituents to assume responsibilities at every level, rather than manipulating passive followers*
- *Collaborating with other leaders, even former adversaries, as colleagues, rather than as competitors*
- *Nurturing potential leaders, including possible successors*
- *Renewing and building broad-based democratic institutions, instead of creating dynasties and oligarchies*
- *Demonstrating authenticity through consistent dedication to supra-egoistic goals, and*
- *Demanding serious sacrifice first from themselves and only then from others.[18]*

In some ways, connective leaders resemble Robert K. Greenleaf's servant leaders, particularly in their service to the group or society.[19] They behave less self-righteously, however, in their stewardship and more pragmatically in their ethical instrumental action on behalf of the group.

As such, connective leaders act with agency and creativity to stitch together the various connections among people, institutions, visions, and aspirations to achieve important benefits for the society. These are people whom Peter Drucker could admire and encourage.

Achieving the Mission through Connections: A Repertoire of Achieving Styles

Using connective leadership requires a detailed understanding of the behavioral strategies that are available to leaders and anyone else who is interested in being effective in a world that is pulled asunder by diversity and interdependence. While the Connective Leadership Model provides the overarching leadership framework, the *L-BL Achieving Styles Model* describes the underlying behaviors that leaders—and the rest of us, too—actually use in accomplishing their goals.

Drucker insisted that executives should "manage for the mission." Connective leaders do exactly that, recognizing that their larger mission is to integrate the antithetical forces of diversity and interdependence. Yet, they wed a principled pragmatism to ethics and altruism, placing great emphasis upon the group's mission. They do so by calling upon a wide range of behavioral strategies or "achieving styles" to accomplish their goals (see Figure 10-1). Taken together, these encompassing and flexible behavioral strategies provide connective leaders with the tools they need to reconcile diversity and interdependence, that is, to bring together diverse constituencies that need to work harmoniously.

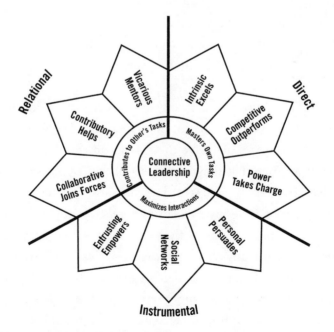

FIGURE 10-1 L-BL Achieving Styles Model

The L-BL Achieving Styles Model

In this section, I shall describe the ninefold L-BL Achieving Styles Model that allows leaders and the rest of us to achieve goals and accomplish tasks effectively.

The leadership profile of connective leaders is structured around a continuum of three major behavioral orientations or sets: *Direct*, *Instrumental*, and *Relational* achieving styles. Each achieving styles set comprises three distinctive, but related, styles, resulting in a full complement of nine achieving styles. Leaders with fully developed connective leadership profiles use multiple styles easily and simultaneously, moving with great agility from one combination to another as they read and adjust to situational cues. For purposes of simplicity, however, let us describe these nine achieving styles as pure or, as Weber would say, "ideal types."[20]

The Direct Achieving Styles Set: Intrinsic, Competitive, and Power

The *Direct* achieving styles set includes three categories of achieving styles: *Intrinsic*, *Competitive*, and *Power*.

Intrinsic: The *Intrinsic* achieving style involves focusing on one's "personal mastery or execution of a task."[21] People who prefer the Intrinsic style perceive the task as an exciting, compelling challenge, one that they must meet or, better yet, surpass. The achievement of the goal is intrinsically satisfying, hence the label. The Intrinsic style involves an *internalized* standard of perfection, one that references that individual's own previous performances (not any external measure of rivals' achievements) as the standard that must be met or exceeded. Being the best is less important than achieving perfection. Most people with a predilection for Intrinsic behavior derive an aesthetic sense of beauty and satisfaction from accomplishing the task—whether it be the discovery of a new planet or the design of a political campaign. They relish having full autonomy over their work, the freedom that accompanies self-reliance, unlimited options for creativity and innovation, and the possibility of perfection.

Competitive: *Competitive* is the second achieving style within the Direct set. The Competitive achieving style, as its name implies, involves an *external* standard of comparison, that is, the measurement of one's own performance against that of relevant others. Beating the competition and being the best, regardless of the task or level of performance, is what really sets Competitive achievers' juices flowing. For Competitive achievers, however, doing their best is never good enough; true satisfaction comes only from doing better than everyone else in the game.[22]

Power: The third member of the Direct achieving styles set is *Power*, which involves taking charge and bringing order out of chaos. People who prefer this style enjoy controlling and coordinating people, resources, situations, and tasks. They direct and delegate parts of the task to others, offering both suggestions and instructions for how the task should be accomplished by others, whom they simply expect to implement their orders.

Connective leaders have little compelling need to be the "leader of leaders." As we shall see, they are content with collaborating on a group mission, contributing behind the scenes to others' success, or simply taking pride when "their people" succeed. They seek to take the lead only when their own skills are the ones required to keep the work on track.

All three of the Direct achieving styles involve maintaining control over both the means and the ends desired. The locus of control over means and ends, as we shall see, changes as we progress around the Achieving Styles Model. As the reader has probably noticed, the three Direct achieving styles are familiar holdovers from the Geopolitical

Era's focus on command and control. Yet connective leaders are neither obsessed with, nor limited to, these achieving styles that are so characteristic of the Geopolitical Era. Nonetheless, they know how to use them when circumstances demand. In fact, connective leaders tend to focus more on the additional six styles encompassed in the remaining two sets of achieving styles: Instrumental and Relational.

The Instrumental Achieving Styles: Personal, Social, and Entrusting

The *Instrumental* set also comprises three achieving styles: *Personal*, *Social*, and *Entrusting*.

> **Personal:** Leaders who prefer the *Personal* style use themselves and everything about them as instruments for accomplishing their goals. They call upon their own intellect and wit (including self-deprecating humor); their physical attractiveness and eloquence; their charm and persuasiveness; their past achievements (e.g., educational, athletic, and so on); as well as their genealogy (drawing sympathy for humble beginnings or awe for high-status ancestry) to attract others to their cause.
>
> If you are beginning to sense the possibility of charismatic leanings in this style, you are right on target. Connective leaders use their charisma to attract others to their cause. Whether their cause involves building institutions for world peace or organizations that produce computers, people who prefer Personal Instrumental behaviors openly and ethically use themselves and others as instruments to achieve known and valued ends. Here we see that connective leaders do not shrink from principled charisma, but use it merely as one element in their repertoire of connective leadership strategies. I think Peter Drucker would have sanctioned this ethical use of charisma, deployed without deceit and without narcissism.

Leaders who tend to select Personal Instrumental strategies have a flare for using symbolism, ritual, costume, timing, and theatrics (all part of charismatic action) to communicate their vision. With great effect, leaders who excel in the Personal achieving style strategically engage in "counter-intuitive gestures."[23] As you might suspect, counterintuitive gestures are those unexpected actions, such as reaching out to a former enemy, that take others by surprise. The unanticipated nature of the action makes it more likely that its target will respond spontaneously and, in most cases, positively, as well. For example, as of this writing, in the few short months of the Obama administration, the new president has unexpectedly reached out to a variety of groups and nations, including Republicans, Muslims, Iran, and Turkey, as well as others that his predecessors would have treated as the "enemy."

Social: Leaders who are skilled in the second style within the Instrumental set, the *Social* achieving style, use their own and others' social connections and experience to create chains of individuals linked together in successful action. They recognize and use the connective tissue that binds individuals and groups inside and beyond organizations and communities. They build, maintain, and share large social networks sometimes creating shifting coalitions of associates, whom they call upon as the situation requires. Faced with a task, people who are drawn to Social Instrumental behavior identify a specific individual with the most appropriate experience or connections for that particular assignment.

Leaders who prefer the Social achieving style masterfully navigate the informal system. As Weber and others have suggested,[24] the informal system is that vast network of interpersonal relationships on which various resources, from friendship, to discretionary time, to solace, political advice, and gossip, are exchanged. The informal system is the actual birthplace of most organizational decisions. Consequently, skilled connective leaders use their Social expertise to test and refine their agenda in the byways of the informal system. They build interpersonal capital by various means of communication, from the numerous blogs and social networks on the Internet to direct e-mail, phone, fax, and even the now-cherished handwritten note, as well as face-to-face communication.

Entrusting: The third Instrumental style is *Entrusting*, whereby the leader empowers another individual to carry out an important task without concern for that individual's previous relevant experience or contacts. Here, we begin to see how the Entrusting achiever (in sharp contrast to previously described achievers) lets slip the reins on the means selected, while still sharing the ultimate ends or goal with the person to whom the task is entrusted.

For example, where the Power achiever would outline and control the means to the end, the Entrusting achiever leaves that up to the person he has chosen to attain the shared goal. Granted, the use of the Entrusting style usually rests on a larger, more general evaluative process. That is, the Entrusting achiever relies upon the fact that the group from which she is selecting the implementer (e.g., the members of a particular organization, the students admitted to a certain university, or some similar group) has been previously vetted by some selective process. In addition, the one who is entrusted with this potentially unfamiliar task has a reputation to maintain within that larger milieu. Thus, the Entrusting achiever operates within certain generally known parameters of excellence and reciprocal relationships, but pays little attention to the specific relevant experience, talents, or contacts the chosen one may have.

We might think of the Entrusting achieving style as "leadership by expectation." Here, the leader and the entrusted individual share the goal, but choice of the specific means to accomplish that goal is left to the implementer. That is the case as long as the implementer meets the connective leader's ethical and legal standards. As Robert Cialdini suggests, the underlying mechanism that makes this seemingly casual, even risky, style of leadership work is the "principle of reciprocation."[25] More specifically, to maintain balance in an ongoing relationship, the leader's gift of trust and confidence in the one entrusted with an important task must be reciprocated by the implementer's fulfillment of those expectations. More often than not, that grant of confidence is fully repaid by the implementer's outstanding, creative results—frequently exceeding even the implementer's own expectations.

The Relational Achieving Styles Set: Collaborative, Contributory, and Vicarious

The third and last set of achieving styles, the *Relational* set, also encompasses three individual styles: *Collaborative*, *Contributory*, and *Vicarious*. This triad completes the nine-factor Achieving Styles Model.

Here, let me inject a brief cautionary note: *Relational*, in this context, does not refer to liking or needing relationships—merely to the willingness to contribute either actively or passively to the tasks or goals of others with whom the individual has some relationship, be it close or distant. This contrasts sharply with the orientation of the three Direct achieving styles, which focuses primarily on one's own tasks.

Collaborative: The first Relational style, *Collaborative*, involves preferring to work actively with others on a common goal rather than laboring alone on one's own task. The goal might be one that has been jointly created or merely mutually agreed upon, as in winning a game with preestablished rules and outcomes, such as an athletic contest. Collaborative achievers enjoy the stimulation of interacting with one or more others.

They expect to share both the rewards of success and the pain of defeat with their teammates. Collaboration can occur either among equals or among individuals with different talents and statuses, such as the members of a football team, who have different, but related, skills and positions. Creating and sustaining the circumstances in which former foes can collaborate in interdependent systems is one of the talents of connective leaders. Collaboration, like most of the other achieving styles, is best built on trust, reciprocity, and mutual goals.

Contributory: The second Relational style, *Contributory*, calls for contributing, often behind the scenes, to another individual's success. Contributory achievers recognize and support the goals established by others. They not only are willing to help others achieve their goals, but also derive a sense of achievement and satisfaction from putting their shoulder to the wheel of another individual's or group's task. Sociologists would say that they participate in the actual "role tasks" of another achiever. For example, a speechwriter who writes a talk for the leader to present is an individual whose role calls for contributory behavior. You will probably recognize the Contributory style as one set of behaviors commonly associated with the traditional wife and mother roles, in which women dedicated their achievement efforts to helping those they loved accomplish their goals. Typing a family member's term paper is an example of contributory behavior.

Vicarious: The third Relational achieving style, *Vicarious*, involves indirectly or passively deriving a sense of accomplishment from the achievements of others with whom the Vicarious achiever identifies. The individual may be someone the vicarious achiever knows personally, such as a family member, or simply someone admired from afar, such as a celebrity. The Vicarious achieving style is another behavioral strategy that was traditionally linked to women's roles, in which adult females presumably met their own needs for achievement indirectly by taking pride and satisfaction from the accomplishments of their children and husbands. Unlike Contributory achievers, Vicarious achievers do not participate directly in the role tasks of others. Rather, they participate passively and indirectly, or vicariously, hence the style's label. People who prefer the Vicarious style simply identify with, encourage, and possibly advise other achievers. A mentor advising a protégé offers one example of vicarious behavior. Sports fans who cheer on their team from the stands provide another.

In the Relational set, we see three types of behavior in which the choice of means and the setting of goals move along a continuum from mutual activity to relatively passive observation and encouragement. That is, the individual achiever or actor who is the focus of our attention moves along a continuum from active participation in a mutually set or previously established group goal (Collaborative), to active, but secondary, participation in achieving a goal set by another (Contributory), to passive observation or encouragement of other individuals, with whom the actor identifies (Vicarious). Yet, within each of the three achieving styles in the Relational set, as in the other six achieving styles, the achiever who is the focus of our attention can derive a genuine sense of achievement satisfaction.

Taken together, the nine achieving styles, grouped in triads within the Direct, Instrumental, and Relational sets, constitute the full complement of behavioral strategies that are available to individuals engaged in goal-oriented activity. Connective leaders use these achieving styles adroitly to link their vision to those of their own constituents, as well as to the dreams of other leaders and their supporters. Moving adeptly from one combination of styles to another, always aware of situational demands and the tensions between diversity and interdependence, connective leaders enlarge their support base in important and powerful ways. In the process, they envision and accomplish goals that their more limited Geopolitical predecessors never could have imagined.

Inventories for Measuring Connective Leadership: Individual, Organizational, Situational, and 360° Assessments

As suggested earlier, fully developed connective leaders can easily access all nine achieving styles. They call upon these behavioral strategies individually and in various, kaleidescopic combinations, as the situation demands. But how do we know this?

Since 1984, we have been measuring the connective leadership profile of *individuals* by administering the *L-BL Achieving Styles Inventory (ASI)*, a 45-item survey, with each item scored on a 7-point Likert scale. At the present time, our database contains information on more than 25,000 managers, leaders, and business students from the United States and countries throughout the world. More than 150 dissertations have been written on different aspects of achieving styles and connective leadership in the United States, Finland, South Africa, and other countries around the globe.

Beginning in 1984, we developed an *organizational* version to measure the connective leadership profiles and the underlying achieving styles rewarded by organizations. We call this inventory the *L-BL Organizational Achieving Styles Inventory (OASI)*. In addition to its use as a measure of the organizational reward system, the OASI may be used to measure the underlying values or culture of an organization.

By 1989, we had also designed and tested a third related instrument, the *Achieving Styles Situational Evaluation Technique (ASSET)*. ASSET may be used to determine the most appropriate connective leadership profile for success in a specific *role/position*, *task*, or *project*. Using the data from ASSET in combination with the individual data (ASI) from a group of relevant candidates, we are able to select the individuals who are most likely to succeed in specific roles, projects, and tasks on the basis of their ASI/ASSET convergence or match. Both the ASI and the OASI have been translated into numerous languages.

A fourth instrument, the 360° *Achieving Styles Assessment Inventory (ASAI)*, is currently under development. As the title suggests, ASAI allows a focal person to take the individual ASI for herself. Two additional gender-specific instruments allow peers, direct reports, supervisors, and other relevant individuals and groups to evaluate the focal person's connective leadership profile. Used in various combinations, these instruments provide useful feedback to the focal targets regarding other people's perceptions of their leadership behavior. These instruments can be used both inside organizations and beyond their boundaries with other appropriate individuals and groups, such as clients, family members, and so on.[26]

Leadership for What? Dealing with the Serious Issues of Life

Before closing this chapter, we need to confront the proverbial elephant in the room. At least, let us raise the larger question: leadership for what? Given the near-universal yearning for leaders, what exactly do they offer that truly enhances our lives? Clearly, leaders take responsibility for many rather mundane things that we could arrange for ourselves if only we were willing to engage in the "valuable inconvenience of leadership."[27]

The Dangerous Trade-Off

When we view leadership through Peter Drucker's lens—as responsibility and performance, rather than as privilege—leadership means taking responsibility not only for our own fortunes, but for others' as well. Such responsibility demands time and effort that many of us prefer to devote to "doing our own thing." So, we eagerly delegate the responsibility for those dull, but necessary tasks to someone else who is willing to develop the budget, arrange for resources, and take care of all the other life-sustaining, but laborious and unglamorous, aspects of existence.

At first glance, the trade-off seems like a no-brainer: we give up onerous burdens and performance on behalf of the group in exchange for time and freedom to indulge our own interests. Only later, do we notice the danger embedded in relinquishing to others authority for major aspects of our lives.

We discover, sometimes too late, that our very freedom is at stake. By then, of course, we can't complain when these leaders make decisions that we don't particularly countenance or, worse yet, that harm us and others. Avoiding the "valuable inconvenience of leadership" is a trap, but one into which we lazily fall until leaders blatantly display their toxic predilections, leaving us worse off than they found us.[28] By then, however, the damage is usually hard to undo, if not totally irreparable.

One Critical Leadership Contribution

Aside from making the proverbial trains run on time, I think there is one critical contribution that truly thoughtful leaders can make: they can help us deal with the serious issues of life, death, and the search for the meaning of our lives.[29] Most humans ultimately seek to confront these existential questions, and the answers are different for each of us. Yet, the journey is one that is better undertaken in the company of others, with a decent, intelligent, thoughtful, ethical, and altruistic leader pointing the way.

This is a huge topic, one that is more fit for a volume of its own. Still, a chapter on leadership would be remiss indeed if it did not point the reader to a larger set of issues that are far beyond the confines of this chapter, or even this volume.

The duality of human nature—our entwined physical and symbolic selves—evokes many questions for us to ponder. How do we fulfill our symbolic, our more ethereal selves when we know that we are destined to succumb to our physical finitude, returning to dust and leaving behind something, we know not exactly what?[30] What is our earthly journey all about, and how do we console ourselves that it must end?

One way of dealing with these questions is to ask ourselves what we wish to leave behind as evidence of our having taken that journey. This is precisely where leaders have an important role to play if they are willing and dedicated to a larger goal than their own power.

We recognize as leaders those who lift our sights to consider important issues. Such leaders invite us to participate in life-expanding experiences and identify noble enterprises to which we can devote ourselves, and through which we can also find the complex, satisfying meaning of our lives. Good leaders help us to turn our "attention away from our personal death and direct it instead to a conscious discourse about pervasive societal issues, a discourse that allows us to deal symbolically with our unconscious personal fears."[31]

This—and much more—is something that connective leaders seriously try to do. They act from the depths of their character, not their ego. They understand the existential angst that we now find ourselves confronting against the turbulent backdrop of the Connective Era. They recognize that the "thick description" of our lives that we all eventually seek comes from a dedication to a cause greater than ourselves.[32] And, along with that "thick description," perchance we experience happiness and success. As Viktor E. Frankl noted in his classic work, *Man's Search for Meaning*:

> *Success, like happiness, cannot be pursued; it must ensue, and it only does so as the unintended side-effect of one's dedication to a cause greater than oneself.*[33]

One obvious benefit of dedication to a cause greater than ourselves is the possibility of reconciling the global tensions of diversity
and interdependence. Serendipitously and simultaneously, we can
also put to rest the parallel tension between self and other. Without
the rapprochement of these powerful parallel forces, there is no life-
sustaining path to the future.

Charisma cannot suffice. The challenges of the Connective Era demand far more. At this pivotal historical moment, we need to return
to the bedrock of character and its companions: integrity, authenticity, accountability, trust, and performance. We also need a new, more
appropriate form of leadership, untrammeled by the thirst for power
and privilege, leadership that can reconcile the needs of the many.
That is why we, too, must proclaim, "A pox on charisma." That is
why connective leadership and character count.

I suspect Peter Drucker would agree.

11

Knowledge Worker Productivity and the Practice of Self-Management

Jeremy Hunter, Ph.D., with J. Scott Scherer

More and more people in the workforce—and mostly knowledge workers—will have to MANAGE THEMSELVES.

—Peter F. Drucker, *Management Challenges*
for the 21st Century

Toward the end of his life, Peter Drucker asserted that making knowledge workers productive was "the biggest of the 21st century management challenges."[1] Other scholars support Drucker's position. Tom Davenport, a leading thinker on knowledge workers, underscores why this productivity is so important: "If our companies are going to be more profitable, if our strategies are going to be successful, if our society is going to become more advanced—it will be because knowledge workers did their work in a more productive and effective manner."[2] The task of improving knowledge worker productivity is immense, and so are the consequences of failing to do so. In fact, Drucker warned that improving knowledge worker productivity is the "first *survival requirement*" of developed nations.[3] Failure carries dire consequences for a nation's economy and society.

Significant efforts have been made in this quest, with varying degrees of success. Most endeavors have focused on the logical suspects—work process, managerial practice, organizational structure, information technology, and workplace ergonomics.[4] Despite these efforts, quantum gains in productivity have not flooded the workplace. In his blog, Davenport wondered why more headway wasn't being made, even going so far as to ask, "Was Drucker wrong?"[5] Alas, Drucker's twenty-first-century challenge is proving to be a tricky lock to pick.

Perhaps the key lies hidden elsewhere. Thus far, most energy has focused on the worker's external environment. If, according to Drucker, the primary asset of a knowledge economy lies "between the ears" of its knowledge workers,[6] then maybe the key to enhancing productivity lies *within* the workers themselves.

Productivity from the Inside Out

An internally based exploration of productivity asks different questions about how to optimize it. An inner approach examines how a knowledge worker manages—or mismanages—her internal experience and helps her to see how her internal processes have a direct impact on her outward behavior. Some questions to ask are:

- How do knowledge workers use their attention to focus on and engage with work and one another?
- How can rigid, judgmental mindsets be shifted toward the openness, learning, and transformation that are the heart of innovation and problem solving?
- How do negative emotional reactions derail the work process or corrode the morale of a work group?

Losses in productivity can often be traced to momentary events inside a person—events whose outward expression disrupts clear thought and effective social interaction. In short, visible behavior results from invisible processes that occur within a person's inner black box, often with negative consequences:

- A senior executive's emotional volatility makes him a scary person to report to. As a result, bad news does not get delivered, and the right decisions are not made. The organization begins to reel off course. Defusing the inner churn that precedes his eruptions quells his outbursts and, in turn, changes how his people relate to him.
- A team leader's penchant for judgmental and sarcastic comments erodes team morale and performance. Talent leaves the organization, along with the knowledge capital that the company needs if it is to thrive. Teach the leader not to utter his acerbic thoughts and to be more supportive, and watch team performance improve.
- An up-and-coming manager's multitasking BlackBerry addiction compulsively distracts her attention in meetings. She misses key points, her colleagues feel disrespected, and decision making takes longer. Her chances for promotion are diminished. If the manager keeps her attention focused, decisions proceed more smoothly and her team feels more respected.

In each example, maladaptive behavior can be traced to an event inside the worker that affects outward performance. But why should management be concerned?

The answer becomes clear upon reflection. Drucker reminded us that "knowledge workers must be considered a *capital asset*."[7] If an organization is seeking to grow its assets and to maximize its return, and if knowledge workers' productivity is deeply influenced by the workers' inner states, then helping knowledge workers to cultivate optimal internal states becomes the responsibility of management and, in effect, becomes an exercise in *asset management*.

If we know that internal states affect behavior, then the productivity challenge shifts to how to manage these states effectively and how to improve them. In *The Practice of Management*, Drucker "illuminated the dark continent of management"[8] and made conscious the inner workings of the organization. Analogously, the practice of *self*-management, as I have coined the phrase, allows the worker to shine a light into his own inner black box to illuminate his internal processing, and then to transform these processes to enhance his effectiveness.

The practice of self-management builds directly on recent advances in neuroscience, medicine, and psychology. The model melds Drucker's classic themes of change and continual transformation with contemporary views on human development, providing a systematic framework of theory and practice to help knowledge workers better manage themselves, their work, and their relationships. In the process, workers transform their individual and collective productivity and, in turn, generate more capital for the organization.

Creating the Practice of Self-Management

I developed the practice of self-management after conducting a research study that involved interviewing prominent, successful professionals who were dedicated to practicing mindfulness. Mindfulness practices are a method of attention development that enhances self-awareness, self-regulation, and self-transformation. I'll say more about what that means later.

In recent years, mindfulness practices have received considerable scholarly attention. Research studies have demonstrated that these practices improve numerous measures of well-being, including mental and physical health, self-regulation, and the quality of relationships.[9]

Outside of academia, mindfulness practices produce tangible results in a variety of professional settings. Such methods inform stress management programs used in hospitals in more than 26 countries around the world.[10] Mindfulness has been incorporated into legal training,[11] and it has been applied successfully in professional sports, notably by coach Phil Jackson in his NBA championships with the Chicago Bulls and Los Angeles Lakers.[12]

The professionals I interviewed in the research study included a Fortune 500 CEO, a well-known architect, a financier, senior corporate managers, medical researchers, a film director, and a host of other prominent knowledge workers. Most of the time, I met these people in person. Without fail, they were open, relaxed, and attentive. They were not the stereotypical picture of the stressed-out but "successful" professional.

Our conversations revealed a common refrain: "My life is so complex and demanding—if I didn't have these mindfulness practices, I think I'd be dead." Often they meant this literally. They produced medical records showing their previous high blood pressure, heart problems, and overweight conditions, or they shared stories of divorces and broken relationships.[13] Each person attributed her sustained success and well-being to a regular mindfulness practice. Their sustained internal training had resulted in significant transformation.

During this time, I too was using these practices to confront a personal challenge. I had been diagnosed with a terminal illness at the age of 20 and told that I had a 90 percent chance of dying within 5 years. Having outlived that prognosis by decades, I knew the power of these methods intimately.

One day, in a conversation about this research, my colleague Jean Lipman-Blumen pointed out, "We rarely train managers to manage themselves." Her comment crystallized an insight for me: the inner world of the executive remained largely neglected. How ironic this all seemed to me, since my study had suggested that internal self-management was the source of both professional effectiveness and professional failure.

The notion of "managing oneself" was already present in Drucker's work.[14] I realized that mindfulness could be the basis of a systematic discipline in self-management. The impulse to create a scientifically-based method of self-management for an expanding audience of knowledge workers was born. Recent discoveries in neuroscience would help to explain why mindfulness works, providing a biological description for this seemingly mystical process. Understanding the function of the human nervous system would be the first step in transforming it for greater professional and personal effectiveness.

Self-Management Means Managing Your Nervous System

Self-management begins with the human nervous system, including (and especially) the brain. The brain lies at the center of knowledge work. Knowledge workers use their brains to focus, to decide, and to act. Unfortunately, few knowledge workers understand how their brain works. Self-management examines how the brain and the nervous system function, explores their limits, and demonstrates how these limits can be effectively managed and transformed. Making knowledge workers more productive means helping them to use their brains better.[15]

From this point onward, I will examine specific internal processes involved in self-management. The starting place for this examination is *attention*. Attention informs how we process experience and, at the same time, attention powers performance. So I will explore how attention can be used as a tool in a variety of applications, including how to transform nonperforming mindsets and how to manage emotional reactivity—two elements that can deeply affect professional performance.

Attention Is the Foundation for Self-Management

Attention and our experience of the world are intimately linked: you are what you attend to. Attention powers our ability to perceive the outside world as well as to perceive our own actions, thoughts, and emotions. The first step toward self-awareness, self-control, self-transformation, and connection with others is to master attention. Attention is fundamental.

Over a hundred years ago, the great American psychologist William James recognized the essential role that attention plays in self-management. James cited attention as "the very root of judgment, character and will," and warned that people could not be masters of themselves if they failed to first control their attention. Furthermore, James declared that an education that enhances attention would be "the education *par excellence.*"[16]

At this point in the conversation, many people furrow their brows and say: "Huh? Attention? If it's so important, why haven't I heard of it before?"

Good question. Here's why. There are two reasons. First, modern education has usually favored the conceptual and abstract over the perceptual, which is one reason that attention and its development seem foreign to most of us. Second, although Western psychology after James created theories of development for cognition and emotion, it failed to create a theory of attention development.

"Not paying attention to attention" is a massive cultural blind spot. The modern West has ignored the importance of preserving and developing attention, to its peril. Japan, for example, has a well-developed cultural heritage of "attention-developing arts," including the tea ceremony, calligraphy, flower arrangement, martial arts, and archery. The fundamental purpose of these methods is to develop focus, awareness as well as mental and emotional stability. A person is considered mature and civilized if she has at least one of these under her belt. Drucker, incidentally, was one of the United States's foremost collectors of Japanese art, a hobby that he used to train his perceptive capacities.

Drucker and the Vital Need to Train Perception

Peter Drucker recognized the West's perceptual blindness when he wrote: "Descartes said, 'I *think* therefore I am.' We will now have to say also, 'I *see* therefore I am.'"[17] Drucker realized that modern management had overemphasized analysis and underappreciated perception. (In this discussion, Drucker used *perception* as a synonym for attention.) He echoed James's century-old declaration: "[P]erception is at the center. And it can—indeed it must—be trained."[18]

Why is perception important? The greater facility I have in perceiving, the more and more subtle forms I am able to see. A well-developed perception allows a person to see hidden assumptions as well as new possibilities. In *Innovation and Entrepreneurship*, Drucker reminds us that "when a change in perception takes place, the facts do not change. Their meaning does."[19] How we see things influences how we understand them and how we can respond to them.

Concentrated Attention: Focus Is Power

For the knowledge worker, focused attention is what gets work done. It is the engine of productivity. Complex mental operations cannot happen without a focused mind. Mihaly Csikszentmihalyi's studies of optimal experience find that focused attention is the basic ingredient for those exhilarating moments of flow when a person performs to his highest limits.[20]

Conversely, distraction decreases cognitive efficiency. Interruptions in the flow of thought break momentum, which then takes time to reestablish. Scattered and distracted attention wastes energy and results in less productive action. Thus, management should design work systems that help knowledge workers focus their attention.

In terms of brain structures, attention is associated with the prefrontal cortex (PFC), also known as "the inner CEO." This brain part is associated with directing and allocating attention. This area can be strengthened through systematic practice, just as a muscle can be strengthened through exercise. A more developed prefrontal cortex is associated with an increased ability to concentrate, connect, learn, and make decisions. However, it can also be weakened through another "systematic practice": multitasking.

Multitasking Damages Your Productivity, Your Relationships, and Your Brain

Multitasking, or simultaneously splitting one's attention across many tasks, has become an all-too-common résumé boast. Many people erroneously believe that doing multiple things at once makes them more efficient. After all, if the PC on my desk can multitask, why can't I? Workers look over their shoulder at their colleagues who are simultaneously talking on the phone, writing a report, and eating a sandwich. They wonder to themselves, "Is that what it takes to survive?" The good news is: no.

In fact, research shows that multitasking both slows performance and increases errors.[21] Multitasking also reduces the available attention and increases the chance that disorganizing emotions, like fear and anxiety, will overwhelm brain function. Chronic multitaskers report feeling "out of control." Over time, regular multitasking can lead to a state of panic. By the end of the day, many chronic multitaskers feel that they have accomplished little and are completely spent.

Multitasking also damages relationships. Consider this scenario: when your boss is pecking away at his keyboard as you attempt to discuss your pay raise, do you feel heard and respected? Probably not. Attention is the bridge of relationships, and the quality of a relationship is proportionate to the quality of attention. When attention is split or scattered, the quality of connection diminishes, and with it goes the productivity of a team.

It gets worse. Multitasking has a negative effect on how well people learn. UCLA researchers found that divided attention impairs complex learning and thus negatively affects decision making, adapting, and a host of other essential knowledge worker skills.[22] In their study, multitaskers demonstrated a superficial understanding of issues. Brain scans showed that they had become habituated to using a more primitive part of the brain—a part that is responsible for creating rote, inflexible memories (the basal ganglia). Conclusion: multitaskers use a part of the brain that leaves them less capable of applying the principles they have learned.

Study participants who focused their attention, however, relied on a different brain structure, namely, the hippocampus, a part that creates more flexible memories and allows for a deeper, more robust knowing. The focused students were able to apply a more nuanced understanding when facing problems. Chronic multitasking, therefore, leads to a form of neural "de-evolution." That's not a good recipe for high productivity.

Breaking the Cycle of Multitasking

Reducing multitasking means increasing effectiveness. Here is an example. After I asked her to limit her multitasking for a week, one finance executive I worked with reported the following:

> When I made a concerted effort not to do it, I was actually very effective. I finished quite a few tasks. I was able to better prioritize and minimize distractions. I was more focused. I didn't get overwhelmed with all the things I had to do and waste time just thinking about them in circles. I kept things in perspective. I stayed in the moment, and things that usually feel insurmountable were actually manageable.

After making a conscious effort to reduce multitasking, many people say that both their productivity and their quality of work increase significantly. They report connecting more meaningfully with their colleagues and loved ones, and becoming better listeners all around. Becoming aware of the high costs of multitasking and gradually stepping away from the habit helps people to preserve attention, concentrate, and be more productive. Multitasking is the opposite of concentrating. The good news is that there are other ways to improve concentration as well.

Concentration Meditation: Strengthening the Inner CEO

There are numerous methods for developing focused attention or concentration. Consider a tried-and-true way of developing attention: concentration meditation practice.[23] For many, meditation conjures up images of New Age incense and candles. However, for centuries, meditation served as the "basic training" of the fierce Japanese samurai warrior. Meditation gave the samurai an intense, unwavering focus to face a deadly enemy. Meditation can be useful for corporate warriors, too.

Plenty of scientific evidence proves that concentration meditation practice is beneficial. Concentration meditation lowers blood pressure, helps the stressed body to relax, and decreases difficult emotions.[24] Brain research at Harvard Medical School found that the prefrontal cortex in mindfulness meditators was significantly thicker than in non-meditators. As people age, the prefrontal cortex thins out, but the study showed that the cortex of older meditators was substantially thicker than that of their nonmeditating counterparts.[25] A thicker cortex is thought to mean greater strength in attention. Meditation strengthens the brain's ability to focus and is the antidote to multitasking.[26]

Attention, Mindfulness, and Systematic Abandonment: Learning to See in Order to Change

Once attention is strengthened through developing concentration, it can be used as a tool for other tasks, such as bringing things into awareness. Mindfulness, introduced earlier, is a way of directing attention to become increasingly more aware of our emotions, beliefs, and actions. Awareness leads to the possibility of choice. Choice gives us greater conscious influence over our subsequent actions. As I will demonstrate, directed attention is closely related to Drucker's advocacy of systematic abandonment.

Drucker prescribed that organizations should regularly and dispassionately examine their habitual processes and even whole businesses to determine whether they are still effective, or even necessary. Nonperforming elements should be *systematically abandoned* to free up resources for new, more productive ventures.

The process of systematic abandonment holds true for the knowledge worker as well. Because much of the brain's processing happens nonconsciously, or outside of awareness, workers unknowingly cling to maladaptive habits. For example, a colleague of mine habitually makes wisecracks in meetings, which often offend people. When I gently mentioned this to him, I found that he had no idea how frequently he did it, even though he wisecracked nearly every day. Attention training expands the scope of what we notice. Again, attention powers awareness. Mindfully directing attention makes conscious the nonconscious, enabling us to "see" (perhaps for the first time) and make more conscious choices about the invisible, ineffective behaviors that need to be "systematically abandoned" to achieve greater productivity.

To understand why systematic abandonment is necessary, let's explore the neurobiology behind how conscious actions and assumptions become nonconscious habits and beliefs. The neural root of the need for systematic abandonment lies in an old part of the brain called the basal ganglia. In the interest of efficiency and saving cognitive resources, the brain moves a repeated action or belief from the conscious control of the evolutionarily newer and more complex prefrontal cortex to the instinctual and much older basal ganglia.

This transfer to the basal ganglia makes conscious and intentional behavior gradually become nonconscious and automatic—a sort of behavioral default position. The newly formed habit becomes, literally, unthinking and nonadapting. Once a habitual action is triggered, it will play out rigidly, automatically, and often unknowingly. And, yes, frequently *unproductively*.

The basal ganglia's habitual patterning reflex explains why people often fall into a routine of relying on yesterday's successes to meet today's conditions, showing why "old habits die hard." These mindless habits are wired into the basal ganglia. Training and mindfully directing attention helps the worker to observe and shift out of default habitual thinking patterns and behaviors, creating the possibility for more productive effort.

Neuroplasticity: Rewiring the Network

If the shift to the basal ganglia is one cause of "mindlessness," the antidote lies in another well-established neural operation: neuroplasticity.[27] This term refers to the brain's ability to rewire itself. Though scientists previously thought that the brain did not change radically after adulthood, we now know that this is untrue. Furthermore, not only is the brain capable of change, but the change can be intentionally self-directed—call it self-directed transformation. By altering their neural pathways, it is possible for people to radically alter how they engage with the world. The automatic operations of the basal ganglia are not permanent and can be undone through practice.

The kicker? Attention is thought to be what holds the neural circuitry in place. You get the brain you practice. If you direct attention to a new behavior by breaking the pattern of the old one, the old behavior will gradually dismantle. Neuroplasticity is the biological basis for personal transformation and greater productivity. This can be achieved through mindfulness practice.

Mindfulness Means Directing Attention

The process of mindfulness is analogous to Drucker's systematic abandonment. Mindfulness directs the attention flashlight inward and examines what's working and what isn't. By illuminating the inner black box, it creates the possibility of abandoning an unwanted behavior.

Mindfulness and Adam Smith

Earlier in the chapter, I introduced the idea of mindfulness as a means of self-awareness, self-regulation, and self-transformation. You may be surprised to learn that no less a figure than the founding father of capitalism, Adam Smith, advocated cultivating *mindfulness*. Yes, Adam Smith.

In *The Theory of Moral Sentiments*, Smith counseled, *"We must become the impartial spectators of our own character and conduct."*[28] The impartial spectator is the part of you that dispassionately observes your behavior. This is mindfulness, pure and simple.

A helpful metaphor: imagine the mind as a raging river. Normally, we're caught in the river and taken for a wild ride by our thoughts and emotions. To take the perspective of the impartial spectator means to step out of the river and watch its flow from the shore. The shift in perceptual stance is critical, fostering the ability to watch our thoughts from an objective position. You are not your thoughts. Training his attention helps the knowledge worker to make a separation between what he thinks and feels and *how he acts*. To repeat, the impartial spectator creates the possibility of witnessing a thought or emotional reaction erupt inside without it translating into a destructive outward action. This distinction, as we shall see, provides a crucial pivot point for increasing the effectiveness of the knowledge worker.

If someone repeatedly recognizes an internal impulse, but does not act on it or suppress it, the neural connections between, say, a flash of anger and verbally lashing out gradually become disentangled. In time, the impulse to act no longer holds its gripping charge. The result: the knowledge worker's earlier destructive reactivity is now converted into a considered response. Productivity increases.

Employing the Impartial Spectator

Smith's impartial spectator turns out to be a powerful ally in responding to Drucker's knowledge worker productivity challenge, so let's take an in-depth look at how to employ this tool. First, I'll explore workers' mindsets, and second, I'll look at their emotional reactivity.

Mindsets for the Status Quo and Mindsets for Growth

Internal narratives are the ideas, stories, or explanations that we have about our experience, including the experience of ourselves. Taken as a whole, they form a mindset. Mindsets serve as an unconscious filter that predetermines what we see and how we see it. Think of a mindset as a meta-software program that runs underneath your conscious awareness but "preprograms" your perception and response.

The implications of a mindset for workplace productivity are readily apparent. A manager who automatically thinks about how new ventures could fail (and reflect poorly on him) and a counterpart who explores what the possibilities are for moving into an untapped market are two examples of how mindsets function at work. One mindset shuts down opportunity; the other creates it.

Luckily, the impartial spectator can help you uncover which mindsets are guiding your behavior and shift to a mindset for growth and productivity. But first, let's take a closer look at these mindsets.

Stanford psychologist Carol Dweck, after 30 years of research, identified two forms of mindset: fixed and growth.[29] (Bear in mind that both forms of mindset can exist within the same person and can be activated depending on the circumstances.)

The fixed mindset is rigid and judgmental. It holds that people either are or are not born with talent. Subsequently, this mindset will go to great lengths to protect an ego identity that disallows admitting mistakes, since "mistakes = failure." Perfection rules, and, unfortunately, learning, risk taking, and adapting stop. In a networked knowledge work environment, improvement efforts are unconsciously blocked, and productivity suffers.

The growth mindset, in contrast, is flexible and generative. It views talent as something that can be grown with effort. Instead of trying to *impress*, this mindset will try to *improve*. The growth mindset is curious and views mistakes not as a cause for condemnation, but as information—as an opportunity to learn and develop. In the collaborative world of knowledge work, such a mindset fertilizes new thought, encourages risk taking, and creates stronger bonds of connection among team members.

The growth mindset exemplifies Drucker's notion of continual learning. By being curious and open to the world, this mindset allows people to take on a wider, empathic, and more hopeful view that rationally focuses on possibilities and opportunities. Such a mindset is essential in a knowledge work environment.

Mindfulness practice illuminates how these mindsets operate, enabling the worker to learn how to "switch tracks" from the rigid world of the fixed mindset to the open and receptive way of the growth mindset. Take the example of Jack, a banking executive who, after applying mindfulness practice, had this self-observation:

A fixed mindset definitely played a role in my reactivity, which was a problem for me at work. It caused me to make assumptions about a situation from a negative belief that I held about a coworker's motives, and that belief was not based on any real information but derived purely from my own mindset. Had I been more curious, I could have asked, "What is causing him to respond in that way?" Instead of

learning something useful about the situation, I reinforced my exist-
ing prejudices about the person and ended up in an argument with no
better understanding of the situation.

The fixed mindset does not learn. Instead, it seeks to support what it already knows. Furthermore, feelings of tension, threat, and fear often accompany the fixed mindset. A stance of defense or attack is by nature stressful and makes productive interaction difficult.

By contrast, a growth mindset approaches a situation with greater calm and openness. Listen to Shirley, an accounting executive, explain how she successfully employed the growth framework:

In working with a client, I put myself in a more inquiring state of
mind by asking questions from a growth and learning point of view
instead of assuming that this person was acting selfishly and egotis-
tically. First, I sensed a calmer state of mind while I was in an in-
quiring mode. Consequently, it stemmed the urge to feel frustrated or
indignant. In addition, I could see that the other person, although at
first defensive, could sense that I really wanted to understand his
point of view. He gradually opened up to me with a more authentic
and honest manner. We were able to come to common ground that we
didn't know we had.

By becoming mindful of both orientations, fixed and growth, a person becomes aware of her operative mindset and its ramifications. People are often astonished that a simple change in mindset can produce dramatically positive results. Consciously shifting to a growth orientation opens up unforeseen possibilities and solves problems. The alternative fixed position results in an ego-driven, intractable emotional battle about right and wrong that goes nowhere. Changing the mindset opens opportunities to improve productivity.

Now, let's move to the second application of Smith's impartial spectator—the area of reactive emotions.

Being Mindful of Reactive Emotions

Reactive emotions happen automatically, without will or effort. They are nearly always motivated by self-defense or self-gratification—anger, fear, anxiety, lust, and desire are some examples. Reactive emotions generally do their jobs well, protecting us, feeding us, and so on. However, from time to time, these emotions hijack us and precipitate actions that lead to unwanted results.

Strong reactive emotions affect productivity because they shut down the brain's ability to be rational, objective, and adaptive. Reactive emotions distort perception, as the person interprets events to confirm, support, and maintain the emotional state. The brain of a knowledge worker who is in the grip of a reactive emotion cannot accept information that challenges her thinking or emotional state.

The attention of the impartial spectator can be a powerful tool to catch the emotional reaction before it has a chance to lead to destructive behavior. Paul Ekman, the pioneering researcher agrees: "When we are being *attentive* . . . we are able to observe ourselves during an emotional episode. . . . We recognize that we are being emotional and can consider whether or not our response is justified. We can reevaluate, reappraise, and if that is not successful, then direct what we say and do. This occurs while we are experiencing the emotion, as soon as we have become conscious of our emotional feelings and actions."[30] Let's consider a practical example to observe how the mindful impartial spectator relates to emotional reactivity.

The Case of the Anxious Engineer

I once worked with a respected and technically brilliant engineer who was affiliated with a large defense contractor. Call him Marv. Though he was very well liked, he was known to erupt verbally when he was presented with bad news. This reaction overwhelmed whoever delivered the news. To make matters worse, Marv's eruptions took place in meetings with his superiors, and they were negatively affecting his prospects for promotion. So, he sought my help.

Marv learned how to train his impartial spectator to become aware of how the verbal eruption actually worked. With some practice and observation, he realized that his verbal explosion was actually the *result* of something else that he hadn't noticed before. He perceived something new.

Preceding the eruption, Marv clearly sensed a rush of energy in his chest that came out in the form of a panicked verbal reaction. Armed with this information, he could become mindful of the emergence of the energetic impulse. When he sensed that an eruption was imminent, that was his signal to take a deep breath and pause for a moment. The impulse would rise, come to a peak, and then subside. With practice, he became increasingly able to catch the reaction before it erupted verbally. Marv used his attention to perceive the situation and make a different choice. That resulted in better relationships with his colleagues and higher productivity.

What Marv did was to use the principle of neuroplasticity to decouple the rush in his chest from verbal action. In time, by using his attention, he became better able to stop himself. He said he felt a sense of control and confidence that he had never experienced before. Without the weight of this debilitating reaction, he was freer to put his brilliant mind to work for the firm.

Drucker, the Great Liberator

We have only scratched the surface of how self-management improves knowledge worker productivity. There is much more to explore. We have seen how enhanced perception (or attention) plays a pivotal role in the process, and we have discussed some basic ways in which perception can be trained to focus as well as manage the knowledge worker's mindset and emotional reactivity.

Peter Drucker was gifted with an exceptional perceptive power—a capacity to see what was already there, but remained largely invisible to most. The author of 39 books and numerous articles, a one-time apprentice in the cotton trade, journalist, university professor, and sought-after consultant, Drucker was a highly productive knowledge worker. The issue of making other knowledge workers productive was a central concern of his work for almost 50 years.

In her work *The Definitive Drucker*, Elizabeth Haas Edersheim mentioned that a core characteristic of Peter's personality was his ability to liberate people.[31] By asking the right question, challenging a closely held assumption, and pushing person after person to see something that was previously unseen, he liberated them from their self-imposed boundaries. By shifting our perceptions ever so slightly, he revealed a new world full of possibilities. Because Drucker is no longer here to liberate us from our own limitations of thought, emotion, and action, we—guided by his work—must adopt new tools and learn to liberate ourselves.

12

Labor Markets and Human Resources: Managing Manual and Knowledge Workers

Roberto Pedace

In the better use of human resources lies the major opportunity for increasing productivity. . . . The management of men should be the first and foremost concern of operating managements, rather than the management of things and techniques.

—Peter Drucker, *The New Society*

Although it was not always central to Peter Drucker's thoughts, much of his work has described the importance of managerial decisions concerning employee recruitment, training, incentives, and compensation. In addition, the significance that Drucker placed on history and institutions is particularly critical in understanding labor-market behavior and outcomes. The objective of this chapter is to explore some intersections between Drucker's ideas on labor markets and human resource management with the tools that economists utilize in addressing issues in these areas. Later, I will also use an example from my own research to illustrate how Drucker's ideas shed light on an important empirical puzzle.

The subsequent material in this chapter is organized into three sections. The first section covers broad concepts in the economics of labor and human resources. Specifically, this section develops some general principles about worker-firm interaction, illustrating how labor economics utilizes the basic tools of microeconomics, but has evolved to analyze scenarios that are unique to markets in which labor services are bought and sold. Following that section, I describe the role of management in dealing with issues of employee productivity. Here, I focus on integrating Drucker's work with some important elements of human resource and personnel economics. The third section illustrates how some of Drucker's insights can shed light on a practical and important question in the area of labor economics. The chapter concludes with a summary of the most important ideas.

Conceptual Foundations and the Importance of Labor Markets

The elasticity of the total wage bill is the key factor in the enterprise's ability to survive a business setback.

—Peter Drucker, *The New Society*

Drucker had an uncanny ability to make complicated, theoretical concepts applicable in the real world. The statement just given was no exception, but without an understanding of some fundamental microeconomic theory, it is difficult to envision precisely what is implied by his words and the conditions that most influence the relevance of those ideas.

The *total wage bill* is defined as the wage rate (cost per unit of labor) multiplied by the total number of labor units employed by the firm. For a particular type of labor (e.g., machine operator), the wage paid is determined by the market (the number of people in this line of work and the number of firms seeking this type of worker), along with numerous worker-specific factors (e.g., education and experience) and job characteristics (e.g., working conditions and nonwage benefits). After evaluating these existing conditions, potential workers will determine the lowest wage at which they are willing to accept employment, and firms will determine the highest wage that they are willing to pay. The firm continues to hire workers as long as the additional revenue generated by hiring another worker exceeds the wage at which those seeking employment are willing to work. When the firm cannot make more profit by hiring an additional worker, it has reached its optimal labor input allocation and accordingly determined its total wage bill.

The *elasticity* of the wage bill is the ratio of the percent change in the labor costs to the percent change in the firm's production. The larger the ratio, the more responsive (or elastic) is the firm's wage bill. Drucker's focus on the elasticity of labor costs suggests that the ability of a firm to constantly adjust its wages and/or the number of workers it employs is a critical component of its long-term success. In response to declining sales of a product or service, a firm will seek cutbacks in the size of its labor force and in its use of raw materials and physical capital. Since labor is typically the largest component of variable production costs, it is sensible that attention would be focused there.

However, a couple of factors must be considered when examining a firm's ability to swiftly adjust its wage bill in the face of a "business setback." One is the production technology that is utilized by the firm or available in the industry. This will determine the firm's ability to substitute capital for labor or higher-wage labor for lower-wage labor. The other element is existing institutional constraints. This can result from union contracts (which may have predetermined wage bill targets) or, in the case of knowledge workers, long-term employment and compensation agreements. Finally, direct government intervention in labor markets with work-time restrictions and minimum wage laws can directly affect the elasticity of the wage bill. Consequently, as Drucker often emphasized, an understanding of the precise conditions in which firms operate and the practicality of exercising various options is critical for managing an organization's human resources effectively.

Human Resources and the Role of Management

Management everywhere faces the same problems. It has to organize work for productivity; it has to lead the worker towards productivity and achievement.

—Peter Drucker, *Management:*
Tasks, Responsibilities, Practices

He (the worker) *needs above all predictable income on which he can plan and budget. Hence the worker's own insistence on "security" as his first need and as vastly more important than the wage rate.*

—Peter Drucker, *The New Society*

One reason that labor economics became a specialized field of microeconomics is that scholars and practitioners recognized the need to analyze worker-firm interactions beyond the brief and impersonal transactions characterizing most markets. For example, if I visit the local convenience store to purchase a candy bar, the store owner will not know anything about me, but will not care as long as I pay for the product. Similarly, I will not have any information about the store owner, but I will not be troubled by this as long as I can purchase the product there. These types of market transactions, in which buyers and sellers are not concerned about each other's personal characteristics, are sometimes called *spot-market* transactions. Unlike transactions in most product markets, a job involves an ongoing personal relationship between the employer and the employee. These long-term relationships make spot-market models of labor substitution incomplete because they ignore the characteristics and outcomes of "internal labor markets" (ILMs). Generally, ILMs contain job ladders with an inventory of all jobs; job evaluations based on the degree of supervision, skill, and importance of the tasks; and promotional paths that provide opportunities for professional development and wage growth. The ILM provides the "security" that Drucker describes by defining seniority rules and rewarding workers for good performance.

While this long-term worker-firm relationship is valuable for workers in easing anxieties related to unemployment and future earnings, the development of ILMs can also benefit employers. First, imperfect information in the labor market typically results in the use of interviews, tests, and other screening measures, which increase the costs associated with hiring new workers. Second, once they are on the job, workers acquire specific skills; this increases the costs of turnover, since new workers will not have the same productivity levels. Third, an even more radical view argues that when workers began seeking the protection of unions with industrialization, firm owners responded with ILMs as a divide-and-conquer tool. That is, the creation of job categories and hierarchies divided the interests of the workers, reduced solidarity, and made workers more submissive to the firm's demands. A common theme in all of these explanations, which contrasts with Drucker's statement, is that the development of ILMs was largely beneficial to firms.

The reality is likely to lie somewhere in between. In other words, ILMs improved workers' well-being by providing them with increased job security and promotional opportunities, while firms could now also be more efficient in retaining workers with industry- and job-specific skills. The benefits of long-term attachment between workers and firms make it possible and, in many cases, sensible for firms to offer wages that exceed those that the worker can obtain elsewhere.

> *A high wage rate may in effect constitute a very much lower wage cost per unit of production; it may bring forth much greater productive effort and efficiency.*
>
> —Peter Drucker, *The New Society*

It is in this dimension of labor and personnel economics that Drucker's idea that managers should pay workers a wage above the market rate was truly innovative. While many managers understand that it makes sense to consider the influence of pay on workers' sense of value to their organization, commitment, and productivity, this was initially resisted by mainstream economists. The idea, now known as the *efficiency wage hypothesis*, was first utilized by political economists as a complement to Marx's notion of subsistence wages during the initial stages of industrialization and the positive relationship among wages, nutritional intake, and worker productivity. This was later formalized in the context of developing economies and low-wage, manual-labor markets, where models predicted that, up to a point, productivity increases would outweigh the higher costs incurred through wage increases.

It was not until later, however, that the relevance of this concept in a market for knowledge workers was explored. In this labor market, two of the most important hiring issues are *adverse selection* and *moral hazard*. Adverse selection occurs when it is not possible to observe the *abilities* of job applicants to perform the required tasks, and moral hazard results when it is not possible to observe the *actions* of employees when they are "on the clock." As we increasingly move to a knowledge-based economy, both adverse selection and moral hazard contribute to the asymmetric information difficulties in hiring and retention decisions concerning knowledge workers. This is something that Peter Drucker saw well ahead of its time.

Efficiency wages mitigate adverse selection problems because higher wages attract more capable job seekers, and this allows managers to choose workers from an applicant pool that generally consists of more productive candidates. While piece rates and commission compensation schemes solve the moral hazard problem in situations in which worker output is easily measured, these techniques will not suffice for most knowledge work, where productivity is not directly observable. Here, efficiency wages, combined with productivity and seniority rewards in the earnings profile of an ILM, increase the cost of job loss for workers, induce a greater degree of effort (less shirking) and more productivity, and simultaneously minimize supervising costs. Moreover, these higher wages boost morale and reduce turnover, which in turn create additional cost savings in hiring and training activities.

Undoubtedly, Drucker had similar views about the positive effects of paying "high wages." What is striking, however, is that, while his observations in labor markets had typically drawn on existing theories of worker-firm interaction, there are no references to efficiency wage effects on "productive effort" that predate Drucker's statement earlier in this section. Furthermore, he has never been appropriately recognized for this idea.

Using Drucker's Insights to Understand the Labor-Market Impact of Immigration in the United States

One specific area of my research on labor markets estimates the impact of immigration on workers in the United States. A major concern in the United States is that immigrants will increase the competition for jobs and, as a result, reduce the wages and employment opportunities available for native-born workers. Since the concentration of immigrants varies considerably across the United States, the fear is that wages and employment of the native-born are disproportionately affected in high-immigration areas. A classification of metropolitan areas between 1985 and 1990 revealed that six out of ten high-immigration metropolitan areas were located in the southern or western regions of the country. Furthermore, in 1980 and 1985, three cities (New York, Los Angeles, and Miami) accounted for more than half of the immigrants who had arrived in the previous decade. Even data with a longer time horizon show that only six states (California, Florida, Illinois, New Jersey, New York, and Texas) have received the bulk of immigrants over the last 40 years.

While these states must deal with the direct labor-market impacts of immigration, any migratory response of native-born workers will transfer some of the effects to numerous labor markets, and therefore deserves national public policy attention. The debates on this issue are typically quite emotional, but before joining any mass appeals for policy change, it is important to review the facts in this area and understand their relationship to some of the concepts previously discussed in this chapter.

Many studies have estimated the effects of immigration on wages and employment. The most common method is a regional or area approach. This approach typically compares the effects of immigration on the wages of native-born workers across regions by introducing a variable that accounts for immigration as a percentage of the total labor force in a given geographical area, while simultaneously controlling for human capital characteristics (education, work experience, and so on). In most studies, the metropolitan area is used as the level of aggregation for measuring immigrant concentration.

In studies that have used this approach, there is a small relationship between increased immigration and labor-market outcomes. Early studies found that a 10 percent increase in the percentage of immigrants reduces the earnings of the native-born by less than 0.5

percent and employment of the native-born by a maximum of 1 percent. However, there is also evidence that these effects vary by demographic group, and that some even experience increases in earnings when there are larger concentrations of immigrants.

More recently, research has focused on controlling for the migratory response of native-born workers and better identifying the extent of immigrant competition for specific jobs. Measures of the proportion of immigrants in a metropolitan area may not accurately capture the extent of immigrant labor-market competition for most workers, since immigrants are not equally distributed across various jobs in these local labor markets. However, after using metropolitan area– and occupation-specific immigration and internal migration measurements, studies continue to find that the effects of immigration are small. The largest negative effects estimate that a 10 percent increase in the immigrant population share reduces wages by only 0.5 percentage point for lower-skilled workers. On the other hand, these studies also find that wages for some higher-skilled workers are positively affected by increases in immigration and often offset the negative effects on lower-skilled workers.

Overall, there is only limited evidence that immigration exerts downward pressure on wages for native-born workers. Until recently, many researchers believed that the small effects of immigration were due to the failure of studies to explicitly control for the internal migration of native-born workers. Several studies have now incorporated this into the analysis, but evidence of any convincing negative effects of immigration remains elusive. Most of the immigration effects on native-born workers' wages not only remain positive but also tend to outweigh the occasional negative effects.

The large number of immigrants who are employed or seeking work in lower-skilled jobs generates expectations of finding negative impacts on native-born workers that are much larger than those that are actually observed. The manual labor employed in these jobs tends to be highly substitutable, since the tasks tend to require the acquisition of physical skill, but less "knowledge work." The result is that the demand for labor is highly responsive to changes in wages.

> *If the demand for labor in secondary sector occupations is relatively elastic, an increase in immigration will initially reduce wages and employment levels for natives, but the increase in total employment will outweigh the reduction in wages.*
>
> —Roberto Pedace, "Immigration, Labor Market Mobility, and the Earnings of Native-Born Workers: An Occupational Segmentation Approach"

The increase in the total wage bill simultaneously generates a series of demand effects (from increased aggregate income) that benefits both lower- and higher-skilled workers. This would ultimately result in higher wages and employment levels. Consequently, some of the same theoretical tools that Drucker used to understand a firm's labor demand response during the business cycle can also be used to understand this important public policy issue.

Many immigrants have also been working in higher-skilled jobs. While we would not expect the same degree of labor substitutability in these jobs, where knowledge becomes the worker's primary contribution to the production process, the traditional theory of labor markets would predict at least some wage decreases with increased competition in this labor market. The absence of negative wage effects is not due to any lack of immigrant competition for jobs in this sector. In fact, in the Los Angeles, Miami, New York, San Francisco, and Washington, D.C., metropolitan areas, more than 10 percent of the workers in higher-skilled occupations are foreign-born. In some industries, this percentage is considerably larger. The persistent results in empirical studies, indicating that the wage outcomes of native-born workers in these occupations are improved with higher levels of immigration, demonstrate that other insights into worker and firm behavior in labor markets may be useful.

Once again, Drucker's ideas also shed some light on the observed immigration effects on higher-skilled workers. Specifically, the existence of ILMs and efficiency wage structures plays a more important role in those labor markets in which knowledge workers are most prevalent. In these circumstances, the diversity and specialization of knowledge, the accumulation of firm-specific human capital, and the seniority rules of ILMs provide some shelter from the downward wage pressures caused by increased labor-market competition. In addition, immigration allows firms to screen job seekers from a more diverse labor pool, where they are more likely to find workers with knowledge and skills that are complementary to those of the existing workers. Wage increases for these workers result from these complementarities combined with efficiency wages that create better job matches, reduce incentives to shirk, lower hiring costs, and increase returns from on-the-job training.

Conclusion

This chapter began with some general concepts of labor and human resource management and proceeded to a discussion of some specific tools utilized in labor economics, their relationship with Drucker's work, and their relevance to my own research.

The fundamental ideas can be summarized by the following:

1. Management's understanding of labor markets is essential for the performance of the most important human resource tasks: who and how many workers to hire, how much to pay, and how to motivate employees for maximum productivity.
2. Since labor and knowledge are the most valuable production assets in the firm, the human resource management tasks

should not be delegated to departments that are not directly responsible for strategic decisions on production, pricing, growth, and mission; general managers must take the initiative and be responsible for aligning the human resource decisions with the objectives of the firm.

3. Managers must "look out the window" and attempt to understand how economic conditions, demographic trends, and government policies affect labor-market outcomes in order to better support the goals of the firm with their human resource decisions.

Author's Notes: I am indebted to Joe Maciariello and Hideki Yamawaki for their support and feedback during the Drucker Difference lectures and to Craig Pearce for his willingness to critique an earlier draft of this chapter. I would also like to thank the students who have taken my course on labor and personnel economics; their questions and comments helped me better integrate Peter Drucker's ideas with labor economics generally and my own research specifically.

13

Peter Drucker:
The Humanist Economist

Jay Prag

We have an approach that relates economics to human values.

—Peter F. Drucker, *The Daily Drucker*

Introduction

Having taught economics for 25 years, I have had occasion to engage with a student or colleague who volunteers (usually with a curious sense of pride) that he doesn't like or doesn't believe in economics. It was with that perspective that I used to think about Peter Drucker. After all, he said in Jack Beatty's *Atlantic* magazine article "The Education of Peter Drucker" that "there's one thing economists and I agree on, I'm no economist."

Typically, people who don't believe in economics also don't believe in free markets or individual rights, yet they do believe in—or have a lot of faith in—big governments. So I was surprised when I first read Drucker's book *The New Realities* and found that he and I have virtually identical perspectives on practically everything economic. But how is that possible? I am a tried-and-true, card-carrying

(University of Rochester Ph.D.) economist, and Peter was an avowed noneconomist. Having considered his positions and thoughts and my own on many issues, I have found the answer, and I declare the great man to be a humanist economist.

Peter Drucker: The Early Years

In "The Education of Peter Drucker," Jack Beatty writes:

> *During his four-year stay in England, Drucker sat in on John Maynard Keynes's economics seminar at Cambridge University and made an important discovery: He "suddenly realized that Keynes and all the brilliant economics students in the room were interested in the behavior of commodities while I was interested in the behavior of people."*

With that, Peter Drucker left his early career as an economics teacher, and many people, including Peter himself, believe that he left economics itself. While any informed reader of Drucker would disagree with that overstatement, it is clear that Peter had a serious discomfort with the abstractions that economists and their models make.

Economics is a social science. I tell students that repeatedly and make them think about those words carefully. Economics uses the tools of mathematics, physics, engineering, and other "hard sciences" in its models, but what economics is modeling is very human and very social behavior. Put differently, economics uses mathematical precision to explain human behavior in the same way that particle physicists use it to explain the unobservable. From Aristotle to Newton to Rutherford to Bohr, particle physics became more refined and, in many scientists' opinions, more accurate. They predicted, tested, proved, and disproved conjectures about the structure of matter. They could do this because, over time, their tools for observing the minuscule particles that they postulated became more discerning and more sophisticated.

Economists took that cue and also modeled the unobservable with great mathematical precision. A wonderful example that Drucker mentions in *The New Realities* is utility theory. Observations of human behavior show us that consumers don't usually consume a huge quantity of any one good at any one point in time. When I teach this to students, I ask them to think about something simple like eating donuts. The first donut makes you very happy, but the sixth donut adds very little additional happiness to your total. If asked to explain this, we would simply say that we are sick of donuts, having already eaten five of them. This behavior is modeled by economists with a mathematical expression that recreates that pattern.

We invent a utility function $U(x)$ with properties that mimic the aforementioned human behavior, happiness rises with every additional unit of consumption, but it rises at a decreasing rate. Over the objections of most microeconomic purists, I usually teach this with a chart that explicitly measures my happiness:

Donuts	U(Donuts) = Happiness	Change in Happiness
1	20	20
2	35	15
3	47	12
4	55	8
5	58	3
6	59	1

There's nothing wrong with this abstraction, and it does model simple consumer behavior reasonably well. But when we discuss utility theory in advanced economics classes, we do so with calculus, derivatives, and lots of rules about how consumers *must* behave. Peter Drucker would say that's putting the cart before—or maybe even on top of—the horse. The math isn't right; the consumer is. These microeconomic, math-based rules are a wrongheaded approach to teaching and understanding economics. This is where one can truly see Drucker's "humanist" approach.

When he said that economists are "interested in the behavior of commodities," Peter Drucker likely meant that economists were thinking too much as scientists and not enough as sociologists. They wanted to explain something as well as their hard science colleagues did, and that something had to be tangible, measurable, and testable—like the price of commodities. There is nothing wrong with that desire, but in explaining the price of commodities elegantly, you have to have the humility to admit that you have explained only *that* well.

In *The New Realities*, Drucker quite accurately skewers Keynesian macroeconomic policy for its uneven track record in curing our economy's ills. Drucker likens countercyclical macroeconomic policy to a drug and says, quite correctly, that if we assessed that drug the same way we do others, it would probably not be accepted by the FDA. He also says, again with incredible insight, that the rampant use of this policy drug during the Great Depression changed the expectations of the electorate. Even though the effectiveness of this policy is limited, we now expect the government to do something when the economy slows or declines. Macroeconomic policy is thus the social version of the cure for the common cold: a largely useless set of drugs that do not speed recovery and, at best, treat a few symptoms.

Our addiction to spurious macroeconomic policy has a curious connection to the government's response to our current economic crisis. Like most economists today, Drucker would have said that bailing out firms that made bad decisions, as in the government's bailout of the banking sector, leads only to more bad decisions down the road and an expectation of another bailout. Perhaps the biggest irony in the current economic crisis is the near-death and subsequent government takeover of General Motors. Drucker famously advised GM on a long-term success strategy in 1946, but the company largely ignored his advice. One can only guess that GM would have been in better shape today if it had heeded his advice (it certainly couldn't be in worse shape!).

Abstracting from Drucker a bit, there is a good example of overelegance in the related field of finance: efficient markets. This is taught in finance classes as a theory or hypothesis with proofs that are based on the mathematics of random numbers and information. These proofs show that you cannot beat the market (you cannot do better than buying and holding the market portfolio), and thus, the theorists conclude, investors should not waste their time trying to beat the market. It's all very precise. But once again, that's putting the math before the reality. Markets probably are efficient, but they are made so by people who find and invest in mispriced stocks. Put differently, if people didn't try to beat the market (if you take people out of the process), markets would not *be* efficient!

Peter Drucker, the social scientist, wanted us to remember that the people are always part of the result. But like it or not, he was a very astute economist. He discusses incentive structures, productivity, and motivation as often as the famous economists Alfred Marshall, Joseph Schumpeter, and Paul Samuelson. Peter just didn't feel obliged to model these things with mathematical, overelegant equations. And while he didn't rely on first-order conditions derived from constrained maximizations in his books and articles, history has proven that his economic intuition was correct far more often than that of many of my fellow economists.

Drucker's ability to assimilate and interpret a wide array of scholarly work (from an even wider array of disciplines) and his keen sense of observation allowed him to predict changes in the economy that no narrowly trained economist could have fathomed. To wit, Drucker noted that he had seen the future of industrial organization in the empowered American workforce of World War II, and his "responsible worker" from 1942 is, in many ways, the first sighting of Craig Pearce's "shared leadership" of 2004.

And because he was a truly integrated thinker, he could see that the parts of the economy that were easily reducible and easily modeled by mathematics were also limited and, in many ways, limiting. These economic models, and their brethren in related fields like finance, were empowering decision makers to view their businesses as abstract entities that could be tweaked to perfection. Drucker never lost sight of the people. He knew that no set of equations ever produced a single product and no amount of money could make an employee a happy cog in an uncaring corporate machine.

Drucker also reinvigorated the largely dormant economic concept of human capital. His astoundingly accurate concept of the "knowledge worker" (from 1959!) predicted the time when the typical employee would use education and training as much as he did machinery and land. He saw the growth potential in human capital, especially as it became augmented by things like technology. Furthermore, Drucker understood and predicted that this human capital would allow the worker to get the fair share of the business profits that Marx coveted. Marxism never imagined the technological shift in which the machine would become slave to the worker—but Peter Drucker did.

Peter Drucker: Groups and Governments

This humanist approach explains Drucker's insight into the power of groups. While Drucker knew that the human element would often dictate the final results in the corporate setting, he also appreciated the power that was created when that human element banded together. A major theme of Drucker's *The New Realities* is that the economic and political power of the individual is magnified when people stop being individuals. He abstracts from Mark Hanna's late-nineteenth-century innovations in politics that mobilized the power of special-interest groups in both business and government.

This too is a well-known economic concept. But there are two factors at work here: the collective versus the individual and the power of bigness. Peter Drucker showed his economic instincts when he said that collective groups have more power than the sum of their parts. Unions, clubs, corporations, and other special-interest groups apply a collective decision-making mentality to get more than the sum of what they would get as individuals. All of these collectives were created with good intentions, but all of them are susceptible to the corruption that is often associated with power.

Unions were formed to prevent large employers from artificially lowering wages by using individual workers' incentives against them: if you don't take this job at low wages, someone else will. By forming a union, the workers all agreed that none of them would work at unfairly low wages, thus forcing the firm to be fairer to all of its workers. But from that noble beginning, the unions used their collective bargaining power to extort an ever-larger share of the pie. The flaw in the logic then appeared: unless all workers around the world are members of the group, this wage demand isn't going to work. As we have repeatedly seen in recent years, goods can be imported or jobs can be relocated to places that don't have unions or where wage demands are more reasonable. And then the union becomes a political group rather than an economic group, offering its massive voting bloc to any candidate who agrees to protect its jobs from "cheap foreign labor."

The corporation itself is a collective of people. Because it has its own legal standing, we often ascribe life to the corporation, and to a large extent, Peter Drucker's life's work was undoing that animation. In reading Drucker on almost any business topic, you hear his mantra: what about the people? Thus, the corporation doesn't try to make profits, or compete, or survive—its people do. But this human element has two sides, as the often misused concept of sustainability shows. When asked, many executives will say that the corporation must find a way to survive. Why? Because it employs a lot of people—most notably the executives, who want to keep *their* jobs. But the corporation does not exist except as a legal protection for its investors. And therefore, it should exist only if its investors are being well served. When the firm's technologies and products become outdated, the firm needs to allow its capital, labor, and other resources to move into more productive industries. As a matter of good business practice, Peter Drucker would be appalled by the now popular concept of "too big to fail." As a student of political power and economic history, however, he would most certainly predict its assertion.

But the power of groups, like the precision of the mathematical models we discussed earlier, has limits. The supergroup known as the government is often ascribed superhuman power by voters, by macroeconomists, and even by itself. Keynesian macroeconomics placed government in its own separate category, like the 800-lb gorilla that sleeps wherever it wants. By its nature, government is big, but why should its size change the rules that apply to it or the expectations that we have for it?

As Drucker points out, one reason that we ascribe great power to the government is specifically because it makes the rules, and thus it can make them in such a way as to create power. A good example of that is the government's two primary revenue sources: taxation and seignorage.

We probably think we understand taxation pretty well because we all pay taxes. But consider the ways in which taxation is different from other payments in our lives. Income taxes, for example, are not optional payments for most people. If you don't think that an apple is worth its price, you don't pay the price, and you don't get the apple. But once the government decides on taxes, it's illegal for citizens not to pay them. If you refuse to pay, you go to jail. So taxes are not a choice in the same way that other prices are. Seignorage, or paying for its expenditures with newly printed money, is similar. If the government decides to pay for its expenditures by printing money, individuals have little choice other than to keep using money and pay the subsequent inflation tax.

Given this mandatory aspect, the "how" part of taxation is critical. Representative government is supposed to work like this: we send a small group of people to the seat of government to decide for all of us what the right amount of government spending is and how the things we collectively need should be paid for. This sounds pretty straightforward. But deferring for a moment the question of what the government should be doing, consider the problem of paying for it. In theory, you should allocate taxes like any other price: people pay what the government services are worth to them. But that approach will almost certainly tax poor people too much and rich people too little.

Thus, we have progressive taxes, estate taxes, and other "deep pockets" taxes that arise from the reality that it's faster, easier, and more politically astute to tax a few rich people a lot rather than to try to find a tax system that's completely fair. But reiterating the Oliver Wendell Holmes quote that Drucker uses, "The power to tax is the power to destroy." Soak-the-rich taxes probably started when wealth was associated with property and other fixed resources. In that world, taxes couldn't change the income that they were taxing very much. Put differently, the size of the pie that the government was trying to take a slice from was roughly fixed, so how it took its slice didn't matter much.

Today, most high-income people are highly educated, highly productive, and loaded with choices. If the government says that it's going to tax away 75 percent of the income that your last hour of work generates, your incentive to work that hour falls—and by extension, output falls and society is harmed. That's also true of the last dollar that you decide to invest if investment returns are taxed. And if taxes change the size of the pie, and there's every indication that they do beyond some point, then the size of the government's slice and its method of paying for that slice have a potentially negative effect on the economy.

So how does the government decide what it does? Drucker believes that the government should provide only what economists call public goods. It is known that there are goods that the free market simply won't produce on its own—goods like national defense and public parks have what's called a free-rider problem. Once these things are provided by someone, everyone can use them without paying for them. Given this free-rider problem, no individual has an incentive to buy these public goods, since every individual knows that he'll be able to use them once someone else buys them. So we need the group known as government to buy the correct amount of public goods, and to charge everyone a fair price.

All of this works fine until we realize that the government, like the corporation, is a social construct. It isn't a machine, a monster, or a force of nature. It's an invention of people that is operated entirely by people. Government, as our collective and representative, does vital things. But government is also a job and a business and, at heart, just a very large collective of people. It reacts to the same forces that all other groups of people react to. It wants to succeed, but success is a difficult thing to measure here. For the government, is success building a better mousetrap or getting reelected? That matters a lot. Those with one of these beliefs see the government as a special, large business. Those with the other see it as a self-interested special-interest group. And the correct answer is that government is both of these things.

Like any business, government cannot be unproductive and inefficient forever if it expects to survive, but it doesn't have stockholders and traditional customers that keep it in line with its competitors. It has lots of voters with lots of reasons to vote. As Peter Drucker points out in *The New Realities*, governments respond to groups of voters more than they do to individual voters. A group with a lot of votes gets much more of what it wants from the government than the same number of unorganized individuals. Drucker understood that the power of the special-interest group comes from the fact that the government is itself people—elected officials—with well-paying jobs that they want to continue doing.

Peter Drucker had great respect for the power of government to affect societal outcomes. He saw a lot of different governments do a lot of different (sometimes terrible) things. But despite its size and its concentrated economic power, government is not superhuman. The recent financial bailout and economic stimulus package have again revitalized the perspective that government will save us and protect us. The brutal fact is that government *is* us. It doesn't know more just because it is bigger. It doesn't see the future any better than we do, and it can't undo the past. It is our collective wisdom on its best day, but it is never a deity. We need a government to do the things that no one of us can do or would do well. We need the government to purchase—although not necessarily to produce—public goods. And as Peter Drucker pointed out, we need the government to regulate and control our markets to be sure that there isn't too much economic power or influence in any one entity's hands.

One well-known compelling case for government regulation was put forth by Nobel Prize–winning economist George Akerloff in what's called "The Market for Lemons."

> *Suppose there are an equal number of two types of used car: good ones worth $10,000, and lemons worth $2,000. Suppose further that only the seller knows which type he has. If you're a potential buyer faced with this asymmetric information problem, your best approach is to offer the average value, $6,000, for a used car. But only the lemon owner will be willing to sell his car at that price. This result implies that a poorly informed market often brings forth lower-quality goods.*

Here, the need for government regulation in even the simplest market is clear. Consumers (and, in fact, the earlier-mentioned utility theory) need accurate information if they are to function well. On the other hand, ethically challenged firms in an unregulated market have come up with many famous shady business strategies, such as "bait and switch" and what I call "price confusion" (advertised prices such as 7 for $19.95, a difficult per unit calculation for most customers).

Another rationale for regulation can be found in the classic game theory case known as "Hot Dog Stands on the Beach."

Suppose there is a one-mile stretch of beach with people equally distributed along it. Suppose further that there are two equally popular hot dog stands that are trying to determine their optimal location. Most people believe that the two stands would locate at the quarter-mile and three-quarter-mile points—the socially optimal locations (assuming that people walk to the closest stand). But strategically, either stand can see that it would improve its position by moving next to the other stand, thus taking some business away from its competitor (because people walk to the closest stand). When the strategic moves are done, the stands will be located next to each other, but in the center of the beach. This strategic solution means that consumers have to walk further for a hot dog, and thus it is an inferior outcome for society.

Here, a zoning regulation that forces the stands to stay at the quarter-mile and three-quarter-mile locations will make consumers better off without making either firm worse off, since neither stand is allowed to move.

There are many practical applications of this famous game theory result. I relate this game to the firm's decision to provide its employees with education or training programs. If Firm A provides training, Firm B can save the training cost and use the money to hire away the trained workers from Firm A! The result is that (strategically), no firm will be willing to provide enough training. The government can undo this strategic result by requiring all firms to provide a certain level of training.

Now consider the well-known circumstance in which government regulation is considered necessary: the natural monopoly. Because it knows that it is able to affect the market price, a monopoly restricts its output, raises its price, and usually makes excess profits. Competition can control this incentive, but some markets (electric utilities, for example) simply can't support competing firms and thus are called natural monopolies. Faced with this economic reality, the government usually forms a commission to set the price for these firms, in theory, at the competitive equilibrium price. But where does the government get the information that allows it to determine that price? Again, governments aren't omniscient. They usually rely on the firm being regulated for much of the necessary information.

Adding some strategic thinking to this problem, we can get a wide range of outcomes. If the firm provides false information—say, higher costs—it might get a higher price from the regulator. But the regulator knows that, and it might assume some cost overstatement when it determines the regulated price. But what if the firm provides accurate information and the regulator sets the price as if the firm's cost information were inflated? The regulated price will be too low, and the regulator will have had an adverse effect on the market. Again, the government, well-meaning though it might be, is not omniscient.

We also observe that well-meaning government-determined prices frequently start to have a life of their own. People forget that markets exist and begin to believe that some prices simply *have* to come from the government. Minimum wages began as a Depression-era check on labor markets that were overrun with unemployed people. Since there were far more job seekers than there were jobs, employers could play job seekers against each other and drive wages down. The minimum wage is thus a government union of low-skilled workers that sets a floor on the wage rate to take away that strategic incentive. Now, 80 years since the beginning of the Great Depression, people have come to believe that wages are determined by the government.

Put differently, they forget that wages—even minimum wages—have to line up with a market.

Our current economic problems and the solutions that are being enacted and proposed also remind us that the maker of the rules has the ability to rewrite the rules if that serves its purpose. A government by the people, for the people, but made up *of* the people can choose to wipe the slate clean anytime it sees fit. It can take or give, enforce or forgive, incentivize or protect. But it had better look forward before it panders to the masses too much. The current administration could order every bank to renegotiate the terms of every distressed mortgage until all current homeowners can keep their homes. But if it does so, after this crisis is over, will any bank ever issue another mortgage to a risky borrower? Rewriting the rules will always have other—and sometimes unintended—consequences.

One of the biggest challenges for the government and for the U.S. economy is the health-care industry. High-quality health care, it is said, is a right and a public good, and thus it should not be left to the market. Drucker talks about the issues and problems surrounding the health-care industry, but again he notes that there are "people" issues on both sides. No doubt there are some excess profits being made in health care, and thus it might be possible to regulate parts of the health-care industry, but which profits are excess? Doctors' salaries? Drug companies' earnings? Insurers' profits? Payments to hospitals? Guess wrong and regulate poorly, and the market will suffer. And, as Peter Drucker would say, we *are* the market.

Markets, like governments and corporations, are social inventions. They are people performing a role. When we think of these creations as separate, freestanding entities, we often imbue them with extraordinary power and a certain mystique. But, as Peter Drucker always reminded us, these entities are just people acting, perhaps in concert, with predictable, comprehensible human behavior.

14

The Drucker Vision and Its Foundations: Corporations, Managers, Markets, and Innovation

Richard Smith

[D]epressions are not simply evils, which we might attempt to suppress, but, perhaps undesirable—forms of something which has to be done, namely, adjustment to previous economic change. . . . There is no reason to despair—this is the first lesson of our story. Fundamentally the same thing has happened in the past. . . . In all cases . . . recovery came of itself. . . . But this is not all: our analysis leads us to believe that recovery is sound only if it does come of itself.

—Joseph Schumpeter, "Depressions: Can We
Learn from Past Experience?" In *Essays on
Entrepreneurs, Innovations, Business Cycles,
and the Evolution of Capitalism*

On the Foundations of the Drucker Vision

Perhaps no contemporary thinker and writer on management has had a more profound and far-reaching impact on the practice of management than Peter Drucker. It would be hard to find any organization that does not profess to embody at least some "Drucker management principles." Whether one respects Drucker for his scholarship or dismisses him on the grounds that his scholarship generally does not conform to academic conventions, it is hard to find anyone who does not respect and appreciate his influence and insights—particularly his ability to peer into the future with clarity.

The focus of this chapter is on the foundations—historical and intellectual—upon which Drucker built his ideas. Drucker's vision and his management principles are products of his uncompromising application of economic principles, tempered by a broad grasp of history and by his exposure, early in his life, to a particularly turbulent sequence of socioeconomic events. The purpose of the first section of this chapter is simply to review some of the more important historical and intellectual foundations of his ideas. In the second section, I draw upon these foundations to show their influence on his thinking and writing and to provide a useful framework for understanding Drucker's meaning.

First, I provide a brief review of the historical context that was important in shaping Drucker's views of the roles of businesses, social-sector entities, and government. Second, I review the influence of economics on his views. On many occasions, Drucker was critical of economics as being overly theoretical and disconnected from reality. However, we find that his criticisms are directed only at certain aspects of the discipline and that he relies heavily on the core principles of the Austrian School of economics.

Historical Context

One can neither fully appreciate nor understand Drucker's perspectives on management without knowing something of the context that contributes to his emphasis on the centrality of the individual, the importance of the corporation as an institution of society, and his advocacy of limited government, legitimacy, and the rule of law. Early in his life, Drucker experienced massive failures of government, the rise of a disaffected working class, a cataclysmic world war, and an economy that oscillated between prosperity and severe depression.

At the time of Drucker's birth, in Vienna in 1909, Austria-Hungary was already heading toward war. The country was an agglomeration of diverse and geographically separated ethnicities, nationalities, and cultures. During the late 1800s and early 1900s, the Hapsburg monarchy was largely focused on internal dissension.[1]

World War I pitted Austria-Hungary and Germany against the Allied Powers. Before its end in 1918, the war had decimated the Austrian population and brought about the fall of the Hapsburgs. Drucker experienced not only the devastation of war, but also a protracted postwar period of recession and hyperinflation. Much of Austria's manufacturing capacity had been destroyed and, in an effort to rebuild the country's infrastructure, service its war debt, and support its population of unemployed workers, the new democratic government resorted to printing money. As a result, between the end of the war and 1923, the Austrian crown lost 99.9 percent of its value, and much of the private wealth of the population was lost. Government, it appeared, had failed Austrian society in three ways: getting it into a war that it would ultimately lose, bringing on the postwar recession, and lacking the discipline to manage the currency.[2]

The war and what followed it in Europe were outgrowths of socioeconomic changes that had begun much earlier. The Industrial Revolution led to falling wages in sectors where workers found themselves competing with machines. Industrialization gave rise to a massive dislocation of the workforce.[3] While the direct impacts were immediately negative for workers who were involved in labor-intensive, repetitive work, the impetus that drove the changes was the pursuit of the opportunity to create wealth through innovation. These innovations made goods and services more affordable to those who were not directly harmed by the dislocations and enabled some innovators to become extremely wealthy.

Drucker experienced only the fallout from the Industrial Revolution. Although the pie grew dramatically, many people initially were left out. Economic dislocation fostered the growth of a disaffected labor force that saw itself as the ultimate source of wealth creation for those who were benefiting from the technological changes. The dislocations attracted the attention of academic economists and political scientists and provided a medium on which divisive ideas could thrive. Karl Marx articulated the view that wealth creation flows from the value created by labor, a view that implies that labor-saving innovations are expropriations of the value created by labor. (Marx died in 1883, 25 years before Drucker's birth. *The Communist Manifesto* was published in 1848. *Das Kapital* was published in 1867.)

Under Marx's view of capitalism, laws protect the wealthy to the detriment of workers, but capitalism has inherent contradictions that will lead to revolution. Marx articulated a labor theory of value in which workers are not paid the full value of what they produce. The excess, the capitalist's profit, is what Marx calls the "unpaid labour of the working class." Marx argued that capitalism leads to working-class poverty. The final stage of the Marxian paradigm is "communism," with the working class overthrowing the capitalist system and ushering in a socialist system based on working for the common good.[4]

Particularly in Europe, economic dislocation, catalyzed by Marxist political philosophy, fostered support for "social democracy," that is, an ideology of using regulation and state-sponsored programs to redress the perceived injustices of capitalism. Proponents of social democracy included Marxist or revolutionary socialist groups that sought to introduce socialism in democratized countries and democracy in undemocratized countries, including Austria-Hungary. Social democrats claimed to uphold a reformed version of Marxism that was less revolutionary and less critical of capitalism. They argued that socialism should be achieved through evolution rather than revolution.[5]

The Industrial Revolution, Marxism, and the rise of social democracy are all part of the backdrop to the outbreak of World War I. Opinions at the time concerning the ultimate causes of the war varied, but all drew upon these earlier developments. One view was that in countries like Germany and Austria-Hungary, war was a consequence of the desire for wealth and military power and a disregard for democracy. Supporters called for an end to aristocratic rule. Drawing upon Marxist theories, Vladimir Lenin asserted that capitalist imperialism was responsible for the war. This argument resonated with the social democratic ideology and supported the rise of Communism. Both views argued for greater reliance on democratic political systems. They differed in their perspectives on capitalism. During his childhood in Austria, Drucker would have been exposed to these differing views. The Drucker family was aligned with the Hapsburg monarchy, as his father was an economist and government official in the prewar era.

During the war, the effects of the decimation of the workforce and the destruction of means of production were severe. In Austria and other warring European countries, gross domestic product declined by almost half. The production that did occur was focused on the war effort. To harness the power of the country's industrial resources in a wartime effort, laissez-faire policies gave way to command and control. New taxes were levied and new laws enacted, all ostensibly to aid the war effort. The war strained the abilities of large and bureaucratized governments such as that of Austria-Hungary, where much of the bureaucracy was based in Drucker's Vienna, and the postwar shrinkage of the empire did little to shrink the bureaucracy.[6]

In the aftermath of the war, some European economies resorted to further bursts of inflation to meet the postwar demand for government spending, given the diminished tax base and the burden of wartime borrowing and reparations. The populace demanded government aid, but as there was little productive activity, there were almost no tax revenues available. The solution that many elected governments found was to print money. The first hyperinflation took place in Austria. Before the war, the Austrian crown had been worth about 20 cents. By the summer of 1922, it was worth $\frac{1}{100}$ of a cent. In *Adventures of a Bystander*, Drucker recalls how the Austrian hyperinflation wiped out his family's wealth.

The war and the postwar recession provided impetus for the growing distrust of capitalism that was manifested in rising support for the agenda of the Social Democratic Party. Drucker left Austria for Germany in 1927 to study and started a career in journalism related to business and finance.

While Austria and Germany were struggling with hyperinflation and low productivity, countries that had been less harmed by the war benefited as exporters to the rest of the world. The "Roaring Twenties" in the United States and the "Golden Twenties" in Europe were the result. The Great Depression (Great Slump in the United Kingdom) began with the market crash of 1929 but was caused by inadvertently contractionary monetary policies engineered by the U.S. Federal Reserve Bank. While the Depression began in the United States, it quickly spread to Europe. It lasted for many years, with devastating effects both in industrialized countries and in those that exported raw materials.[7]

At issue was the question of whether the Depression was a failure of free markets or a failure of government. Those who favored a large role for government believed that it was mostly a failure of free markets, and those who favored markets believed that the failure of government exacerbated the economic problems.

From 1927 through 1933, Drucker was in Germany. He experienced the German hyperinflation and the increasing militancy of Germany's labor class. With the growing strength of the Social Democratic Party and the more militant National Socialist German Workers Party (Nazi), Drucker left Germany for London in 1933.

There, at the depth of the recession, he was exposed to the debate over laissez-faire economics and the interventionist arguments of John Maynard Keynes. Keynes argued against the self-equilibrating tendency of the economy, and provided a rationale for government management of economic activity. He argued that severe recession could cause consumers to become overly cautious in their saving/spending behavior. He called this the "paradox of thrift"— the more people try to save, the poorer they become. Accordingly, an economy can emerge from a decline only if spending increases. The argument for activist government is that if consumers won't spend, then government must (like priming the pump).[8]

Keynes argued in his *General Theory of Employment, Interest and Money* that lower aggregate expenditures contributed to a massive decline in income and to employment that was well below the norm. He argued that the economy could reach equilibrium at a point of high unemployment. Keynesian economists called upon governments to pick up the slack during times of economic crisis by increasing spending and/or cutting taxes. It is important for understanding some of Drucker's observations that Keynes developed his *General Theory* in a classical economic model that did not provide for innovation and ignored the reactions of individual consumers to aggressive government spending.

The *General Theory* was published in 1936. In 1937, Drucker moved to the United States. Franklin D. Roosevelt, a proponent of Keynesian economics, had been elected president in 1932. Echoing the sentiments of the Social Democrats, he blamed the Depression on big business and capitalist avarice. Roosevelt's New Deal was intended to address the perceived deficiencies of laissez-faire capitalism by empowering labor unions and farmers and by raising taxes on corporate profits. The Securities and Exchange Commission, the Federal Trade Commission, and Social Security all are products of the New Deal.

Although the U.S. economy grew from 1933 through 1937, much of the growth was in public-sector projects that competed for resources with private-sector demand. Drucker arrived in the United States at a time when dissatisfaction with the New Deal was growing. In the face of this growing dissatisfaction, conservatives were able to form a coalition to stop further expansion of the New Deal. By 1943, most New Deal relief programs had been abolished.[9]

World War II began in Europe in 1939, a consequence, in large part, of the failure of the German economy to recover from the aftermath of World War I, partly because of unrealistic demands for reparations after the war. By 1940, the U.S. GDP still had not returned to 1929 levels, and the unemployment rate was still about 15 percent. The United States was drawn into the war in late 1941. The unemployment problem was "solved" by the outbreak of World War II, when about 12 million men were drafted and taken out of the labor market. In addition, war goods production programs brought millions of new workers into the labor markets. Wartime production in the United States was managed by the private sector with public financing. Drucker witnessed the ability of the highly industrialized U.S. private sector to innovate and quickly make the transition to the needs of wartime production.

Economic Foundations

The other important aspect of Drucker's background is his exposure to leading thinkers of the Austrian School of economics. Drucker grew up in Vienna during a time when the Austrian School was particularly influential in giving perspective on then-recent economic history and trends. Proponents of the Austrian School advocate adherence to strict methodological individualism. They hold that to be valid, economic theory must be logically derived from principles of human action. Alongside a formal approach to the theory of human action (i.e., praxeology, the science of human action), the school advocates a deductive/interpretive approach to history. The praxeological method allows for the discovery of economic laws that are valid for all human action, while the interpretive approach addresses specific historical events.

The Austrian School espouses a rationalist approach that is different from the positivist approach of classical economics (i.e., that the only authentic knowledge is scientific knowledge that can come only from affirmation of theories through strict scientific method). The school is sometimes criticized for its rejection of the scientific method in favor of "self-evident" axioms and verbal logical reasoning.

Just as Marxism was a by-product of the Industrial Revolution and a reaction to classical economics, the Austrian School was a by-product of social democracy and a reaction to Marxism and later to Keynesianism, in particular with regard to the role of markets and prices as the alternative to central planning, the role of interest rates and capital in intertemporal allocation, and the role of government in managing the economy.[10]

As revealed in his writings, Drucker was deeply influenced by both the methodology and the ideas of the Austrian School, particularly the ideas of Schumpeter, with whom he had a long-lasting personal relationship.

Carl Menger (1840–1921) In 1871, with the publication of his *Principles of Economics*, Menger became the "father of the Austrian School." In this work, he challenged the labor theory of value with his own theory of marginality. Think of a firm that hires workers to search for diamonds. Some will be found with little effort, but others will take a great deal. Wages will depend on the productivity of the least productive worker (the marginal worker) and the value of the diamonds that this worker is able to find. Other workers will be paid the same, even though what they find is more valuable.[11]

In 1883, with the publication of his *Investigations into the Method of the Social Sciences with Special Reference to Economics*, Menger challenged the classical (German Historical School) method of research in economics, which was based on an exhaustive examination of history. In response, members of the German Historical School derisively called Menger and his students the "Austrian School." They did so to emphasize the departure from what was then mainstream economic thought.[12]

Eugen von Böhm-Bawerk (1851–1914) Though he was never Menger's student, Böhm-Bawerk was an enthusiastic disciple. In Books I and II of *The Positive Theory of Capital*, *Capital* and *Interest*, he criticized Marx's worker exploitation theory. Böhm-Bawerk argued that capitalists do not exploit workers. Rather, they provide employees with income in advance of the receipt of revenue from the goods produced—think of a long production chain. Only the final sale is not an advance to labor. Thus, he concluded, "Labor cannot increase its share of the pie at the expense of capital." He argued that the Marxist theory of exploitation ignores the time dimension of production and that redistribution from capitalist industries would undermine the importance of interest rates in intertemporal allocation and as a tool for monetary policy. From this, it follows that the full value of a product is not produced by the worker. Rather, labor can be paid only the present value of foreseeable output.[13]

Books III and IV, *Value* and *Price*, extended Menger's ideas of marginal utility to develop the idea of subjective value as related to marginalism, in that things have value only insofar as people want them. This means that we cannot infer that maximum dollar value is the same as maximum social value and that there is no calculus that central planners can use to decide what to produce.

Ludwig von Mises (1881–1973) Mises has been called the "Dean of the Austrian School." He was a visiting professor at New York University from 1945 until 1969, overlapping with Drucker. In his treatise Human Action, Mises introduced praxeology as the conceptual foundation of the science of human action.[14]

Many of his works were on the differences between government-controlled economies and free exchange. Mises argued that (as was true in the 2008 economic collapse) significant credit expansion would cause business cycles. He held that socialism must fail because of the impossibility of a socialist government's making the economic calculations needed to organize a complex economy. Mises projected that without a market economy, there would be no functional price system, which he held essential for achieving rational allocation of capital. Socialism would fail because without prices to guide productive activity, demand cannot be known.

Friedrich von Hayek (1899–1992) Hayek is best known for his defense of free-market capitalism against socialist and collectivist thought. Although Hayek enjoyed a reputation as a leading economic theorist in the 1930s, his models were not well received by followers of Keynes. In his popular book *The Road to Serfdom* (1944), Hayek claimed that socialism requires central planning, which could lead to totalitarianism because the central authority would have to be endowed with powers that would affect social life as well.[15]

Hayek argued that in centrally planned economies, an individual or a select group must determine the distribution of resources, but that planners can never have enough information to carry out the allocation reliably. The efficient exchange and use of resources, Hayek claimed, can be maintained only through the price mechanism in free markets. In "The Use of Knowledge in Society" (1945), Hayek argued that the price mechanism serves to share and synchronize local and personal knowledge, allowing society's members to achieve diverse, complicated ends through spontaneous self-organization.[16]

In Hayek's view, the role of the state is to maintain the rule of law, with as little intervention as possible. Hayek viewed the price system not as a conscious invention (intentionally designed by people), but as spontaneous order, "the result of human action but not of human design."

In his *Prices and Production* (1931) and *The Pure Theory of Capital* (1941), Hayek explained the origin of the business cycle in terms of central bank credit expansion. The "Austrian business cycle theory" has been criticized by advocates of rational expectations and neoclassical economics, who point to the neutrality of money and to real business cycle theory as providing a sounder understanding.[17]

Joseph Schumpeter (1883–1950) Schumpeter was a friend of the Drucker family in Austria. In 1919–1920, during the postwar hyperinflation, he served as the Austrian minister of finance. He resigned because of his frustration with the failure of the Austrian government to control the money supply. He moved to Harvard in 1932 and taught there until 1950.

Schumpeter criticized Keynes for his reliance on models that ignore the complexities of human nature. According to Schumpeter, Keynes developed his models by freezing all but a few variables, which led to the mistaken belief that one could deduce policy conclusions directly from highly abstract theoretical models.

Schumpeter's most important contributions are his theories of business cycles and economic development. In *The Theory of Economic Development*, he starts with a treatise on circular flow that, since it excludes innovation, leads to a stationary-state equilibrium. He regards this as the essence of classical economics. He then introduces the entrepreneur, who disturbs the equilibrium and is the cause of economic development, which proceeds in a cyclical fashion of boom and bust.[18]

To Schumpeter, innovation is disruptive in that the pursuit of profit, while making some part of the population better off, simultaneously results in economic dislocation of others. Think of the Industrial Revolution—while per capita GDP rose dramatically, basic workers became unemployed. Schumpeter sees capitalism as a process of "creative destruction," in which old ways are endogenously destroyed and replaced by new ones. He argues that the importance of the entrepreneur depends on his having access to the capital necessary to develop and exploit innovations.

Schumpeter rejected Keynesianism on the ground that public programs intended to address cyclic downturns actually impede long-run growth and prosperity through innovation. He argued that the Great Depression would have been shorter and ended better if the New Deal programs had not been implemented.

Schumpeter is sympathetic to Marx's conclusion that capitalism will collapse, but his reasoning is different. In *Capitalism, Socialism and Democracy*, he concluded that capitalism could be replaced by socialism because of failures of the democratic process. The success of capitalism could foster the popular growth of values that are hostile to capitalism, especially among intellectuals. The intellectual and social climate needed to allow entrepreneurship to thrive might not exist in advanced capitalism. Rather than a revolt of the working class, there could be a tendency to elect candidates from some form of social democratic party. Thus, capitalism would collapse from within as democratic majorities voted for the creation of a welfare state and placed restrictions upon entrepreneurship.

Schumpeter disputed the idea that democracy is a process by which the electorate identifies the common good and politicians carry it out for them. He argued that this is unrealistic, and that people are largely manipulated by politicians, who set the agenda. He advocated a minimalist model of government in which democracy is simply the mechanism for competition between leaders.

The concept of entrepreneurship cannot be fully understood without Schumpeter's contributions. He offered two theories. In the earlier one, he argued that innovation and technological change come from entrepreneurs, or wild spirits. Individuals are the ones who make things work in the economy. In the latter theory, he pointed out that the ones who really move innovation are the big companies, which have the resources and the capital to invest in research and development.

Schumpeter's influence on Drucker, and particularly on Drucker's views of entrepreneurship and innovation, was profound.

Synthesis

In his early life, Drucker witnessed a number of failed states and totalitarianism in Europe. Both were to direct his life's work. When he called the twentieth century "the wasted century," it was because of the two world wars, hyperinflation, genocide, the nanny states, and the human waste. He did not see a much better situation as he looked at the world in 2000.

Throughout his intellectual life, Drucker was focused on people and the human condition. Fearing the consequences of economic dislocation and social polarization, he pursued organizational and social models that he believed had the potential to achieve harmonious growth. While he accepted the Austrian School's rejection of government as the solution, he was fearful of the style of laissez-faire capitalism that characterized the Industrial Revolution and its aftermath. His first attempt to reconcile his economic principles with his concern for the individual was the idea of the "plant community," of which post–World War II Japan is probably the best example. He later proposed refinements, such as his emphasis on managing innovation, and alternative models, such as his views of the new society and the postcapitalist society.[19]

The Drucker Vision

Business enterprises . . . are organs of society. They do not exist for their own sake, but to fulfill a specific social purpose and to satisfy a specific need of a society, a community, or individuals. (Management: Tasks, Responsibilities, Practices)

Peter Drucker has written enough and on so many topics that one can invoke passages that appear to support almost any position. He is often quoted in support of the proposition that management has a social and ethical responsibility that transcends the classical economic notion of profit maximization, and that survival of the enterprise, per se, has intrinsic value. But are these accurate characterizations of what Drucker sees as the legitimate responsibility of management?

Understanding what Drucker meant is of interest as a means of limiting the potential for the power of his words to distort the evolution of the dialogue. My thesis is that Drucker's vision and his management principles derive from his uncompromising application of Austrian School economic principles (reliance on prices to direct economic activity and distrust of central planning as an alternative; the importance of the individual as an economic actor and the consequent rejection of overly abstract economic models; the importance of capital to support the role of innovation as an engine of growth, and the resultant inevitability of economic downturns when innovation slows; and the narrow social responsibility of business management and the limited role of government), tempered by a broad grasp of history and by his exposure to a particularly turbulent sequence of socioeconomic events. Understanding Drucker in this context allows today's business leaders to apply his management principles correctly to the issues and decisions they face and to avoid overly broad interpretations of the social responsibility of management. These foundations are reviewed in "On the Foundations of the Drucker Vision" at the beginning of this chapter.

Drucker's views are interdependent, but some of his central themes can be organized under four headings:

- Classical economics and the profit motive

- Corporate social purpose and the value imperative
- Corporate social responsibility and managerial ethics
- Corporate purpose and innovation

In the final section, I draw upon the analysis of his writings to offer some conjectures as to how he might have viewed the financial and economic crisis of 2008–2009.

Classical Economics and the Profit Motive

On Keynesian Macroeconomics Consistent with the Austrian School view, Drucker was critical of economic models that are overly mathematical and dismissive of the role of the individual. Keynes was a particular and recurring target. In 1946, Drucker wrote,

> *Keynes' work was built on the realization that the fundamental assumptions of nineteenth-century laissez-faire economics no longer hold true in an industrial society. . . . But it aimed at the restoration and preservation of . . . the basic institutions of nineteenth-century laissez-faire politics; above all . . . at the preservation of the autonomy and automatism of the market. The two could no longer be brought together in a rational system; Keynes's politics are magic—spells, formulae, and incantations, to make the admittedly irrational behave rationally.* (The Ecological Vision)

In conceding that laissez-faire economics does not function in industrialized society, Drucker accepts the idea that the propensity of the economy to restore full employment through price adjustments may not hold when the economic actors are large industrial firms, labor unions, and others, who are bound through long-term contracts. Since policy instruments merely create the illusion of rational behavior, it does not make sense to stimulate the economy by artificially increasing labor demand or by tricking people into working by inflating. While he argues against the Keynesian solution, he does not favor government intervention.

On the Profit Motive Drucker consistently regarded economic performance as the overriding social responsibility of an enterprise.

> *In any society . . . the first and overriding social function and responsibility of the enterprise is economic performance. . . . The demands of economic performance which society makes on the enterprise are identical to the demand of the enterprise's self-interest: the avoidance of loss. . . . There is no conflict between the social purpose and the survival interest of the enterprise.* (The New Society)

Drucker acknowledges that a business that is profitable is doing what society demands. He does so without superimposing normative judgment about values that are different from prices. While there may be reasons to suppress the price mechanism, Drucker holds that it is not the responsibility of business leaders to make such choices. This is exactly the Austrian view.

Drucker's view of profit derives directly from economic principles.

> *Profit serves three purposes. It measures the net effectiveness . . . of a business's efforts. . . . It is the "risk premium" that covers the cost of staying in business. . . . Finally, profit insures the supply of future capital for innovation and expansion.* (The Practice of Management)

Thus, Drucker accepts the role of prices in directing activity and the role of profit in directing resource allocation. He articulates the Austrian School view (in direct challenge to Marx) that profit is the return to capital. Profit compensates those who have already paid for the labor services embedded in capital. In saying that profit ensures the supply of capital for innovation, Drucker is voicing Schumpeter's premise that capital is essential for innovation and growth.

Drucker always speaks of business purpose in a social welfare context, and he always means the creation of value for society. Profit (i.e., economic profit) validates that the business is achieving its social objective.

> *Business enterprises . . . are organs of society. They do not exist for their own sake, but to fulfill a specific social purpose and to satisfy a specific need of a society, a community, or individuals. They are not ends . . . but means. . . .*
>
> *. . . In business enterprise, economic performance is the rationale and purpose. . . . Business management must always . . . put economic performance first. . . . A business management has failed if it does not produce economic results. It has failed if it does not supply goods and services desired by the consumer at a price the consumer is willing to pay. It has failed if it does not improve, or at least maintain, the wealth-producing capacity of the economic resources entrusted to it. And this . . . means responsibility for profitability.* (Management: Tasks, Responsibilities, Practices)

In 1946, Drucker acknowledges the profit motive as a mechanism for social efficiency:

> *The profit motive has a very high . . . social efficiency. All the other known forms in which the lust for power can be expressed offer satisfaction by giving the ambitious man direct power and domination over his fellow men. The profit motive alone gives fulfillment through power over things.* (The Concept of the Corporation)

The profit motive is at the core of Austrian School reasoning. Unless people are focused on profits, prices cannot direct human activity. Drucker expressed antipathy for central planning, which the Austrians criticize as unworkable. He had seen, firsthand, the consequences of failed attempts at central planning.

But his respect for the profit motive in practice gives rise to a tension with his disdain for formal economics. Drucker questions the very existence of the profit motive as a theoretical construct.

> *Whether there is such a thing as a profit motive at all is highly doubtful. The idea was invented by the classical economists to explain the economic reality that their theory of static equilibrium could not explain. . . . The profit motive and . . . maximization of profits are . . . irrelevant to the function of a business . . . and the job of managing a business. In fact, the concept . . . does harm.* (Management: Tasks, Responsibilities, Practices)

The contradiction between this and Drucker's earlier view is apparent. In the first, his focus is on individual behavior. In the second, he means "equating marginal cost and marginal revenue."

References to static equilibrium and the profit motive are pure Schumpeter. Schumpeter argued that, because there is no innovation in the classical model, classical economics cannot explain growth or business cycles. Drucker believed that the neoclassical concept does harm because it takes the focus off innovation.

Drucker's views on profit are easy to misinterpret because he distinguished between profit as a measure of performance and profit maximization as a behavioral orientation. Drucker said that the root of confusion about business purpose is the mistaken belief that the profit motive is a guide to right action.

> *The concept of profit maximization is . . . meaningless. . . . Profit and profitability are, however, crucial—for society even more than for the individual business. . . . Profit is not the . . . rationale of business behavior and business decisions, but rather their validity. . . . The root of the confusion is the mistaken belief that the motive of a person—the so-called profit motive . . . is an explanation of . . . behavior or . . . guide to right action.* (Management: Tasks, Responsibilities, Practices)

This emphasis on human behavior rather than abstract principles like profit maximization is at the core of Austrian School economics. There is a tendency to interpret Drucker as supporting stakeholder rather than shareholder value. What he meant, however, is different. It is consistent with stakeholder value, but not with interpretations that imply that managers can legitimately make trade-offs among stakeholder groups. In fact, Drucker argued that an emphasis on restraining the profit motive leads to bad public policy.

> *It [the profit motive] . . . and . . . deep-seated hostility to profit . . . are among the most dangerous diseases of an industrial society. It is largely responsible for the worst mistakes of public policy . . . which [are] squarely based on the failure to understand the nature, function, and purpose of business enterprise. . . . Actually, a company can make a social contribution only if it is highly profitable.* (Management: Tasks, Responsibilities, Practices)

This position is shaped by Drucker's experience with the repercussions of the Industrial Revolution. If the public believes that shareholders profit at the expense of employees, they will fight to eliminate the profits. Policy mistakes (such as price controls and artificial job creation programs) deprive business of what Drucker (and Schumpeter) believed are the resources to fund real economic growth.

Another subtlety that is easy to misconstrue is Drucker's distinction between profit maximization and profit sufficiency.

> *Profit is . . . needed to pay for attainment of the objectives of the business . . . a condition of survival. . . . A business that obtains enough profit to satisfy its objectives . . . has a means of survival. A business that falls short . . . is a marginal and endangered business. . . . The minimum needed may well turn out to be a good deal higher than the profit goals of many companies, let alone their actual profit results.* (Management: Tasks, Responsibilities, Practices)

One can best understand this passage by recalling Schumpeter's notion of dynamic competition. Minimum necessary profitability does not mean that once a firm achieves this, it can do what it wants with the rest. The minimum must include a normal return on capital. A firm that temporarily achieves a high return is not sustainable unless it continues to innovate successfully.

Corporate Social Purpose and the Value Imperative

Schumpeter expected capitalism to fail because of the inability of democratic processes to restrain the use of monetary and fiscal policy to create short-run benefits, and because an increasingly wealthy electorate would favor social programs that would undermine innovation.

Early Views on the Plant Community In his early writings, Drucker looked to the corporation as a "solution" to Schumpeter's prediction. He argued that business needed to create a sense of community within the firm (the "plant community") to curtail the conflict between labor and investors. In 1946, Drucker argued that every member of an enterprise must be seen as being equally necessary.

> *The corporation must be organized on hierarchical lines. But also everybody from the boss to the sweeper must be seen as equally necessary to the success of the common enterprise. At the same time the large corporation must offer equal opportunities for advancement.*
> (The Concept of the Corporation)

Drucker recalled the dehumanizing conditions and catastrophic consequences of the Industrial Revolution. The appeal to mutual respect and equal opportunity reflects his concern with the polarization of society around the misperception that labor is not a stakeholder in a capitalist regime. Moreover, it is important for workers to believe in the rationality and predictability of the forces that control their jobs.

Insecurity . . . leads to a search for scapegoats. . . . Only if we restore the worker's belief in the rationality and predictability of the forces that control his job, can we expect any policies in the industrial enterprise to be effective. (The New Society)

This writing followed the resurgence of labor unrest in the post-World War II era. By "scapegoats," Drucker means managers and capitalists. His concerns about adversarial relationships between workers and business are natural extensions of his experience. Thus, he sought to foster the recognition that workers cannot benefit unless the business is profitable.

Later Views on the Plant Community and the "New Society" The plant community was essentially the model in post–World War II Japan, as championed by Drucker. The model worked well as long as Japan had a cost advantage relative to the West and was free of competition from countries with lower labor costs. Once competition intensified, many Japanese firms were unable to adhere to the organic model of the firm, with lifetime employment and internal promotion. Confronted with this reality in the 1990s, Drucker sought other means of individual fulfillment.

Fifty years ago I believed the plant community would be the successor of the community of yesterday. I was totally wrong. We proved totally incapable even in Japan.[20]

I argued . . . that . . . large business enterprise would have to be the community in which the individual would find status and function. . . . This . . . has not worked. . . . The right answer to the question "Who takes care of the social challenges of the knowledge society?" is neither the government nor the employing organization. The answer is a separate and new social sector. ("How Knowledge Works," Atlantic Monthly)

Undaunted by having been wrong about a central tenet of his early work, Drucker's concern remained: how do we avoid the divisive impacts of economic change that were so traumatic in the first half of the twentieth century? When the plant community model proved not to be able to withstand competitive pressure, Drucker sought solutions in other dimensions.

Later Views on Purpose and Performance In his later writing, Drucker equivocated on questions related to corporate purpose and performance assessment. At least in accounting terms, he saw business as focusing too narrowly on profit and with too short-run a view— the results of management's being too oriented toward accounting performance rather than the creation of true shareholder value.

> *Neither the quantity of output nor the "bottom line" is by itself an adequate measure of the performance. . . . Market standing, innovation, productivity, development of people, quality, financial results— all are crucial to an organization's performance and survival.* (The New Realities)

Terms like "bottom line" are decidedly different from the notion of economic profit, which Drucker espouses as the true measure of enterprise success. Accounting profit, in contrast, is short-run and does not provide for capital cost.

> *[W]hat we generally call profits, the money left to service equity, is usually not profit at all. Until a business returns a profit that is greater than its cost of capital, it operates at a loss. . . . The enterprise still returns less to the economy than it devours in resources. . . . Until then, it does not create wealth, it destroys it. By that measurement . . . few U.S. businesses have been profitable since World War II.* (Managing in Times of Great Change)

Ultimately, Drucker comes down squarely behind economic profit as the driver of economic growth.

> *One may argue (as I have) that the present concentration on "creating shareholder value" as the sole mission of the publicly owned business enterprise is too narrow. . . . But it has resulted in improvement in these enterprises' financial performance beyond anything an earlier generation would have thought possible—and way beyond what the same enterprises produced when they tried to satisfy multiple objectives, that is, when they were being run (as I have to admit I advocated for many years) in the "best balanced interests" of all the stakeholders. ("The New Pluralism," Leader to Leader)*

Drucker's view of profit as the measure of whether a business is serving society's needs evolved because of his perception that accounting profit is too short-run and because of the pressures of the corporate control market. However, he adhered to the shareholder value model (economic profit) as the evidence of fulfilling social purpose.

Pension Funds and the Market for Corporate Control During the hostile takeover era of the 1980s, Drucker expressed concern about the increasing concentration of equity ownership in the hands of institutional asset managers.

> *To whom is management accountable? And for what? On what does management base its power? What gives it legitimacy? These are not . . . economic questions. They are political questions. Yet they underlie the most serious assault on management in its history—a far more serious assault than any mounted by Marxists or labor unions: the hostile takeover. . . . What made it possible was the emergence of the employee pension funds as the controlling shareholders of publicly owned companies.*
> *. . . The pension funds, while legally "owners," are economically "investors." . . . They have no interest in the enterprise and its welfare.*

In fact, in the United States at least they . . . are not supposed to consider anything but immediate pecuniary gain. What underlies the takeover bid is the postulate that the enterprise's sole function is to provide the largest possible immediate gain to the shareholder. In the absence of any other justification for management and enterprise, the "raider" . . . prevails—and . . . often immediately dismantles or loots the going concern, sacrificing long-range, wealth-producing capacity for short-term gains. (The New Realities)

The core of Drucker's concern was his perception that there is an inconsistency between short-run and long-run value. Since his vision for management was based on long-run value, significant ownership by short-run investors threatens his prescription that managers focus on long-run value creation.

Corporate Social Responsibility and Managerial Ethics

On Responsibility for "Impacts" Drucker's view of corporate social responsibility as the pursuit of economic value was strained when this pursuit is coupled with the production of externalities ("impacts").

The third task of management is managing the social impacts and the social responsibilities of the enterprise. . . . Free enterprise cannot be justified as being good for business; it can be justified only as being good for society. . . . Business exists to supply goods and services to customers, rather than to supply jobs to workers and managers, or even dividends to stockholders. (Management: Tasks, Responsibilities, Practices)

How the conflict is resolved is not a matter of managers weighing stakeholder interests. While economic value is the yardstick, business does not exist narrowly to provide returns to stockholders. Rather, it must provide returns to stockholders by producing what society values. What this implies for management is where things become confused.

> *One is responsible for one's impacts. . . . The first job of management is, therefore, to identify and to anticipate impacts. . . . Wherever the impact can be eliminated by dropping the activity that causes it, that is . . . the best . . . solution. . . . In most cases the activity cannot . . . be eliminated. . . . The ideal approach is to make the elimination of impacts into a profitable business. . . . More often eliminating an impact means increasing the costs. . . . It therefore becomes a competitive disadvantage unless everybody in the industry accepts the same rule. And this, in most cases, can be done only by regulation. . . .*
>
> *. . . Whenever a business has disregarded the limitation of economic performance and has assumed social responsibilities that it could not support economically, it has soon gotten into trouble. . . . This, to be sure, is a very unpopular position to take. It is much more popular to be "progressive." But managers . . . are not being paid to be heroes in the popular press. They are being paid for performance and responsibility.* (Management: Tasks, Responsibilities, Practices)

Thus, Drucker's view of responsibility for managing impacts was highly circumscribed. If eliminating an impact would be costly, the only real issue is whether eliminating it unilaterally would make the firm noncompetitive. Here, the only viable solution is cartelization through regulation. Drucker's view of limited government clashed at times with his argument here. For example, there are better ways to encourage the use of ethanol than by subsidizing farmers and mandating ethanol use, both of which distort prices and obfuscate the evidence of whether businesses are producing social value.

On the Social Responsibility and Ethics of Managers   What is the responsibility of business managers for dealing with social problems? According to Drucker, the manager is responsible for the success of the business—not for activities that detract from it. A manager who devotes effort to nonbusiness activities is taking resources from the firm and distorting the profit measure of the firm's success.

> *The manager who uses a position . . . to become a public figure and to take leadership with respect to social problems . . . is irresponsible and false to his trust. . . . The institution's performance . . . is also society's first need and interest. . . . Performance of its function is the institution's first social responsibility. Unless it discharges its . . . responsibility, it cannot discharge anything else. A bankrupt business . . . is unlikely to be a good neighbor. . . . Nor will it create the capital for tomorrow's jobs and the opportunities for tomorrow's workers. . . .*
>
> *. . . But where business . . . is asked to assume . . . responsibility for . . . the problems or ills of society . . . management needs to think through whether the authority implied by the responsibility is legitimate. Otherwise it is usurpation and irresponsible. . . . Every time the demand is made that business take responsibility for this or that, one should ask, Does business have the authority and should it have it? . . . Management must resist responsibility for a social problem that would compromise or impair the performance capacity of its business. . . . It must resist when the demand goes beyond its own competence. It must resist when responsibility would . . . be illegitimate authority.* (Management: Tasks, Responsibilities, Practices)

Drucker was concerned with management losing its focus on its responsibility to society and with the competency of managers to deal with problems that are beyond their expertise. His concern was shaped by his experiences with the illegitimate use of power in Europe and the United States.

Drucker saw ethics as important, but he did not see business as involving unique ethical choices.

> *Countless sermons have been preached . . . on the ethics of business. . . . Most have nothing to do with business and little to do with ethics.*

. . . The problem is one of moral values and moral education. . . . But neither is there a separate ethics of business, nor is one needed. . . . All that is needed is to mete out stiff punishments to those . . . who yield to temptation. . . .

. . . [M]anagers, we are told, have an "ethical responsibility" . . . to . . . give their time to community activities. . . . Such activities should, however, never be forced on them, nor should managers be appraised, rewarded, or promoted according to their participation. . . . It is the contribution of an individual in his capacity as a neighbor or citizen. And . . . [it] lies outside the manager's job and . . . responsibility. (Management: Tasks, Responsibilities, Practices)

As with impacts, the Austrian view is that intense competition prevents a business from adhering to a higher ethical standard than its rivals. In such an environment, only legal restrictions with appropriate punishment can align business conduct with ethical norms.

Corporate Purpose and Innovation

On the Importance of Innovation Schumpeter first saw innovation as resulting in the continuous displacement of existing businesses by new ones. He later focused on the ability of businesses to renew themselves through innovation. The second view is the basis for Drucker's aspiration that such innovations can be aligned with the interests of employees.

[T]he business enterprise has two . . . basic functions: marketing and innovation. . . . It is not enough . . . to provide just any economic goods and services; it must provide better and more economical ones. . . .

Sooner or later even the most successful answer to the question, What is our business? becomes obsolete. . . .

. . . Just as important as the decision on what new and different things to do, is planned, systematic abandonment of the old that . . .

no longer conveys satisfaction to the customer or customers, no longer makes a superior contribution. (Management: Tasks, Responsibilities, Practices)

Schumpeter was interested in the economic dislocations caused by innovative activity. Drucker, who was much closer to practice, saw the economic downturns that are derived from innovative waves as problematic. He hoped for a world in which the innovative efforts of existing businesses can mitigate the negative impacts of the dislocations. Then, possibly, some of the divisiveness that followed the Industrial Revolution can be avoided.

On the Role of Profit in Innovation Drucker, like Schumpeter, emphasized that profit is essential to the pursuit of innovation, but he argued that innovative activity is guided more by perceived opportunity to create value than by the pursuit of profit per se.

> *Schumpeter's . . . "creative destruction" is the only theory . . . to explain why there is something we call "profit." The classical economists . . . did not give any rationale for profit. Indeed, in the equilibrium economics of a closed economic system there is no place for profit. . . . As soon . . . as one shifts . . . to Schumpeter's dynamic, growing, moving, changing economy, what is called "profit" . . . becomes a moral imperative.* ("Schumpeter versus Keynes," Forbes)

In one of his later efforts to strike a balance between corporate objectives and individual well-being, Drucker tied economic progress and social well-being to the presence of entrepreneurial management and attributed differences in growth across nations to differences in the entrepreneurial orientation of management.

> *Any existing organization . . . goes down fast if it does not innovate. Conversely, any new organization . . . collapses if it is not managed. Not to innovate is the single largest reason for the decline of existing*

organizations. Not to know how to manage is the single largest rea-
son for the failure of new ventures. (The New Realities)

Every institution . . . must build into its day-to-day management four
entrepreneurial activities that run in parallel. One is the organized aban-
donment of products . . . that are no longer an optimal allocation of re-
sources. . . . Then any institution must organize for systematic, continuing
improvement. . . . Then it has to organize for systematic and continuous
exploitation, especially of its successes. . . . And finally, it has to organize
systematic innovation. ("Management's New Paradigms," Forbes*)*

Drawing upon Schumpeter, Drucker recognized that creative destruction will make the current business of the enterprise obsolete. Based on
Schumpeter's second model of entrepreneurial activity, he emphasizes
systematic innovation as part of the responsibility of the business. He
credits continuous innovation with enabling firms and economies to
avoid the very long economic downturns that Schumpeter focused on.

Schumpeter argued that "creative destruction" is what drives economic growth and prosperity. The economy necessarily goes through
periods of rapid growth precipitated by transformational innovation,
followed by inevitable economic downturns when the rate of innovation slows. Drucker accepted Schumpeter's view that important
innovations are likely to be developed by large corporations that
have access to the necessary capital. However, by emphasizing innovation as a responsibility of management, Drucker hoped to develop
a constructive means of dampening economic downturns. He accepted the idea of creative destruction, but he still saw the corporation as having survival value if, through innovation, it could mitigate
the impact of economic downturns on its employees.

Recap

Drucker concluded that the social responsibility of business is to produce goods and services that are valued by society at more than the

costs of the inputs and that economic profit is the best measure of whether a business is achieving what society demands of it. Based on the Austrian School's praxeological approach, he advanced the view that economic reasoning and predictions must begin with a focus on the individual rather than with abstract concepts like profit maximization.

Based on economic principles and on his views of power, authority, and legitimacy, Drucker held that a manager's purpose is to focus on achieving the profit objectives of the business by creating value for consumers, not on solving social problems that exist outside the organization. He emphasized legal and political approaches to dealing with externalities. In the face of competitive pressure, a business cannot make ethical choices that involve costs for some stakeholders and gains for others.

Based on his experience with the disruptions of the post-Industrial Revolution period and not trusting government to address these problems, Drucker envisioned the possibility of aligning value creation with a culture of belonging. Though he was eventually forced to abandon this view, he continued to seek the same objectives through his emphasis on corporate entrepreneurship and his discussions of the "new social reality."

A Conjecture on Drucker's View of the Economic Collapse of 2008–2009

According to the Case-Shiller Housing Index, U.S. housing values increased 123 percent from 2000 through 2006. Driving the increase, two U.S. government-sponsored enterprises, Fannie Mae and Freddie Mac, along with other institutions, aggressively expanded the availability of funds for home mortgages. To reduce their exposure to housing market risks, primary lenders, investment banks, and insurance companies engaged in a complex array of risk-shifting tactics. The arrangements worked as long as housing prices were rising and homeowners continued to make their payments. However, from mid-2006 through mid-2008, housing values declined by 21 percent. The declines more than wiped out the homeowners' equity in many markets, even for conforming loans.

Faced with rising defaults, the failures of some counterparties, and similar repercussions, some banks were confronted with losses of regulatory capital that forced them to dramatically curtail their lending activities. The housing-sector decline and the contraction of the banking sector precipitated a global economic downturn.

Government in the United States responded in a variety of ways, including capital infusions for some financial institutions, purchases of underperforming assets to restore banks' ability to lend, revisions of mark-to-market rules, capital infusions to support troubled firms, and aggressive government spending to offset the perceived unwillingness of consumers to spend.

It is natural to ponder what Peter Drucker would have had to say about this financial and economic collapse. While conjecture is open to easy criticism, conjecture based on the foundations of history, economics, and Drucker's own writings is not fundamentally different from the methodology of economic forecasting.

Drucker would probably see the collapse as a failure of both management and government. Concerning management, he might reiterate his concern that its incentives were too short-run to align its decisions with long-run value creation, which would benefit not only shareholders, but also customers and employees. Concerning government, he might fault policy makers for overreaching in ways that created incentives for the managers of financial firms to focus their lending decisions in ways that would not be sustainable.

Government, according to Drucker, is best if it is limited to providing an infrastructure of rules and enforcement that can enable economic enterprises to thrive by offering products and services that customers demand. Though Drucker was frustrated in his search for enterprise models that could achieve complete harmony between customer service and employee satisfaction, he never proposed that government has a legitimate role in trading off labor-market and consumer-market interests. In fact, Drucker was fearful of government usurpation of economic power.

Based on his critiques of economic models that are not grounded in human behavior, Drucker would probably have been critical of financial engineering models that were based on statistical arbitrage and were disconnected from such basic questions as: How will people respond if housing values decline and mortgage payments are sharply increasing? And what will happen to the financial sector if declining housing values and rising unemployment lead to significant defaults? Drucker might argue that if the housing market had been viewed through the lens of the underlying demographics and household consumption and investment choices, it would not have been difficult to anticipate the market decline and predict its impact.

Drucker, as a proponent of the rule of law, did not favor direct government intervention in the survival of financial firms or specific industrial firms. The notion of "too big to fail" might have carried little weight with him, as long as the interests of consumers and counterparties could be protected.

It seems likely that Drucker would argue, along the lines of Schumpeter, that some U.S. automobile producers have failed the market test. Therefore, perhaps they should be permitted to fail quickly so that their resources can be redeployed to activities that society values more highly.

Based on his experience in Austria, Drucker might be concerned about the growth of government. He might also have challenged the efficacy of the regulatory bodies that were supposed to be preventing the crisis in the first place. Mark-to-market accounting, which was championed by regulators, actually magnified the impact of the defaults. Following the Austrian School, Drucker might observe that participants in competitive markets will always find the weaknesses of any regulatory infrastructure, so that unintended consequences are inevitable.

Based on his exposure to Schumpeter and his experience with the Great Depression, Drucker would be critical of Keynesian-style attempts to use government spending to restart economic activity. Government inevitably acts politically, and using government spending to deal with downturns retards the incentives and ability of the economy to recover through innovation.

Along with Schumpeter and others of the Austrian School, Drucker might be critical of government efforts to influence the course of innovation through direct involvement in such matters as the environment. While government may provide incentives to help deal with recognized externalities, there is little evidence to indicate that it is very effective as a venture capitalist. In contrast, the venture capital industry, which at its highest point invested only about $100 billion in a single year and is only about 30 years old, is linked to economic enterprises that, as of 2007, accounted for 10 percent of non-government jobs and 17 percent of U.S. GDP.[21]

15

Drucker on Marketing: Remember, Customers Are the Reason You Are in Business

Jenny Darroch

Marketing is so basic that it cannot be considered a separate function within the business . . . it is, first, a central dimension of the entire business. . . . It is the whole business seen . . . from the customer's point of view.

—Peter F. Drucker, *The Practice of Management*[1]

The aim of marketing is to make selling superfluous. The aim of marketing is to know and understand the customer so well that the product or service fits him and sells itself.

—Peter F. Drucker, *Management: Tasks, Responsibilities, Practices*[2]

Although Drucker is often referred to as the "father of modern management," his work also had a profound effect on the field of marketing. For example, as the two opening quotes illustrate, Drucker reminded those within an organization that customers were the reason that the organization was in business, and so he argued that marketing was the responsibility of all employees, not just those within the marketing department. He integrated marketing principles into his work on management to such an extent that the question of where marketing begins and management stops is "more a matter of taste."

The purpose of this chapter is to explore Drucker's work on marketing. As such, I have organized the chapter around three themes. First, in order to give a context to Drucker's work, I will provide a brief history of marketing relevant to the time at which he wrote about marketing and management. Second, I will discuss Drucker's key contributions to the field of marketing. And third, I will examine the relationship between marketing and innovation, organizational performance, and societal welfare, all themes that were central to Drucker's work.

Rather than update Drucker's work, I have chosen to showcase it as a reminder to all of us that his advice is as appropriate today as it was decades ago when he first started writing about marketing. I remember once asking Drucker whether he thought managers were better at blending marketing or innovation; he responded that most companies do neither well. So, with this in mind, I will use this chapter to revisit Drucker's work, using a number of verbatim Drucker quotes, in order to remind us all about marketing—marketing the Drucker way.

The History of Marketing

The discipline of marketing is relatively new. In fact, in 1935, the American Marketing Association (AMA) first defined marketing as, "The performance of business activities that direct the flow of goods and services from producers to consumers."

This definition was, of course, appropriate to the times. The Great Depression of the early 1930s had ended, and the United States was facing a period of economic expansion that lasted until 1937. Managers were preoccupied with mass production and distribution efficiencies: making large quantities of product, bringing down production costs, and moving products to consumers in order to meet a growing demand.

Another recession hit in 1937, which was followed by World War II. Immediately after World War II, households were encouraged to consume as a way of facilitating a postwar economic recovery; being a good consumer became synonymous with being a good citizen, and organizations put strategies and programs in place to encourage consumption. During this period, the selling concept dominated.

But the selling concept is a very organization-centric approach to doing business. It means that organizations engage in aggressive selling and promotional techniques to sell what they make, rather than make what the market wants. Consumers, however, started to rebel—they simply did not enjoy having products pushed on them so aggressively. In response, we saw the rise of the consumer movement as consumers began to unite with a common voice, feeling empowered to push back against producers.

The early 1950s provided an inflection point in marketing history. In response to rising consumer advocacy, organizations became more customer-focused, customers were increasingly consulted by managers, and the customer viewpoint became central to business definition. During this time, terms such as "the consumer is king" or the "center of the universe" emerged. This was also the time period when Drucker began to write prolifically on the practice of marketing.

Drucker on Marketing

Looking at the Organization from the Customers' Point of View

One of Drucker's most influential marketing pieces is a chapter from his 1964 book, *Managing for Results*, called "The Customer Is the

Business." This chapter brings together much of what Drucker wrote about marketing and is still very relevant today. In fact, I use this chapter as an assignment in many of my marketing management classes at the Drucker School and ask students to apply one or a few of Drucker's central themes to an organization in which they are interested. The students enjoy this assignment immensely (if assignments are ever truly enjoyable), and the unanimous positive feedback from students is an element of surprise that something written in 1964 still applies today. I will draw heavily from this chapter as I examine the field of marketing through a Drucker lens.

The first area in which Drucker made a substantive contribution to marketing was teaching managers to look at the organization from the customers' point of view, something that Drucker referred to as the marketing view. As he eloquently put it,

> *Attempting to understand seemingly irrational customer behavior forces the manufacturer to adopt the marketing view rather than merely talk about it.*[3]

and

> *Forcing oneself to respect what looks like irrationality on the customer's part, forcing oneself to find the realities of the customer's situation that make it rational behavior, may well be the most effective approach to seeing one's entire business from the point of view of the market and customer.*[4]

Drucker added that not only should managers understand the business from the point of view of the customer, but they should also seek to identify what customers value:

> *To start out with the customer's utility, with what the customer buys, with what the realities of the customer are and what the customer's values are—that is what marketing is all about.*[5]

Are Customers Rational or Irrational?

The previous quotes make frequent reference to customer irrationality. At the time Drucker wrote about marketing, there was a lot of discussion about whether customers behaved rationally or irrationally. This interest in rationality arose for a couple of reasons. First, nineteenth-century economist John Stuart Mill had already introduced the concept of the *"Economic Man"* or *"Homo economicus"* to describe how people make decisions. Mill described the *Homo economicus* as a rational person, a person who can process a lot of information to make a decision that will maximize his utility (i.e., satisfaction). Thus, the idea of rationality was certainly central to economics and had made its way to marketing and management.

Second, in 1957, Herbert Simon published his groundbreaking work on what he called "bounded rationality," which described what really happens when people make decisions. What made Simon's work so important was that he spoke of our reality. Simon argued that most consumers simply cannot process enough information to make a decision that will maximize their utility. Instead, they make decisions by combining a rational decision-making approach with a degree of emotion, which makes their decisions appear a little irrational to people who are trying to make sense of them. Drucker's response to the increasing discussion of customer irrationality was:

> The customers have to be assumed to be rational. But their rationality is not necessarily that of the manufacturer; it is that of their own situation. To assume—as it has lately become fashionable—that customers are irrational is as dangerous a mistake as it is to assume that the customer's rationality is the same as that of the manufacturer or supplier. . . . It is the manufacturer's or supplier's job to find out why the customer behaves in what seems to be an irrational manner.[6]

Thus, Drucker cautioned managers who dared to describe customers as irrational. Instead, Drucker urged managers to ask what "is it in his reality that I fail to see?"[7] because, after all, "there is only one person who really knows: the customer."[8]

The "Total Marketing Approach"

In a previous section, I discussed Drucker's notion of the marketing view or total marketing approach. By suggesting that they adopt the marketing view, Drucker encouraged managers to look at the organization from the outside, from the customers' point of view. This means that managers need to take the time to understand the needs and wants that customers seek to satisfy by selecting the organization's products.

Back in 1964, however, Drucker felt that managers had not completely embraced the marketing view because they still made reference to "*our* products, *our* customers, *our* technology."[9] The same holds true today. How often do you see an advertisement for a marketing manager job, only to find that it is really a sales role in disguise? So, while many organizations are very outward-focused in their approach to decision making and can claim to have adopted a marketing view, many others continue to do no more than pay lip service to it. Drucker perfectly captured this sentiment when he said:

> For a decade now the "marketing view" has been widely publicized. It has even acquired a fancy name: The Total Marketing Approach. Not everything that goes by that name deserves it. But a gravedigger remains a gravedigger, even when called a "mortician"—only the cost of the burial goes up. Many a sales manager has been renamed "marketing vice-president"—and all that happened was that costs and salaries went up.[10]

Market Boundaries and Changing Markets

To achieve their organization's goals, Drucker encouraged managers to take an outside-in approach to marketing decision making, which influences the way in which marketers define markets and their boundaries, identify potential competitors, and look for new product opportunities that might result in market evolution. For example, marketers now begin the market segmentation process by grouping "customers into segments based on similar needs and benefits sought . . . in solving a particular consumption problem."[11] And so managers are encouraged to ask, "What is the market for what this product does?" rather than, "What is the market for this product?"[12]

Because Drucker took a very outside-in approach to market definition, he considered competitors to be those organizations that offer customers alternative products that satisfy the same need or want. This means that new products (and therefore new competitors) emerge because they satisfy the same need or want:

> *The customer rarely buys what the business thinks it sells him. One reason for this is, of course, that nobody pays for a "product." What is paid for is satisfaction. Because the customer buys satisfaction, all goods and services compete intensively with goods and services that . . . are all alternative means for the customer to obtain the same satisfaction.*[13]

As Drucker reminded us, taking the time to identify customer needs and wants is central to marketing strategy. The following examples illustrate Drucker's perspective on marketing. When I write and then mail a letter, what is my underlying need—an efficient postal service, or the ability to communicate with friends, family, or business associates? Similarly, if I buy a compact disc, is my underlying need defined as access to a good selection of compact discs at a reasonable price, or the ability to listen to music at home, in the car, or in the office? The point is that if managers were focused on the need I am seeking to satisfy when I consume a product, then the manager of the postal service would have asked, "How else can customers communicate with friends, family, or business associates?" and the manager of a record label would have asked, "How else can customers listen to music at home?" An extension of this might be to ask, "What are the problems associated with mailing letters to communicate with friends, family, or business associates?" or, "What are the problems associated with storing music on compact discs?" By asking such questions, managers avoid being blindsided by new products and competitors and thus position themselves at the forefront of new product development, development that might lead to a shift in product-market boundaries and result in the evolution of markets. Had the postal service or music companies adopted this customer-centric approach, perhaps they would not have been blindsided by e-mail and instant messaging or by Apple's innovative iTunes.

Drucker's view on market boundaries and competition can be summarized by the following quote:

> *What to the manufacturer is one market or one category of products is to the customer often a number of unrelated markets and a number of different satisfactions and values.*[14]

Thus, according to Drucker, markets change and evolve when managers develop new products that satisfy the same underlying needs or wants, or that solve problems that customers have with existing products. This outside-in approach to innovation is also referred to as demand-side innovation.

Drucker also wrote about supply-side innovation and recognized that managers can sometimes drive changes in the market, a phenomenon that Drucker called "innovative marketing." A supply-side approach to innovation is the hallmark of technological new product breakthroughs, entrepreneurship, and entrepreneurial marketing. Says Drucker: "He must adapt himself to the customer's behavior if he cannot turn it to his advantage. Or he has to embark on the more difficult job of changing the customer's habits and vision."[15] Drucker cautioned, however, that even when the ideas for an innovation originate internally, the "test of the innovation is always what it does for the user. Hence, entrepreneurship always needs to be market-focused, indeed, market-driven."[16]

Drucker on Innovation, Organizational Performance, and Societal Welfare

Now we must consider one of Drucker's main contributions to marketing (and to management in general): that is, the relationship between marketing, organizational performance, and societal welfare.

First, a reminder of the importance of the role of marketing: since an organization is in business because it has customers, organizational performance is largely determined by how effectively the organization undertakes marketing activities that ultimately give customers a reason to buy from, or interact with, that organization.

Marketing in Different Contexts

Marketers often want to know how marketing principles apply to charities, utility companies, cities, churches, museums, tourist attractions, and the like. The answer is straightforward: the principles of marketing apply equally to any organization, no matter what the organization's purpose. One of the main differences, however, is that some organizations have a more complicated array of stakeholders with a different set of needs and wants. For example, a charity is likely to have people who use its services, people who provide funding to keep the charity afloat, and perhaps a government agency taking an interest in the services that the charity provides. Irrespective of the context, it is important that you look at your organization from the perspective of each group of stakeholders (the outside), and that you understand the stakeholders' needs and wants, as well as the problems that the stakeholders are seeking to solve by interacting with the organization. After all, any successful organization is characterized by its relevance to its stakeholders. Therefore, marketers must not be overwhelmed by the context, but instead must stay focused on sound principles of marketing.

Marketing and Innovation: The Good and the Bad

Marketing plays a central role in monitoring changes in the external environment, changes in technology, changes in policy and regulations, changes in competition, changes in market segments, and changes in customer needs and wants. Marketers, therefore, must consider how these changes might affect the organization. This is where the relationship between marketing and innovation becomes important. Drucker felt strongly that managers need to be adept at entrepreneurship in order to identify and respond to market opportunities. That is, the organization must constantly adapt, if for no other reason than to remain competitive in a changing world.

The breakdown in the relationship between marketing and innovation is often apparent. For example, the U.S. government has injected billions of dollars into the auto industry and, at the time of writing this chapter, is still deciding what to do next—whether to allow the industry to go bankrupt and then restructure it, or to continue to support it with bailout money. Central to the plight of the auto industry has been its failure to innovate. Sure, consumers can be criticized for continuing to demand large gas-guzzling SUVs, but leaders in the auto industry have to shoulder some of the blame for not, for example, advancing more fuel-efficient vehicles and then leading consumers toward these vehicles by shaping tastes and preferences. While we still don't know what will happen to the auto industry, one thing is certain: the auto industry has a responsibility to innovate because a failing industry is a threat to employment, financial stability, social order, and government responsibility.

Marketing, however, is not without its critics. It is often held responsible for creating demand for unwanted goods—that is, goods for which there was little prior demand—and for contributing to overconsumption and environmental damage. Take housing as an example. Home ownership has always been a priority for American families. Even as early as 1862, the Homestead Act offered land to anyone who was willing to "brave the Western frontier." Over time, however, our concept of how big a home should be has changed. In 1950, the average American home was just 983 square feet, and people thought it was normal for a family to have one bathroom, or for two or three growing boys to share a bedroom. In 2004, the average American home was 2,349 square feet, and normal has, no doubt, been redefined. In fact, 0.5 percent of the homes constructed in 2004 and 2005, or 10,000 homes, were 6,000 square feet or larger, and questions are being raised about the impact of these homes on the environment. It seems that marketing has had a role in portraying larger homes as "normal."

There has always been a tension between marketing and innovation that solve consumer problems and make people's lives easier and marketing and innovation that create needs that result in overconsumption and environmental damage. Striking a balance between the two is challenging. Charles Handy, a Drucker Scholar in Residence at the Drucker School, commented on this tension in a recent radio interview:

> *Drucker saw business as the agent of progress. Its main responsibility, he said, was to come up with new ideas and take them to market. But not just any new ideas, please—only those that bring genuine benefits to the customers, and do not muck up the environment. The market, unfortunately, does not differentiate between good and bad. If the people want junk, the market will provide junk. So we have to fall back on the conscience of our business leaders. Maybe they should all be required to sign the equivalent of the Hippocratic Oath that doctors used to be required to swear, including the commitment, "Above all, do no harm." No, it couldn't be a legal requirement, just an indication of a cultivated responsibility.[17]*

Conclusion

One of the central tenets of Drucker's work on marketing was to encourage managers to adopt the marketing view and therefore look at the organization from the outside, from the customers' point of view. Implicit in this approach is the need to truly understand what need or want your customers are seeking to satisfy by consuming your product or by interacting with your organization.

But marketing alone is not enough. Organizations must pay attention to innovation, if for no other reason than to stay afloat and maintain a vibrant organization that continues to make a positive contribution to society at large. Thus, as Drucker himself stated:

> There is only one valid definition of business purpose: to create a customer. . . . Therefore, any business enterprise has two—and only two—basic functions: marketing and innovation.[18]

That said, managers today should continue to differentiate between marketing and innovation that solve consumer problems and make people's lives easier and marketing and innovation that create needs that result in overconsumption and environmental damage.

As we have seen, as with many other fields Drucker wrote about, Drucker was always ahead of the game. This is clearly illustrated by referring to the various American Marketing Association (AMA) definitions of marketing.

In 1985, the AMA finally dropped the 1935 definition and developed a new definition that focused more on the process of marketing. Marketing is

> The process of planning and executing the conception, pricing, promotion, and distribution of ideas, goods, and services to create exchanges that satisfy individual and organizational objectives.

This definition remained until 2004, when a new definition was developed; it was slightly modified in 2007. The 2007 definition is

Marketing is the activity, conducted by organizations and individuals, that operates through a set of institutions and processes for creating, communicating, delivering, and exchanging market offerings that have value for customers, clients, marketers, and society at large.

What is most interesting, however, is that the AMA only recently acknowledged that marketing is about creating value for customers and other stakeholders, a concept that Drucker wrote about in 1964! Clearly, Drucker was ahead of his time, and remains relevant today.

16

A Closer Look at Pension Funds

Murat Binay

Pension funds are very different owners from nineteenth-century tycoons. They are not owners because they want to be owners but because they have no choice. They cannot sell. They also cannot become owner-managers. But they are owners nonetheless. As such, they have more than mere power. They have the responsibility to ensure performance and results in America's largest and most important companies.

—Peter F. Drucker, "Reckoning with
the Pension Fund Revolution"

In his book *The Unseen Revolution: How Pension Fund Socialism Came to America*, Peter Drucker talked about how the growth in the pension fund industry would change the ownership landscape of American companies. In this book, published in 1976, Drucker accurately prophesied the shareholder structures that we observe in most of the S&P 500 companies today—that is, large pension funds owning most of the outstanding shares. The Berle-Means type of ownership structure, in which atomistic individuals owned companies, has been replaced with a concentrated structure in which the main owners of corporations are large public and private pension funds. Institutional ownership has grown drastically over the last two decades (see Figure 16-1). Today, nearly 60 percent of the U.S. equity market is owned by public and private institutional investors.

This chapter will investigate the pension fund structure in the United States in detail. Substantial sums of money are managed by private pension systems all over the world. Among the major OECD countries, the United States enjoys by far the largest private pension portfolio, equaling over $5.1 trillion. The United States is followed by the United Kingdom, with $1.2 trillion, and Japan, with $800 billion. Naturally, there is a direct relationship between the size of private pension assets and the country's economic level. Therefore, it might be more meaningful to examine the size of private pension assets relative to the country's GDP. When this is done, the Netherlands tops the list, with assets equaling 113 percent of the country's GDP, followed by Switzerland, the United Kingdom, Iceland, and the United States at 102 percent, 85 percent, 83 percent, and 75 percent, respectively.

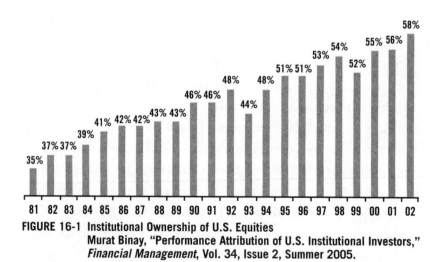

FIGURE 16-1 Institutional Ownership of U.S. Equities
Murat Binay, "Performance Attribution of U.S. Institutional Investors," *Financial Management*, Vol. 34, Issue 2, Summer 2005.

The U.S. Investment Market

According to the Federal Reserve, the equity and debt markets in the United States amount to a total of $31 trillion. About 70 percent of this capital is allocated to corporate investments: 54 percent to equities and 16 percent to corporate bonds. The government sector receives only a 30 percent allocation of this capital. The dominance of the corporate sector, especially corporate equities, is clear from these numbers.

Pension funds have therefore supplied a continuous flow of investment funds to the corporate sector, allowing U.S. corporations to grow, create jobs, and enhance economic growth. The question is, why has the bulk of investable capital flowed into the corporate sector?

When we examine the average returns for different asset classes in the United States over the past 75 years, Ibbotson Associates shows that stocks have earned on average an 11 to 12 percent annual return, while bonds have returned only 5 to 6 percent. Investors have taken on the risk of equities and provided valuable investment capital to corporations. In return, corporate equities have provided handsome returns.

When we investigate the portfolio composition of the U.S. private pension system, we find that 44 percent of the private pension assets are directly invested in equities. Another 18 percent are managed by mutual funds, and most of this is also invested in equities. As a result, more than half of the U.S. private pension assets are now invested in corporate stock. Fixed-income investments make up only 17 percent of private pension fund portfolios, indicating the dominance of equities as the asset class of choice for U.S. private pension investments. It's this preference for corporate stock that supplies readily available sources of financing to U.S. corporations and also provides high returns to pension fund investors.

The U.S. retirement system currently consists of a total of $11 trillion of public and private investments, according to the *Investment Company Fact Book*. Of these funds, 78 percent, amounting to $8.6 trillion, are managed by pension funds, insurance companies, banks, and brokerage houses. The remaining 22 percent, which correspond to $2.4 trillion, are under the management of mutual funds. It's obvious from these numbers that the U.S. pension system has become a financial giant over the past two decades. The pension fund revolution has also changed the ownership structure of companies. The pension funds have become the new owners of U.S. corporations.

Drucker indicates that with this new ownership structure comes new responsibilities. Pension funds must ensure that the CEO and the management team maximize what Drucker calls the "wealth-producing capacity" of the enterprise. In addition, pension funds have to devise systems to maintain management accountability to the new owners. This will entail the detailed analysis and scrutiny of management's performance by the institutional owners, as well as maintaining an effective board of directors. These are the issues that institutional investors have to grapple with currently.

Anatomy of Pension Fund Investors

The growth in the pension fund industry is a direct result of the tectonic shift in the structure of the U.S. retirement system. The first corporate pension fund was founded by GM's legendary CEO, George Wilson, in 1950. Historically, U.S. corporate pension funds have been predominantly defined-benefit plans. Public pension funds, which date back to the Civil War era, have always been defined-benefit systems. In a defined-benefit retirement structure, an employee generally is paid an annual pension payment amounting to the average of his last few years of salary until the end of his life. Under this system, all the risk of providing sufficient funds to fulfill the pension obligations to employees is assumed by the corporation. Over the last two decades, however, there has been a drastic change in the pension systems of private corporations. While public pension systems have remained defined-benefit structures, with the passage of the Employee Retirement Income Security Act of 1974 (ERISA) and the establishment of 401(k) and IRA accounts, most corporations have switched to a defined-contribution system.

Under this system, the corporation makes annual payments into the employees' tax-exempt private pension accounts. Although the corporation determines the investment company that will manage these funds, employees are free to choose their investments from a spectrum of asset classes. This system allows younger employees to assume higher risk levels to earn higher returns, and older employees to invest in more conservative assets, rather than imposing a one-size-fits-all approach. However, the risk of developing a sufficient fund base for a comfortable retirement is shifted entirely to the employee. This change has caused a significant shift in the investment choices of U.S. individuals. This is most apparent in the composition of Individual Retirement Account (IRA) portfolios (see Figure 16-2).

For example, while in 1990, 42 percent of IRA assets were invested in bank and thrift deposits (savings accounts and CDs), by 2001, this amount had decreased to 11 percent. In contrast, while 52

	Mutual Funds		Bank and Thrift Deposits		Life Insurance Companies		Securities Held in Brokerage Accounts		Total Assets (billions)
	Assets (billions)	Share (percent)	Assets (billions)	Share (percent)	Assets (billions)	Share (percent)	Assets (billions)	Share (percent)	
1990	140	22	266	42	40	6	190	30	636
1991	188	24	282	36	45	6	260	34	775
1992	238	27	275	31	50	6	311	36	874
1993	323	33	263	26	61	6	346	35	993
1994	350	33	255	24	69	7	382	36	1,056
1995	476	37	261	20	81	6	471	37	1,289
1996	598	41	258	18	92	6	518	35	1,466
1997	777	45	254	15	135	8	562	33	1,728
1998	975	45	249	12	156	7	770	36	2,150
1999	1,264	50	244	10	201	8	833	33	2,542
2000	1,237	49	252	10	202	8	816	33	2,507
2001	1,173	49	255	11	200	8	779	32	2,407

FIGURE 16-2 IRA Assets and Share of Total IRA Assets by Institutions, 1990–2001

percent of IRA funds were invested in mutual fund and brokerage accounts in 1990, this amount had increased to 82 percent by the end of 2001. This drastic reallocation coincides with the onset of defined-contribution plans in corporate America. The individuals, who are now bearing the brunt of the retirement risk, have decided to allocate a higher percentage of their retirement funds to riskier asset classes in return for potentially higher returns.

The private pension system really took hold after the passage of ERISA in 1974. The U.S. investing public has been through a major shift in its investment preferences. As a result, the shift we see in IRA portfolios can also be seen in the overall household assets (see Figure 16-3).

According to the *Securities Industry Association Factbook*, while in 1985 U.S. households split their liquid assets fairly equally between bank deposits and securities products, including equities and fixed income, in the year 2000 the share of securities in U.S. household portfolios had increased to 79 percent and the share of bank deposits had dropped to only 21 percent. U.S. households are now keeping most of their financial assets invested in exchange-traded fi-

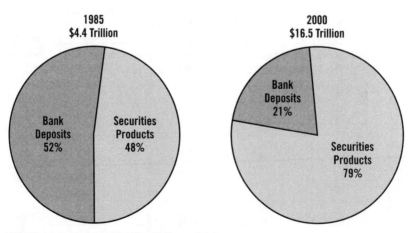

FIGURE 16-3 Households' Liquid Financial Assets

nancial products. This culture shift has also changed the capital allocation distribution channels from banks to securities markets.

The U.S. household portfolio is now an equity-centered one. In fact, 42 percent of the household portfolio is now directly invested in equities, while another 19 percent is invested in mutual funds, and most of this is also invested in equities. Bank deposits still account for a substantial 21 percent. The total fixed-income investments amount to only 12 percent of the household portfolio. The percentage of households that invest their wealth in equities has increased from 19 percent in 1983 to 50 percent in 2002. The number of households investing in equities has tripled over the past two decades, from 16 million to 53 million households. The investment culture shift in U.S. households has introduced 40 million new individuals into the equity markets. Given that the U.S. population is about 250 million, one of every three individuals now has investments in the equity markets. The average U.S. equity investor is 47 years old and invests half of his wealth in equities.

Using the demographic subgroups (Gen X, baby boom, GI generation), even though the amount of funds invested in equities is the lowest for Gen-Xers, they are the group that is investing the highest percentage of its wealth in equities, about 70 percent. As one would expect, as investors age, the weight of equities in their investment portfolios decreases. However, regardless of age groups, about half of all equity investors hold individual stocks and about 90 percent hold mutual funds in their portfolios. More than 80 percent of all equity investors are willing to take on average and above-average risk exposure. Only 15 percent of equity investors target investments with below-average risk. This profile has remained almost constant between the peak of the Internet bubble in 1999 and the third year of the bear market in 2002. U.S. investors include equities in their portfolios in order to have exposure to a high-risk–high-return asset class.

When we study the reasons that investors decide to invest in individual asset classes, we observe that 96 percent of all equity investors perceive stocks as long-term savings vehicles and follow a long-term buy-and-hold investment strategy. Consistent with this behavior, they don't get concerned and panic during short-term market fluctuations. Even after a three-year bear market, 95 percent of equity investors are optimistic about a recovery in their equity investments, indicating their level of confidence in the equity markets. Retirement is the primary goal of 65 percent of all equity investors, followed by education. About 60 percent of investors rely on finance professionals in making investment choices; however, 74 percent of those who interact with a financial advisor make their own fund choices from the alternatives recommended by the professional advisor. In addition, 13 percent delegate all fund purchase decisions to a finance professional. In this regard, it's of the utmost importance that the private pension fund advisors be familiar with the type of information that individual investors are interested in.

In making their purchase decisions, investors are most concerned about the risk level of the funds available for purchase. The expected return of the financial product and the reputation of the fund company are the next most important pieces of information. After making their asset allocation decisions, investors follow the performance of their investments closely. They are interested in getting information about the total wealth accumulated in their account, the returns generated by the financial products in their portfolios, and general economic conditions.

Before investors make their purchase decision, the financial advisor is the most influential source of information for them. The financial media also provide a significant amount of information. As always, word of mouth also appears to be a significant information source that investors use before making purchase and reallocation decisions. Investors utilize financial and media reports to follow the performance of their investments after their asset allocation decisions are made.

Harris Interactive, a major market research firm, has studied the attitudes of pension fund investors toward the securities industry. The results indicate that investors' attitudes toward the securities industry and their brokers are at their lowest levels since the inception of this tracking study in 1995. The percentage holding "very" favorable views of the securities industry has decreased the most. Investors' main concerns have been identified as losing money in their stock investments and dishonesty in the marketplace. Their primary concern is losing money in their retirement accounts. However, investors also point to dishonesty in both corporate accounting practices and the securities industry. Investors believe that the securities industry should be more honest and trustworthy, wrongdoers should be punished, internal controls and regulation should be increased, and a better job of educating investors must be done. Finally, investors have become more risk-averse, and fewer feel knowledgeable about investing. However, most investors continue to embrace a buy-and-hold strategy and do not believe that the past years' unfavorable events reduce the wisdom of this approach to investing.

The U.S. private pension fund system, with its large capital base, supplies investment funds to U.S. corporations and promotes economic growth and job creation. The power and effectiveness of the U.S. private pension fund system are based on the unrelenting trust and confidence of the U.S. investing public in its financial markets and corporations, and the public's willingness to provide capital to the system and maintain a long-term investment focus. When asked if the unfortunate events of September 11 had led them to change their asset allocations, 78 percent of the investors surveyed indicated that they had not touched their portfolios. Of the 22 percent who had changed their allocations, 60 percent had done so for other reasons; for example, cashing out their portfolios to finance college education or a home purchase. Only 40 percent of the 22 percent (that is, only 8.8 percent of the investing public) had changed their asset allocations based on the events of September 11. The investing public's philosophy can be summarized as a goal-oriented, long-term buy-and-hold strategy to attain specific financial objectives, mainly a comfortable retirement.

Notes

Chapter 1

1. Peter F. Drucker, "Teaching the Work of Management," *New Management*, Autumn 1988, p. 5.
2. Bruce A. Kimball, *Orators and Philosophers: A History of the Idea of Liberal Education* (New York: Teachers College Press, 1986).
3. Richard Hofstadter and C. DeWitt Hardy, *The Development and Scope of Higher Education in the United States* (New York: Columbia University Press for the Commission on Financing Higher Education, 1952).
4. Rakesh Khurana, *From Higher Aims to Hired Hands: The Social Transformation of American Business Schools and the Unfulfilled Promise of Management as a Profession* (Princeton, N.J.: Princeton University Press, 2007), pp. 122–125.
5. Kimball, *Orators and Philosophers*.
6. Darren Staloff, *The Making of an American Thinking Class: Intellectuals and Intelligentsia in Puritan Massachusetts* (New York: Oxford University Press, 1998), pp. 91–98.
7. Stephen Innes, *Creating the Commonwealth: The Economic Culture of Puritan New England* (New York: Norton, 1995).
8. Gordon Wood, *The Creation of the American Republic: 1776–1787* (Chapel Hill: University of North Carolina Press, 1998).
9. Thomas Jefferson, "Report of the Commissioners for the University of Virginia," in *Thomas Jefferson: Writings* (New York: Library of America, 1984), p. 460.
10. Peter F. Drucker, "Political Correctness and American Academe," *Society*, November 1994, p. 63.
11. The word *technê* is used repeatedly by Drucker to represent knowledge and craft, but not art. Historically, however, the word has been

used to refer to both knowledge and art. "*Epistêmê* is the Greek word most often translated as knowledge, while *technê* is translated as either craft or art." *Stanford Encyclopedia of Philosophy*; http://plato .stanford.edu/entries/episteme-techne, accessed April 6, 2009. Drucker uses the term *technê* to refer to that part of management that is technology or technique (i.e., specialized knowledge). He uses the word *art* to refer to the application of knowledge to human organizations.

12. Peter F. Drucker with Joseph A. Maciariello, *The Daily Drucker* (New York: HarperCollins, 2004), p. 3.

13. Peter F. Drucker with Joseph A. Maciariello, *Management, Revised Edition* (New York: HarperCollins, 2008), p. 287.

14. Ibid., p. 208.

15. "'Civilization' can surely no longer be equated with the 'Western Tradition' but must be restructured to include the art, wisdom, religions, literature of the East as well." Drucker, "Political Correctness and American Academe," p. 63.

16. Peter F. Drucker, *The Ecological Vision: Reflections on the American Condition* (New Brunswick, N.J.: Transaction Publishers, 1993), p. 213.

17. Transcript of a conversation between Peter Drucker and Bob Buford, Estes Park, Colorado, August 10, 1993, p. 3.

18. See B. F. Skinner, *Beyond Freedom and Dignity* (New York: Knopf, 1971).

19. Peter F. Drucker, *Landmarks of Tomorrow* (New Brunswick, N.J.: Transaction Publishers, 1996), p. 258.

Chapter 2

1. Peter F. Drucker, "*Really* Reinventing Government," *Atlantic Monthly*, February 1995.

2. After the New York Stock Exchange crash of October 1987, Drucker said he had expected it. "Pigs gorging themselves at the trough are always a disgusting spectacle, and you know it won't last long," he said of Wall Street brokers, calling them "a totally nonproductive crowd which is out for a lot of easy money." "The average duration of a soap bubble is known. It's about 26 seconds. Then the surface tension becomes too great and it begins to burst. For

speculative crazes, it's about 18 months," he said, in a rare outburst. AP, Los Angeles, "US management visionary Peter Drucker dies at 95," November 13, 2005, p. 1.

3. Paul A. Volcker, "Public Service: The Quiet Crisis," American Enterprise Institute for Public Policy Research, January 1, 2000.

4. "DoD's High-Risk Areas: Actions Needed to Reduce Vulnerabilities and Improve Business Outcomes," U.S. Government Accountability Office, March 12, 2009, p. 21.

5. Landon Thomas, Jr., "Tax Break Helps a Crusader for Deficit Discipline," *New York Times*, February 15, 2008.

6. For additional information, see http://www.pgpf.org.

7. Laza Kekic, "Index of Democracy 2007," The Economist Intelligence Unit.

8. Proudfoot Consulting, "2008 Global Productivity Report"; http://www.proudfootconsulting.com/productivity/.

9. For additional data, see the Center for Business as an Agent of World Benefit; at http://worldbenefit.case.edu/.

10. See Robert Behn, "The Massachusetts Department of Revenue, A–F," Duke University case study, January 1991.

11. Rakesh Khurana, *From Higher Aims to Hired Hands: The Social Transformation of American Business Schools and the Unfulfilled Promise of Management as a Profession* (Princeton, N.J.: Princeton University Press, 2007).

12. Francesca Di Meglio, "A Crooked Path through B-School?" *Business-Week*, September 24, 2006.

Chapter 3

1. Craig L. Pearce and Henry P. Sims, Jr., "Vertical versus Shared Leadership as Predictors of the Effectiveness of Change Management Teams: An Examination of Aversive, Directive, Transactional, Transformational, and Empowering Leader Behaviors," *Group Dynamics: Theory, Research, and Practice* 6, no. 2 (2002), pp. 172–197.

2. See Brian Dumaine, "Who Needs a Boss?" *Fortune*, May 7, 1990, pp. 52–60; Charles C. Manz and Henry P. Sims, Jr., *Business without Bosses: How Self-Managing Teams Are Building High-Performing Companies* (New York: Wiley, 1993).

3. See Robert C. Ford, Cherrill P. Heaton, and Stephen W. Brown, "Delivering Excellent Service: Lessons from the Best Firms," *California Management Review* 44, no. 1 (2001), pp. 39–56.

4. For a discussion of innovative approaches to employee relations, see E. E. Lawler, III, and D. Finegold, "Individualizing the Organization: Past, Present, and Future," *Organizational Dynamics* 29, no. 1 (2000), pp. 1–15; Jeffrey Pfeffer and John F. Veiga, "Putting People First for Organizational Success," *Academy of Management Executive* 13, no. 2 (1999), pp. 37–48.

5. Susan Albers Mohrman, Susan G. Cohen, and Allan M. Mohrman, Jr., *Designing Team-Based Organizations: New Forms for Knowledge Work* (San Francisco: Jossey-Bass, 1995).

6. See Craig L. Pearce and Jay A. Conger (eds.), *Shared Leadership: Reframing the Hows and Whys of Leadership* (Thousand Oaks, Calif.: Sage, 2002); Craig L. Pearce and Henry P. Sims, Jr., "Shared Leadership: Toward a Multi-Level Theory of Leadership," in Michael M. Beyerlein, Douglas A. Johnson, and Susan T. Beyerlein (eds.), *Advances in Interdisciplinary Studies of Work Teams*, vol. 7, *Team Development* (Greenwich, Conn.: JAI Press, 2000), pp. 115–139; A. Seers, "Better Leadership through Chemistry: Toward a Model of Emergent Shared Team Leadership," in Michael M. Beyerlein, Douglas A. Johnson, and Susan T. Beyerlein (eds.), *Advances in Interdisciplinary Studies of Work Teams*, vol. 3, *Team Leadership* (Greenwich, Conn.: JAI Press, 1996), pp. 145–172.

7. See M. D. Ensley and Craig L. Pearce, "Assessing the Influence of Leadership Behaviors on New Venture TMT Processes and New Venture Performance," presented to the 20th Annual Entrepreneurship Research Conference, Babson Park, Mass., June 2000; Charles Hooker and Mihaly Csikszentmihalyi, "Flow, Creativity and Shared Leadership: Rethinking the Motivation and Structuring and Knowledge Work," in Pearce and Conger (eds.), *Shared Leadership*, pp. 215–234; James O'Toole, Jay Galbraith, and Edward E. Lawler, III, "The Promise and Pitfalls of Shared Leadership: When Two (or More) Heads Are Better than One," in Pearce and Conger (eds.), *Shared Leadership*, pp. 250–267; Pearce and Sims, "Vertical versus Shared Leadership"; Craig L. Pearce, Youngjin Yoo, and Maryam

Alavi, "Leadership, Social Work and Virtual Teams: The Relative Influence of Vertical vs. Shared Leadership in the Nonprofit Sector," in Ronald E. Riggio and Sarah Smith-Orr (eds.), *Improving Leadership in Nonprofit Organizations* (San Francisco: Jossey Bass, in press); Boas Shamir and Yael Lapidot, "Shared Leadership in the Management of Group Boundaries: A Study of Expulsions from Officers' Training Courses," in Pearce and Conger (eds.), *Shared Leadership*, pp. 235–249.

8. Craig L. Pearce, Henry P. Sims, Jr., Jonathan F. Cox, Gail Ball, Eugene Schnell, Ken A. Smith, and Linda Trevino, "Transactors, Transformers and Beyond: A Multi-Method Development of a Theoretical Typology of Leadership," *Journal of Management Development* 22, no. 4 (2003), pp. 273–307.

9. See Charles C. Manz and Henry P. Sims, Jr., "SuperLeadership: Beyond the Myth of Heroic Leadership," *Organizational Dynamics* 19 (Winter 1991), pp. 18–35; and Chester A. Schriesheim, Robert J. House, and Steven Kerr, "Leader Initiating Structure: A Reconciliation of Discrepant Research Results and Some Empirical Tests," *Organizational Behavior and Human Performance* 15 (1976), pp. 197–321.

10. P. J. Guinan, J. G. Cooprider, and S. Faraj, "Enabling Software Development Team Performance during Requirements Definition: A Behavioral versus Technical Approach," *Information Systems Research* 9, no. 2 (1998), pp. 101–125; J. C. Henderson and Soonchul Lee, "Managing I/S Design Teams: A Control Theories Perspective," *Management Science* 38, no. 6 (1992), pp. 757–777.

11. Pearce et al., op cit.

12. This team was a consulting client of mine that preferred to remain anonymous.

13. A. Harrington, "The Best Management Ideas," *Fortune* 104 (1999), pp. 152–154.

14. See Brian D. Janz, "Self-Directed Teams in IS: Correlates for Improved Systems Development and Work Outcomes," *Information and Management* 35, no. 3 (1999), pp. 171–192; and Enid Mumford, "The ETHICS Approach," *Communications of the ACM* 36, no. 46 (1993).

15. See Hooker and Csikszentmihalyi, "Flow, Creativity and Shared Leadership."

Chapter 4

1. Value-based management sets as a goal the transformation of the cultural mindset within the firm to one of maximizing firm value, where success is defined in terms of the increase in shareholder wealth.

Chapter 5

1. Peter F. Drucker, "The Bored Board," in Peter F. Drucker, *Toward the Next Economics and Other Essays* (London: Heinemann, 1981), pp. 116–117.
2. Ibid.
3. See Business Roundtable, "Principles of Governance and American Competitiveness," 2005, p. 2; and Ira M. Millstein, Holly J. Gregory, and Rebecca C. Grapsas, "Six Priorities for Boards in 2006," *Law and Governance* 10, no. 3 (2006).
4. Paul W. MacAvoy and Ira Millstein, *The Recurrent Crisis in Corporate Governance* (New York: Palgrave Macmillan, 2003), pp. 22–23.
5. Colin B. Carter and Jay W. Lorsch, *Back to the Drawing Board: Designing Corporate Boards for a Complex World* (Boston: Harvard Business School Press, 2003), p. 93.

Chapter 6

1. Jim Collins and Jerry I. Porras, *Built to Last: Successful Habits of Visionary Companies* (New York: HarperBusiness, 2004), p. 56.
2. *Introjection* is the unconscious incorporation of attitudes or ideas into one's personality.

Chapter 7

1. *Financial Times*, March 16, 2009, p. 8.
2. *Financial Times*, March 13, 2009, p. 1.
3. *The Economist*, May 8, 2004, p. 64.
4. *Wall Street Journal*, January 10, 2009, p. 1.

5. Drucker refers to "objectives" as "the *fundamental strategy of a business*" [*Management: Tasks, Responsibilities, Practices* (New York: Harper & Row, 1974), p. 99] and thus uses the term to refer to both the ends (goals) and the means (strategy) to achieve them. In keeping with contemporary terminology, objectives are separated from strategy in the POSE framework (Figure 7-1).

6. John W. Bachmann, "Competitive Strategy: It's O.K. to Be Different," *Academy of Management Executive* 16, no. 2 (2002), pp. 61–65.

Chapter 8

1. Frances Hesselbein, "Future Challenges for Nonprofit Organizations," in Ronald E. Riggio and Sarah Smith Orr (eds.), *Improving Leadership in Nonprofit Organizations* (San Francisco: Jossey-Bass, 2004), p. 4.

2. Ibid.

3. Marshall Ingwerson, "Nonprofits Need to be Better Managed to Survive, Drucker Says," *Christian Science Monitor*, November 16, 1993.

4. John W. Gardner was the architect of many social action programs, including the founding of Independent Sector, today a coalition of more than 700 nonprofit organizations, foundations, and corporate philanthropy programs that provides a major meeting ground for organizations in the sector and is a force for advancing the nonprofit and philanthropic community's work. Source: http://www.independentsector.org/about/gardner.html.

5. Peter Drucker, in an introduction of Hesselbein at the February 22, 2002, Kravis-deRoulet Conference hosted by the Kravis Leadership Institute, credited Hesselbein with raising the country's consciousness about the impact and importance of the social sector, and as being the driver to create and provide tools to social-sector leaders and institutions to enable them to perform effectively. As he completed his introduction, he said: "There is no better, no more outstanding, no more significant leader in the nonprofit scene than Frances Hesselbein."

6. Interview with Frances Hesselbein, April 9, 2009.

7. Ibid.

8. Ingwerson, "Nonprofits Need to Be Better Managed to Survive, Drucker Says."

9. Peter F. Drucker, *The Five Most Important Questions You Will Ever Ask about Your Nonprofit Organization* (San Francisco: Jossey-Bass, 1993).

10. Gary J. Stern, *The Drucker Foundation Self-Assessment Tool: Process Guide* (San Francisco: Jossey-Bass, 1999), p. 4.

11. Peter F. Drucker, "What Business Can Learn from Nonprofits," *Harvard Business Review*, August 1989.

12. Peter F. Drucker class lecture, March 21, 2005.

13. *Chronicle of Philanthropy*, April 9, 2009, p. 34.

14. Paul Arnsberger, Melissa Ludlum, Margaret Riley, and Mark Stanton, "A History of the Tax-Exempt Sector: An SOI Perspective," *Statistics of Income Bulletin*, Winter 2008, p. 6; http://www.irs.gov/pub/irs-soi/tehistory.pdf, accessed April 26, 2009.

15. Drucker, "What Business Can Learn."

16. Source: http://www.ashoka.org/social_entrepreneur, accessed April 11, 2009.

17. Source: http://www.michaelorenzen.com/carnegie.html, accessed April 11, 2009.

18. Bill Drayton, CEO and founder of Ashoka, is a social entrepreneur. Ashoka is the global association of the world's leading social entrepreneurs, founded in 1981. With their global community, they develop models for collaboration and design the infrastructure needed to advance the field of social entrepreneurship and the citizen sector. Their Fellows inspire others to adopt and spread their innovations, demonstrating to all citizens that they too have the potential to be powerful change makers.

19. David M. Van Slyke and Harvey K. Newman, "Venture Philanthropy and Social Entrepreneurship in Community Redevelopment," *Nonprofit Management & Leadership* 16, no. 3 (Spring 2006) (Wiley Periodicals, Inc.). Source: www.interscience.wiley.com, accessed April 8, 2009, with reference to J. Gregory Dees, Jed Emerson, and Peter Economy, *Strategic Tools for Social Entrepreneurs: Enhancing the Performance of Your Enterprising Nonprofit* (Hoboken, N.J.: Wiley, 2002).

20. There are seven core principles embodied in Fair Trade Certified: 1. Fair price—farmer groups are guaranteed a minimum floor price

that covers the cost of sustainable production, a "social premium" for community development projects, and an additional price premium when their crops are certified organic. 2. Fair labor—certified farms ensure safer working conditions, better wages, and freedom of association; child labor and forced labor are strictly prohibited. 3. Direct trade—producers develop the business capacity to export their own harvests, bypassing intermediaries and plugging farmers directly into the global marketplace. 4. Access to credit—buyers are encouraged to offer farmers commercial credit, either directly or in collaboration with financial intermediaries. 5. Democratic and transparent organizations—empowerment is a core principle. Small farmers form cooperatives that allow them to process and export their harvests competitively. Workers on larger farms form worker councils that identify, plan, and manage their own community development projects. Both types of organizations are audited annually for transparency, democratic process, and sound financial management. 6. Community development—fair trade premiums allow farmers and farm workers to invest in community development projects, including potable water, education, health-care services, housing, reforestation, and organic certification. 7. Environmental sustainability—standards require environmentally sustainable farming methods that protect farmers' health and preserve ecosystems. http://www .transfairusa.org, 2007 annual report, accessed April 10, 2009.

21. The Kravis Leadership Institute (KLI) is one of a number of research institutes based at Claremont McKenna College, operating within the Claremont Colleges community, which includes the Peter F. Drucker/Masatoshi Ito School of Management and the Drucker Institute. The author of this chapter was conference leader as well as the interim executive director of KLI.

22. Paul Rice reported electronically May 20, 2009.

23. Ibid.

24. Leading Social Change Conference sponsored by the Kravis Leadership Institute, February 27, 2009.

25. Jim Collins, *Good to Great and the Social Sectors, A Monograph to Accompany Good to Great* (New York: HarperCollins, 2005), p. 18.

26. Drucker, "What Business Can Learn."

27. Leading Social Change Conference, 2009.

28. Ibid., p. 1.

29. Ibid., p. 2.

30. George Gendron, "Flashes of Genius," *Inc.*, May 1996; http://www.inc.com/magazine/19960515/2083_Printer_Friendly .html, accessed May 12, 2009.

31. *Chronicle of Philanthropy*, April 9, 2009, and April 21, 2009; http://philanthropy.com/news/updates, accessed April 25, 2009.

32. Ibid., accessed May 12, 2009.

33. Robert Lang, CEO of the Mary Elizabeth and Gordon B. Mannweiler Foundation, is leading the charge to establish the Low-Profit Limited Liability Company (L3C), allowing a for-profit entity to be organized to engage in socially beneficial activities. This structure that would allow foundations to invest by using an alternative to grants: program-related investments (PRIs). The L3C's investment structure would be designed to bring new pools of funds, such as pension and endowment investments, to bear on problems that are normally treatable only by nonprofit dollars. See http://www .philanthromedia.org/archives/2007/10/ lc3_legal_structure.html.

34. Collins, *Good to Great and the Social Sectors*, author's note.

35. Ibid., p. 20.

Chapter 9

1. Peter F. Drucker, *Drucker 20seiki wo ikite: Watashino rirekisho [My Personal History]* (Tokyo: Nihon keizai shinbunsha, 2005).

2. See James P. Womack, Daniel T. Jones, and Daniel Roos, *The Machine That Changed the World: The Story of Lean Production* (London: Macmillan, 1990).

Chapter 10

1. Max Weber, *The Theory of Social and Economic Organization*, trans. A. M. Henderson and Talcott Parsons (New York: Oxford University Press, 1947), pp. 358–392; and Jay A. Conger and Rabindra N. Kanungo (eds.), *Charismatic Leadership: The Elusive Factor in Organizational Effectiveness* (San Francisco: Jossey-Bass, 1988); see also Michelle C. Bligh, Jeffrey C. Kohles, and Rajnandini Pillai, "Cri-

sis and Charisma in the California Recall Election," *Leadership* 1, no. 3 (1988), pp. 323–352.

2. Weber, *Theory of Social and Economic Organization*, p. 358.
3. Joseph A. Maciariello, Personal communication, 2009.
4. Peter F. Drucker, *The Essential Drucker* (New York: HarperCollins, 2001).
5. Peter F. Drucker, "Can There Be 'Business Ethics'?" *Public Interest* 63, no. 3 (Spring 1981), pp. 18–36.
6. Jean Lipman-Blumen, *Connective Leadership: Managing in an Interdependent World* (New York: Oxford University Press, 2000).
7. John Browne, "The G-20 Meeting: What Really Happened in London," April 9, 2009; http://www.dailymarkets.com/economy/2009/04/08/the-g-20-meeting-what-really-happened-in-london/.
8. Lipman-Blumen, *Connective Leadership.*
9. Source: http://www.labnol.org/internet/total-websites-on-internet-worldwide/5206/.
10. Source: http://www.internetworldstats.com/stats.htm.
11. Lipman-Blumen, *Connective Leadership.*
12. Leavitt served as the Walter Kilpatrick Professor of Organizational Behavior at Stanford University Graduate School of Business from 1966 to 1996.
13. Jean Lipman-Blumen and Harold J. Leavitt, "Vicarious and Direct Achievement Patterns in Adulthood," *Counseling Psychologist* 6, no. 1 (1976), pp. 26–32.
14. Lipman-Blumen, *Connective Leadership*, p. 19.
15. Source: http://dictionary.reference.com/browse/Machiavellian.
16. Lipman-Blumen, *Connective Leadership*, p. 17.
17. Niccolò Machiavelli, *The Prince*, ed and trans. Robert M. Adams (1513; reprint New York: W.W. Norton, 1977).
18. Lipman-Blumen, *Connective Leadership*, pp. 17–18.
19. Robert K. Greenleaf, *The Servant as Leader* (Newton Centre, Mass.: Robert K. Greenleaf Center, 1970).
20. Edward A. Shils and Henry A. Finch (eds. and trans.), *Max Weber on the Methodology of the Social Sciences* (New York: Free Press, 1949).
21. Lipman-Blumen, *Connective Leadership*, p. 142.
22. Ibid., p. 151.

23. Ibid., p. 198.

24. Shils and Finch, *Max Weber on the Methodology of the Social Sciences*. See also Chester I. Barnard, *The Functions of the Executive* (Cambridge, Mass.: Harvard University Press, 1964).

25. Robert B. Cialdini, *Influence: How and Why People Agree to Things* (New York: Morrow, 1984).

26. The ASI, OASI, and ASSET may be taken, scored, and retrieved on the Web at www.connectiveleadership.com or www.achieving styles.com under the supervision of Connective Leadership Practitioners trained and certified by the Connective Leadership Institute (formerly the Achieving Styles Institute), Pasadena, California. In addition to English versions of all the current Web-based achieving styles inventories, Thai and Bulgarian versions may be taken on the Web at the same Web site.

27. Jean Lipman-Blumen, *The Allure of Toxic Leaders* (New York: Oxford University Press, 2005), pp. 229–230, 241–242.

28. Ibid.

29. Lipman-Blumen, *Connective Leadership*, Chapter 12.

30. Ernest Becker, *The Denial of Death* (New York: Free Press, 1973).

31. Lipman-Blumen, *Connective Leadership*, p. 352.

32. Clifford Geertz, *The Interpretation of Cultures* (New York: Basic Books, 1973).

33. Victor E. Frankl, *Man's Search for Meaning*, trans. Ilse Lasch (1959; reprint Boston: Beacon Press, 1992), p. 17.

Chapter 11

1. Peter F. Drucker, *Management Challenges for the 21st Century* (New York: HarperCollins, 1999), p. 157.

2. Thomas Davenport, *Thinking for a Living: How to Get Better Performance and Results from Knowledge Workers* (Boston: Harvard Business School Press, 2005), p. 7.

3. Drucker, *Management Challenges*, p. 157.

4. Davenport, *Thinking for a Living*, p. 4.

5. Source: http://www.babsonknowledge.org/2005/12/was_drucker _wrong.htm, accessed April 1, 2009.

6. Drucker, *Management Challenges*, p. 149.

7. Ibid., p. 148.
8. Peter F. Drucker, *The Practice of Management* (New York: Harper-Business, 1993), p. 3.
9. Kirk Warren Brown, Richard M. Ryan, and J. David Creswell, "Mindfulness: Theoretical Foundations and Evidence for its Salutary Effects," *Psychological Inquiry* 18, no. 4 (2007), pp. 211–237.
10. See the University of Massachusetts Center for Mindfulness in Medicine, Health Care and Society Web site at www.umassmed.edu/cfm/mbsr/.
11. Leonard L. Riskin, "The Contemplative Lawyer: On the Potential Contributions of Mindfulness Meditation to Law Students and Lawyers and their Clients," *Harvard Negotiation Law Review* 7 (2002), pp. 1–66.
12. Phil Jackson, *Sacred Hoops: Spiritual Lessons from a Hardwood Warrior* (New York: Hyperion Press, 1995).
13. Jeremy Hunter and Don McCormick, "Mindfulness in the Workplace: An Exploratory Study," paper presented at the 2008 Academy of Management annual meeting, Anaheim, California.
14. Drucker, *Management Challenges*, p. 161.
15. Not to mention putting policies in place that support healthy brain activity, but that is not within the scope of this chapter.
16. William James, *Principles of Psychology*, vol. 1 (New York: Holt, 1890), p. 424.
17. Peter F. Drucker, *The Essential Drucker* (New York: HarperCollins, 2001), p. 345.
18. Ibid., p. 344.
19. Peter F. Drucker, *Innovation and Entrepreneurship* (New York: Harper Perennial, 1985), p. 104.
20. Mihaly Csikszentmihalyi, *Flow: The Psychology of Optimal Experience* (New York: HarperCollins, 1993).
21. Joshua S. Rubinstein, David E. Meyer, and Jeffrey E. Evans, "Executive Control of Cognitive Processes in Task Switching," *Journal of Experimental Psychology—Human Perception and Performance* 27. no. 4.
22. Karin Foerde, Barbara J. Knowlton, and Russell A. Poldrack, "Modulation of Competing Memory Systems by Distraction," *Proceedings of the National Academy of Sciences* 103, no. 31 (2006).

23. Concentration meditation is one of the many varieties of meditation practice.

24. Herbert Benson and Miriam Klipper, *The Relaxation Response* (New York: HarperPaperback, 2000).

25. Sara Lazar et al., "Meditation Experience Is Associated with Increased Cortical Thickness," *NeuroReport* 16 (2005), pp. 1893–1897. If you want to see the data, go here: https://nmr.mgh.harvard.edu/~lazar/. If you want to read the paper, go here: http://surfer.nmr.mgh.harvard.edu/pub/articles/Lazar_Meditation_Plasticity_05.pdf.

26. If you want to know more, I suggest the Web site of the Center for Contemplative Mind in Society (www.contemplativemind.org). It has plenty of resources to help you.

27. The classic work on neuroplasticity is *The Mind & The Brain: Neuroplasticity and the Power of Mental Force* by UCLA professor Jeffrey Schwartz and Sharon Begley (New York: Harper Perennial, 2003).

28. Source: www.adamsmith.org/smith/tms/tms-p3-c2.htm.

29. Carol Dweck, *Mindset: The New Psychology of Success* (New York: Ballantine Books, 2006).

30. Paul Ekman, *Emotions Revealed: Recognizing Faces and Feelings to Improve Communication and Emotional Life* (New York: Times Books, 2003), p. 75.

31. Elizabeth Haas Edersheim, *The Definitive Drucker* (New York: McGraw-Hill, 2007), pp. 9–10.

Chapter 14

1. Leslie C. Tihany, "The Austro-Hungarian Compromise, 1867–1918: A Half Century of Diagnosis; Fifty Years of Post-Mortem," *Central European History* 2, no. 2 (1969), pp. 114–138.

2. For statistical information, see John Ellis and Michael Cox, *The World War I Databook: The Essential Facts and Figures for All the Combatants* (London: Aurum, 2001).

3. The period of time covered by the first wave varies with different historians. See Eric Hobsbawm, *The Age of Revolution: Europe 1789–1848* (London: Weidenfeld & Nicolson Ltd., 1962) and T. S. Ashton, *The Industrial Revolution, 1760-1830* (London: Oxford University Press, 1997).

4. For background, see David McLellan, *Karl Marx: His Life and Thought* (New York: Harper & Row, 1973).

5. See Martin Kitchen, *A History of Modern Germany, 1800–2000* (Malden, Mass.: Blackwell, 2006).

6. See Mark Cornwall, ed., *The Last Years of Austria-Hungary: A Multi-National Experiment in Early Twentieth-Century Europe* (Exeter: University of Exeter Press, 2002) and Ellis and Cox, *World War I Databook*.

7. See Robert F. Himmelberg, *The Great Depression and the New Deal* (Westport, Conn.: Greenwood Press, 2001); and Patricia Clavin, *The Great Depression in Europe, 1929–1939* (New York: St. Martin's Press, 2000).

8. Michael S. Lawlor, *The Economics of Keynes in Historical Context: An Intellectual History of the General Theory* (New York: Palgrave Macmillan, 2006).

9. See Robert S. McElvaine, *Franklin Delano Roosevelt* (Washington, D.C.: CQ Press, 2002).

10. Wolfgang Grassl and Barry Smith, eds., *Austrian Economics: Historical and Philosophical Background* (New York: New York University Press, 1986).

11. Carl Menger, *Principles of Economics*, trans. and eds. James Dingwall and Bert F. Hoselitz (Glencoe, Ill.: Free Press, 1950).

12. Carl Menger, *Investigations into the Method of the Social Sciences with Special Reference to Economics*, ed. Louis Schneider, trans. Francis J. Nock (New York: New York University Press, 1985).

13. Eugen V. Böhm-Bawerk, *Capital and Interest: A Critical History of Economical Theory*, 1890; open source available at http://www .econlib.org/library/BohmBawerk/bbCICover.html. *Capital and Interest* includes Books I and II of *The Positive Theory of Capital*. *Value* and *Price* includes Books III and IV.

14. Ludwig von Mises, *Human Action, A Treatise on Economics* (New Haven, Conn.: Yale University Press, 1949).

15. Friedrich A. von Hayek, *The Road to Serfdom* (Chicago: University of Chicago Press, 1944).

16. Friedrich A. von Hayek, "The Use of Knowledge in Society," *American Economic Review* 35, no. 4 (1945), pp. 519–530.

17. Friedrich A. von Hayek, *Prices and Production*, 2nd ed. (London: Routledge, 1935; reprint New York: A. M. Kelley, 1967), and Friedrich A. von Hayek, *The Pure Theory of Capital* (Chicago: University of Chicago Press, 1952).

18. Joseph Alois Schumpeter, *The Theory of Economic Development: An Inquiry into Profits, Capital, Credit, Interest, and the Business Cycle* (Cambridge, Mass.: Harvard University Press, 1934).

19. See Peter F. Drucker, *The Concept of the Corporation* (New York: New American Library, 1964); *The New Society: The Anatomy of Industrial Order* (New York: Harper & Row, 1962); *Post-Capitalist Society* (New York: HarperBusiness, 1993); and *Innovation and Entrepreneurship: Practice and Principles* (New York: Harper & Row, 1985).

20. Peter F. Drucker, quoted in Tim Stafford, "The Business of the Kingdom," *Christianity Today*, November 15, 1999.

21. Global Insight, "Venture Impact: The Economic Importance of Venture Capital Backed Companies to the U.S. Economy," 2007.

Chapter 15

1. Peter F. Drucker, *The Practice of Management* (New York: Harper and Brothers, 1954), pp. 38–39.

2. Peter F. Drucker, *Management: Tasks, Responsibilities, Practices* (New York: Harper & Row, 1974), p. 64.

3. Peter F. Drucker, "The Customer Is the Business," in *Managing for Results* (London: Heinemann, 1964), p. 128.

4. Ibid., p. 131.

5. Peter F. Drucker, *Innovation and Entrepreneurship* (New York: HarperCollins, 1985), p. 251.

6. Drucker, "The Customer Is the Business," p. 116.

7. Ibid., p. 128.

8. Ibid., p. 113.

9. Ibid.

10. Ibid., pp. 112–113.

11. Philip Kotler and Kevin Lane Keller, *Marketing Management*, 13th ed. (Upper Saddle River, N.J.: Pearson/Prentice Hall, 2008), p. 228.

12. Peter F. Drucker, *The Daily Drucker* (New York: HarperCollins, 2004), p. 225.

13. Drucker, "The Customer Is the Business," p. 114.
14. Ibid., p. 111.
15. Ibid., p. 128.
16. Drucker, *Innovation and Entrepreneurship*, p. 252.
17. Charles Handy, "Finding Drucker's Vision in All That Stuff," interview on *Marketplace*, American Public Media, February 4, 2008; http://marketplace.publicradio.org/display/web/2008/02/04/drucker, accessed March 23, 2009.
18. Drucker, *The Practice of Management*, pp. 39–40.

Sources

Chapter 1

Aristotelian ethics, http://www.experiencefestival.com/a/Aristotelia_ethics /id/1918156; accessed April 6, 2009. Authors' note: For Aristotle, *arête*, or virtue, was not simply a matter of the intellect, but also of virtuous living.

Barnard, Chester I. *The Functions of the Executive*. Cambridge, Mass.: Harvard University Press, 1938.

Drucker, Peter F., with Joseph A. Maciariello. *Management, Revised Edition*. New York: HarperCollins, 2008.

Drucker, Peter F. "Political Correctness and American Academe." *Society* 32, no. 1, November-December 1994, pp. 58–63.

Drucker, Peter F., with Joseph A. Maciariello. *The Daily Drucker*. New York: HarperCollins, 2004.

Drucker, Peter F. *The Concept of the Corporation*. New York: John Day Company, 1946.

Drucker, Peter F. *The New Realities*. New York: Harper & Row, 1989.

Drucker, Peter F. *The Ecological Vision: Reflections on the American Condition*. New Brunswick, N.J.: Transaction Publishers, 1993.

Drucker, Peter F. Transcript of a conversation between Peter Drucker and Bob Buford. Estes Park, Colorado, August 10, 1993.

Drucker, Peter F. *Landmarks of Tomorrow*. New Brunswick, N.J.: Transaction Publishers, 1996.

Fogel, Robert William. *The Fourth Great Awakening and the Future of Egalitarianism*. Chicago: University of Chicago Press, 2000.

Greider, William. *The Soul of Capitalism: Opening Paths to a Moral Economy*. New York: Simon and Schuster, 2003.

Hymowitz, Carol. "Pay Gap Fuels Worker Woes." *Wall Street Journal*,
April 28, 2008. http://online.wsj.com/article/SB120933662693248203
.html?mod=googlenews_wsj; accessed April 4, 2009.

Innes, Stephen. *Creating the Commonwealth: The Economic Culture of
Puritan New England*. New York: Norton, 1995.

Khurana, Rakesh. *From Higher Aims to Hired Hands: The Social Transformation of American Business Schools and the Unfulfilled Promise of Management as a Profession*. Princeton, N.J.: Princeton
University Press, 2007.

Skinner, B. F. *Beyond Freedom and Dignity*. New York: Knopf, 1971.

Staloff, Darren. *The Making of an American Thinking Class: Intellectuals and Intelligentsia in Puritan Massachusetts*. New York: Oxford
University Press, 1998.

Sullivan, Patricia. "Management Visionary Peter Drucker Dies." *Washington Post*, November 12, 2005, p. B06.

Vogl, A. J. "The Real Power."*Across the Board, The Conference Board
Review*™ magazine, January/February 2005.

Wood, Gordon. *The Creation of the American Republic: 1776–1787*.
Chapel Hill: University of North Carolina Press, 1998.

Wuthnow, Robert. *God and Mammon in America*. New York: Free Press, 1994.

Chapter 2

AP, Los Angeles. "US Management Visionary Peter Drucker Dies at 95."
November 13, 2005, p. 1.

Behn, Robert. "The Massachusetts Department of Revenue, A–F." Duke
University case study, January 1991.

Center for Business as an Agent of World Benefit; http://worldbenefit
.case.edu/.

Di Meglio, Francesca. "A Crooked Path through B-School?" *BusinessWeek*,
September 24, 2006.

Drucker, Peter F., with Joseph A. Maciariello. *Management, Revised Edition*. New York: HarperCollins, 2008.

Drucker, Peter F. *"Really* Reinventing Government." *Atlantic Monthly*,
February 1995.

Drucker, Peter F. *The Age of Discontinuity: Guidelines to Our Changing
Society*. New York: Harper and Row, 1969.

Drucker, Peter F. *The New Realities*. New Brunswick, N.J.: Transaction Publishers, 2003.

Heineman, Ben. "G20 Fails to Take on Bribery," Op-Ed. *Harvard Business Review*, April 3, 2009.

Jackson, Ira A., and Jane Nelson. *Profits with Principles: Seven Strategies for Creating Value with Values*. New York: Doubleday, 2004.

Kekic, Laza. "Index of Democracy 2007." The Economist Intelligence Unit.

Khurana, Rakesh. *From Higher Aims to Hired Hands: The Social Transformation of American Business Schools and the Unfulfilled Promise of Management as a Profession*. Princeton, N.J.: Princeton University Press, 2007.

Peter G. Peterson Foundation. http://www.pgpf.org/.

Proudfoot Consulting. "2008 Global Productivity Report." http://www.proudfootconsulting.com/productivity/.

Schulte, Bret. "A World of Thirst." *U.S. News & World Report*, May 27, 2007.

Thomas, Landon, Jr. "Tax Break Helps a Crusader for Deficit Discipline." *New York Times*, February 15, 2008.

U.S. Government Accountability Office. "DoD's High-Risk Areas: Actions Needed to Reduce Vulnerabilities and Improve Business Outcomes." March 12, 2009, p. 21.

Volcker, Paul A. "Public Service: The Quiet Crisis." American Enterprise Institute for Public Policy Research, January 1, 2000.

Chapter 4

Drucker, Peter F. *The Practice of Management*. New York: Harper & Row, 1954, pp. 39–40.

Drucker, Peter F. *Management: Tasks, Responsibilities, Practices*. New York: Harper & Row, 1993, p. 345.

Drucker, Peter F. *Managing in a Time of Great Change*. Butterworth-Heinemann, 2002, p. 84.

Drucker, Peter F. *A Functioning Society*. New Brunswick, N.J.:Transaction Publishers, 2003.

Freeman, Edward. *Strategic Management: A Stakeholder Perspective*. Pitman Publishing, 1984.

Freidman, Milton. *Capitalism and Freedom*. Chicago: University of Chicago Press, 1962.

Goodyear, C. "Social Responsibility Has a Dollar Value." Theage.com, July 27, 2006.

Handy, Charles. "What's a Business For?" *Harvard Business Review*, December 2002, p. 54.

Institute of Management Accountants "Executives Say Corporate Responsibility Can Be Profitable." *IMA Online Newsletter*, October 15, 2007.

Jensen, Michael. "Value Maximization, Stakeholder Theory, and the Corporate Objective Function." *Bank of America Journal of Applied Corporate Finance* 14, no. 3 (2001), pp. 8–21.

Lougee, Barbara, and James S. Wallace. "The Corporate Social Responsibility (CSR) Trend." *Journal of Applied Corporate Finance* 20, no. 1 (Winter 2008).

Martin, John D., J. William Petty, and James S. Wallace. *Value-Based Management with Corporate Social Responsibility*, 2nd ed. Oxford: Oxford University Press, 2009.

Orlitzky, M., F. Schmidt, and S. Rynes. *Organization Studies* 24, no. 3 (2003).

Porter, Michael E., and Mark R. Kramer. "Strategy and Society: The Link between Competitive Advantage and Corporate Social Responsibility." *Harvard Business Review* OnPoint, December 2006.

Smith, Adam. *The Wealth of Nations*. Chicago: The University of Chicago Press, 1976.

Stewart III, G. Bennett. *The Quest for Value*. New York: Harper Business, 1991.

Chapter 5

Barrington, Louise. "Business, Government and Civil Society—Working Together for a Better World." *Asian Review of Public Administration* 12, no. 1 (January–June 2000).

"Big Investors Want SRI Research: European Institutions to Allocate Part of Brokers' Fees to 'Nontraditional' Information." *Financial Times*, October 18, 2004.

Business Roundtable, "Principles of Governance and American Competitiveness," 2005.

Byrne, John A. "The Man Who Invented Management." *Business Week*, November 28, 2005.

Carter, Colin B., and Jay W. Lorsch. *Back to the Drawing Board: Designing Corporate Boards for a Complex World.* Boston: Harvard Business School Press, 2003.

Carver, John. "The Promise of Governance Theory: Beyond Codes and Best Practices." *Corporate Governance* 15, no. 6 (2007), pp. 1030–1037.

Centre for Civil Society and Centre for the Study of Global Governance, London School of Economics. *Global Civil Society 2003*, eds. Mary Kaldor, Helmut Anheier, and Marlies Glasius. Oxford: Oxford University Press, 2003.

Coombes, Paul, and Simon Chiu-Yin Wong. "Chairman and CEO—One Job or Two?" *McKinsey Quarterly*, no. 2 (2004).

de Kluyver, Cornelis A. *A Primer on Corporate Governance.* Williston, Vt.: Business Expert Press, 2009.

Drucker, Peter F. "The Bored Board." *Wharton Magazine*, Fall 1976. Reprinted in Peter F. Drucker. *Toward the Next Economics and Other Essays.* London: Heinemann, 1981.

Felton, Robert, and Pamela Fritz. "The View from the Boardroom." *McKinsey Quarterly*, 2005 Special Edition: "Value and Performance."

Jones, Dale E. "Corporate Crisis: The Readiness Is All. *Heidrick & Struggles Governance Letter*, Second Quarter 2007.

MacAvoy, Paul W., and Ira M. Millstein. *The Recurrent Crisis in Corporate Governance.* New York: Palgrave Macmillan, 2003.

Millstein, Ira M., Holly J. Gregory, and Rebecca C. Grapsas. "Six Priorities for Boards in 2006." *Law and Governance* 10, no. 3 (2006).

"Re-Examining the Role of the Chairman of the Board." Knowledge@Wharton, December 18, 2002.

Saxby, John, and Mark Schacter. *Civil Society and Public Governance: Getting a Fix on Legitimacy.* Ottawa: The Conference Board of Canada, 2003.

"Splitting Up the Roles of CEO and Chairman: Reform or Red Herring?" Knowledge@Wharton, June 2, 2004.

"The State of the Corporate Board, 2007—A McKinsey Global Survey." *McKinsey Quarterly*, April 2007.

World Investment Report 2004: The Shift Towards Services. Geneva: UNCTAD, 2004.

Chapter 7

Christensen, Clayton M. *The Innovator's Dilemma*. Boston: Harvard Business School Press, 1997, p. 133.

Drucker, Peter F. *The Practice of Management*. New York: Harper and Brothers, 1954, pp. 36–37 and 51–56.

Drucker, Peter F. *Management: Tasks, Responsibilities, Practices*. New York: Harper & Row, 1974, p. 99, and Chapter 34.

Drucker, Peter F. "The Theory of the Business." *Harvard Business Review*, September-October 1994, pp. 95–104.

Edward Jones. Harvard Business School Case 9-700-009, pp. 7 and 15.

Edward Jones in 2006. Harvard Business School Case 9-707-497, exhibits 13 and 14.

Sathe, Vijay. *Manage Your Career*. Williston, Vt.: Business Expert Press, 2008, pp. 28–30.

Chapter 9

Bain, Joe S. *Barriers to New Competition: Their Character and Consequences in Manufacturing Industries*. Cambridge, Mass.: Harvard University Press, 1956.

Bain, Joe S. *Industrial Organization*. New York: John Wiley & Sons, 1959.

Caves, Richard E. *American Industry: Structure, Conduct, Performance*. Englewood Cliffs, N.J.: Prentice-Hall, 1964.

Drucker, Peter F. *Managing for Results*. New York: Harper & Row, 1964.

Drucker, Peter F. *The Age of Discontinuity*. New York: Harper & Row, 1968.

Drucker, Peter F. *Innovation and Entrepreneurship*. New York: Harper & Row, 1985.

Drucker, Peter F. *Drucker 20seiki wo ikite: Watashino rirekisho [My Personal History]*. Tokyo: Nihon keizai shinbunsha, 2005.

Mason, Edward S. "Price and Production Policies of Large-Scale Enterprise." *American Economic Review* 29 (1939), pp. 61–74.

Porter, Michael E. *Competitive Strategy: Techniques for Analyzing Industries and Competitors*. New York: Free Press, 1980.

Scherer, F. M. *Industrial Market Structure and Economic Performance.* Chicago: Rand McNally, 1970.

Schumpeter, Joseph A. *Capitalism, Socialism, and Democracy.* New York: Harper & Brothers, 1942.

Womack, James P., Daniel T. Jones, and Daniel Roos. *The Machine That Changed the World: The Story of Lean Production.* London: Macmillan, 1990.

Chapter 10

Barnard, Chester I. *The Functions of the Executive.* Cambridge, Mass.: Harvard University Press, 1964.

Becker, Ernest. *The Denial of Death.* New York: Free Press, 1973.

Bligh, Michelle C., Jeffrey C. Kohles, and Rajnandini Pillai. "Crisis and Charisma in the California Recall Election." *Leadership* 1, no. 3, (2005), pp. 323–352.

Browne, John. "The G-20 Meeting: What Really Happened in London." April 9, 2009. http://www.dailymarkets.com/economy/2009/04/08/the-g-20-meeting-what-really-happened-in-london/.

Cialdini, Robert B. *Influence: How and Why People Agree to Things.* New York: Quill, 1984.

Conger, Jay A., and Rabindra N. Kanungo, eds. *Charismatic Leadership: The Elusive Factor in Organizational Effectiveness.* San Francisco: Jossey-Bass, 1988.

Drucker, Peter F. "Can There Be 'Business Ethics'?" *The Public Interest,* 63, no. 3, Spring 1981, pp. 18–36.

Drucker, Peter F. "Foreword." In *The Leader of the Future.* Frances Hesselbein, Marshall Goldsmith, and Richard Beckhard, eds. San Francisco: Jossey-Bass, 1996.

Drucker, Peter F. *The Essential Drucker.* New York: HarperCollins, 2001.

Frankl, Viktor E. *Man's Search for Meaning.* Translated by Ilse Lasch. Boston: Beacon Press, 1959/1992.

Geertz, Clifford. *The Interpretation of Cultures.* New York: Basic Books, 1973.

Greenleaf, Robert K. *The Servant Leader.* Newton Centre, Mass.: Robert K. Greenleaf Center, 1970.

Lipman-Blumen, Jean, and Harold J. Leavitt. "Vicarious and Direct Achievement Patterns in Adulthood." *Counseling Psychologist* 6(1) (1976), pp. 26–32.

Lipman-Blumen, Jean. *Connective Leadership: Managing in an Interdependent World*. New York: Oxford University Press, 2000/1996.

Lipman-Blumen. Jean. *The Allure of Toxic Leaders*. New York: Oxford University Press, 2005.

Machiavelli, Niccolo. *The Prince*. New York: W. W. Norton, 1977.

Maciariello, Joseph A. 2009. Personal communication.

Shils, Edward A., and Henry A. Finch, eds. and trans. (1949). *Max Weber on the Methodology of the Social Sciences*. New York: Free Press, 1949.

Weber, Max. *The Theory of Social and Economic Organization*. A. M. Henderson and Talcott Parsons, trans. New York: Oxford University Press, 1974.

http://dictionary.reference.com/browse/Machiavellian.

http://www.internetworldstats.com/stats.htm.

http://www.labnol.org/internet/total-websites-on-internet-worldwide/5206/.

www.connectiveleadership.com or www.achievingstyles.com.

Chapter 12

Akerlof, George. "Labor Contracts as Partial Gift Exchange." *Quarterly Journal of Economics* 97, no. 4 (1982), pp. 543–569.

Becker, Gary. *Human Capital*, 2nd ed. Chicago: University of Chicago Press, 1975.

Card, David. "Immigrant Inflows, Native Outflows, and the Local Labor Market Impact of Higher Immigration." *Journal of Labor Economics* 19, no. 1 (2001), pp. 22–64.

Doeringer, Peter, and Michael Piore. *Internal Labor Markets and Manpower Analysis*. Lexington, Mass.: Heath, 1971.

Drucker, Peter F. *The New Society: The Anatomy of Industrial Order*. New Brunswick, N.J.: Transaction, 1993.

Drucker, Peter F. *Management: Tasks, Responsibilities, Practices*. New York: Harper & Row, 1974.

Edwards, Richard. "The Social Relations of Production in the Firm and the Labor Market Structure." In *Labor Market Segmentation*, eds.

R. Edwards, M. Reich, and D. Gordon. Lexington, Mass.: D. C. Heath, 1975.

Kerr, Clark. "Labor Markets: Their Character and Consequences." *American Economic Review* 40, no. 2 (1975), pp. 278–291.

Oi, Walter. "Labor as a Quasi-Fixed Factor." *Journal of Political Economy* 70, no. 6 (1962), pp. 538–555.

Pedace, Roberto. "Immigration, Labor Market Mobility, and the Earnings of Native-Born Workers: An Occupational Segmentation Approach." *American Journal of Economics and Sociology* 65, no. 2 (2006), pp. 313–345.

Stiglitz, Joseph. "The Efficiency Wage Hypothesis, Surplus Labor, and the Distribution of Income in LDCs." *Oxford Economic Papers* 28, no. 2 (1976), pp. 185–207.

Chapter 13

Akerlof, George A. "The Market for 'Lemons': Quality Uncertainty and the Market Mechanism." *Quarterly Journal of Economics* 84, no. 3 (1970), pp. 488–550.

Beatty, Jack. "The Education of Peter Drucker." *Atlantic*, December 15, 2005.

Drucker, Peter F., with Joseph A. Maciariello. *The Daily Drucker*. New York: HarperCollins, 2004.

Drucker, Peter F. *The New Realities*. New York: Harper & Row, 1989.

Drucker, Peter F. *Post-Capitalist Society*. New York: HarperBusiness, 1993.

Fama, Eugene. "Efficient Capital Markets: A Review of Theory and Empirical Work." *Journal of Finance* 25 (1970), pp. 383–417.

Pearce, Craig L. "The Future of Leadership: Combining Vertical and Shared Leadership to Transform Knowledge Work." *Academy of Management Executive* 18, no. 1 (2004), pp. 47–57.

Chapter 14

Ashton, T. S. *The Industrial Revolution, 1760–1830*. London: Oxford University Press, 1997.

Böhm-Bawerk, Eugen V. *Capital and Interest: A Critical History of Economical Theory*. 1890. Open source available at http://www.econlib.org/library/BohmBawerk/bbCICover.html.

Clavin, Patricia. *The Great Depression in Europe, 1929–1939*. New York: St. Martin's Press, 2000.

Cornwall, Mark, ed. *The Last Years of Austria-Hungary: A Multi-National Experiment in Early Twentieth-Century Europe*. Exeter: University of Exeter Press, 2002.

DeLong, J. Bradford. "Restoring the Pre-World War I Economy, Slouching Towards Utopia?: The Economic History of the Twentieth Century." Electronic monograph, University of California at Berkeley, February 1997. Available at http://www.j-bradford-delong.net/tceh/Slouch_Old.html.

Drucker, Peter F. *Adventures of a Bystander*. New York: Harper and Row, 1979.

Drucker, Peter F. *The Concept of the Corporation*. New York: New American Library, 1964.

Drucker, Peter F. *The Ecological Vision: Reflections on the American Condition*. New Brunswick, N.J.: Transaction Publishers, 1993.

Drucker, Peter F. "How Knowledge Works." *Atlantic*, November 1994.

Drucker, Peter F. *Innovation and Entrepreneurship: Practice and Principles*. New York: Harper & Row, 1985.

Drucker, Peter F. *Management: Tasks, Responsibilities, Practices*. New York: Harper & Row, 1974.

Drucker, Peter F. "Management's New Paradigms." *Forbes*, October 5, 1998.

Drucker, Peter F. *Managing in a Time of Great Change*. New York: Truman Talley Books/Dutton, 1995.

Drucker, Peter F. "The New Pluralism." *Leader to Leader*, Fall 1999.

Drucker, Peter F. *The New Realities: In Government and Politics, in Economics and Business, in Society and World View*. New York: Harper & Row, 1989.

Drucker, Peter F. *The New Society: The Anatomy of Industrial Order*. New York: Harper & Row, 1962.

Drucker, Peter F. *The Practice of Management*. New York: Harper and Brothers, 1954.

Drucker, Peter F. *Post-Capitalist Society*. New York: HarperBusiness, 1993.

Drucker, Peter F., quoted in Tim Stafford, "The Business of the Kingdom." *Christianity Today*, November 15, 1999.

Drucker, Peter F. "Schumpeter vs. Keynes." *Forbes*, May 1983.

Ellis, John, and Michael Cox. *The World War I Databook: The Essential Facts and Figures for All the Combatants*. London: Aurum, 2001.

Global Insight. "Venture Impact: The Economic Importance of Venture Capital Backed Companies to the U.S. Economy." 2007. Available at http://www.globalinsight.com/PressRelease/PressReleaseDetail 8726.htm.

Grassl, Wolfgang, and Barry Smith, eds. *Austrian Economics: Historical and Philosophical Background*. New York: New York University Press, 1986.

Hamilton, Richard F., and Holger H. Herwig, eds. *The Origins of World War I*. Cambridge, U.K.: Cambridge University Press, 2003.

Hayek, Friedrich A. von. *Prices and Production*, 2nd ed. London: Routledge, 1935; reprint New York: A. M. Kelley, 1967.

Hayek, Friedrich A. von. *The Pure Theory of Capital*. Chicago: University of Chicago Press, 1952.

Hayek, Friedrich A. von. *The Road to Serfdom*. Chicago: University of Chicago Press, 1944.

Hayek, Friedrich A. von. "The Use of Knowledge in Society." *American Economic Review* 35, no. 4 (1945), pp. 519–530.

Himmelberg, Robert F. *The Great Depression and the New Deal*. Westport, Conn.: Greenwood Press, 2001.

Hobsbawm, Eric. *The Age of Revolution: Europe 1789–1848*. London: Weidenfeld & Nicolson Ltd., 1962.

Keynes, John Maynard. *The General Theory of Employment, Interest and Money*. New York: Harcourt, Brace, 1936.

Kitchen, Martin. *A History of Modern Germany, 1800–2000*. Malden, Mass.: Blackwell, 2006.

Lawlor, Michael S. *The Economics of Keynes in Historical Context: An Intellectual History of the General Theory*. New York: Palgrave Macmillan, 2006.

Lidtke, Vernon L. *The Outlawed Party, Social Democracy in Germany, 1878–1890*. Princeton, N.J.: Princeton University Press, 1966.

Marx, Karl. *Karl Marx: Selected Writings*, ed. David McLellan. Oxford: Oxford University Press, 2000.

McElvaine, Robert S. *Franklin Delano Roosevelt*. Washington, D.C.: CQ Press, 2002.

McLellan, David. *Karl Marx: His Life and Thought*. New York: Harper & Row, 1973.

Menger, Carl. *Investigations into the Method of the Social Sciences with Special Reference to Economics*, ed. Louis Schneider, trans. Francis J. Nock. New York: New York University Press, 1985.

Menger, Carl. *Principles of Economics*, trans. and eds. James Dingwall and Bert F. Hoselitz. Glencoe, Ill.: Free Press, 1950.

Mises, Ludwig von. *Human Action, A Treatise on Economics*. New Haven, Conn.: Yale University Press, 1949.

Schumpeter, Joseph Alois. *Capitalism, Socialism, and Democracy*. New York: Harper and Brothers, 1950.

Schumpeter, Joseph Alois. *The Theory of Economic Development: An Inquiry into Profits, Capital, Credit, Interest, and the Business Cycle*. Cambridge, Mass.: Harvard University Press, 1934.

Sked, Alan. *The Decline and Fall of the Habsburg Empire, 1815–1918*. Harlow, England: Longman, 2001.

Smith, Richard. "The Drucker Vision: Corporations, Managers, Markets, and Innovation," Chapter 14 in this volume. New York: McGraw-Hill, 2009.

Standard & Poor's. "S&P/Case—Shiller Home Price Indices 2008, A Year in Review." January 13, 2009. Available at http:// www2.standard andpoors.com/spf/pdf/index/Case-Shiller_Housing_Whitepaper _YearinReview.pdf.

Tihany, Leslie C. "The Austro-Hungarian Compromise, 1867–1918: A Half Century of Diagnosis; Fifty Years of Post-Mortem." *Central European History* 2, no. 2 (1969), pp. 114–138.

Chapter 15

Adler, Margot. "Behind the Ever-Expanding American Dream House." National Public Radio (2009). http://www.npr.org/templates/ story/story.php?storyId=5525283. Accessed March 23, 2009.

Bartels, Robert. *The Development of Marketing Thought*. Homewood, Ill.: R. D. Irwin, 1962.

Bell, Martin J., and C. William Emory. "The Faltering Marketing Concept." *Journal of Marketing* 35 (1971), pp. 37–42.

Bennett, Roger, and Robert Cooper. "Beyond the Marketing Concept." *Business Horizons* 25 (1979), pp. 76–83.

Cohen, Lizabeth. *A Consumers' Republic: The Politics of Mass Consumption in Postwar America*. New York: Knopf, 2003.

Darroch, Jenny, George Day, and Stan Slater. "A Tribute to Peter Drucker: Editors' Introduction to the Special Issue." *Journal of the Academy of Marketing Science* 37 (2009), pp. 1–7.

Drucker, Peter F. *The Practice of Management*. New York: Harper and Brothers, 1954.

Drucker, Peter F. "The Customer Is the Business." In *Managing for Results*. London: Heinemann, 1964, pp. 110–131.

Drucker, Peter F. *The Age of Discontinuity: Guidelines to Our Changing Economy*. New York: Harper & Row, 1968.

Drucker, Peter F. *Management: Tasks, Responsibilities, Practices*. New York: Harper & Row, 1974.

Drucker, Peter F. *Innovation and Entrepreneurship*. New York: Harper & Row, 1985.

Drucker, Peter F. *The Daily Drucker*. New York: HarperCollins, 2004.

Flanigan, James, and Thomas S. Mulligan. "Prolific Father of Modern Management." *Los Angeles Times*, November 12, 2005. http://articles.latimes.com/2005/nov/12/business/fi-drucker12. Accessed March 23, 2009.

Keith, Robert J. "The Marketing Revolution." *Journal of Marketing* 24 (1960), pp. 35–38.

Kotler, Philip, and Kevin Lane Keller. *Marketing Management*, 13th ed. Upper Saddle River, N.J.: Pearson/Prentice Hall, 2008.

Chapter 16

Drucker, Peter F. "Reckoning with the Pension Fund Revolution," *Harvard Business Review*, March–April 1991.

Federal Reserve Board Flow of Funds Accounts, 2002.

Global Pension Statistics (2002) and OECD.StatExtracts Pensions Indicators (2008) Database.

Harris Interactive for the Securities Industry Association. "Investors' Attitudes Toward the Securities Industry (2003)."

Ibbotson Associates. *Stocks, Bonds, Bills & Inflation (SBBI) Yearbook*. Chicago: Ibbotson Associates, 2002.

Investment Company Fact Book. May 2003.

Investment Company of America and the Securities Industry Association.
"Equity Ownership in America (1999)."

Securities Industry Association (SIA) Factbook. 2003.

Securities Industry Association. "1999 Annual SIA Investor Survey:
Investors' Attitudes Towards the Securities Industry."

"Share Ownership Survey." New York Stock Exchange. 2000.

Index

Page numbers with n indicate note.

About the Contributors

Craig L. Pearce is professor of management at the Drucker School of Management. His research on shared leadership has been featured in the Wall Street Journal. His most recent book, *Shared Leadership*, is published by Sage, and his forthcoming book, Share the Lead, will be published by Stanford University Press.

Joseph A. Maciariello is the Horton Professor of Management at the Drucker School of Management and director of research at The Drucker Institute. He coauthored *The Daily Drucker* and *The Effective Executive in Action* with Peter F. Drucker, and recently carried on Drucker's legacy by revising two existing Drucker books, *Management* and *Management Cases*.

Hideki Yamakawi is professor of management and associate dean at The Drucker School of Management. His most recent book is *Japanese Exports and Foreign Direct Investment: Imperfect Competition in International Markets*.

Professor Murat Binay holds a Ph.D. in finance and an MBA from the University of Texas at Austin. Professor Binay's research interests lie in institutional investors, initial public offerings, payout policy, performance evaluation, and corporate governance. He has taught courses on corporate finance, financial strategy, investments, financial institutions, and derivatives.

Jenny Darroch's research and teaching focuses on marketing strategies that generate growth. She recently coedited a special issue of the *Journal of the Academy of Marketing Science: A Tribute to Peter Drucker* and has a new book coming out in fall 2009 called *Marketing Through Turbulent Times*.

Cornelis A. "Kees" de Kluyver is the former dean and Masatoshi Ito Professor of Management at the Drucker School. His most recent books are *A Primer on Corporate Governance* (Business Expert Press, 2009) and *Strategy: A View from the Top*, 3rd ed. (Prentice Hall, 2008).

Professor Richard Ellsworth's teaching and research have focused on outstanding executive leadership. Before joining the Drucker School he taught at Harvard Business School and held senior management positions with Kaiser Aetna. Publications include *Leadership and the Quest for Integrity* (with Joseph Badaracco) and *Leading with Purpose*. Ellsworth received his doctorate from Harvard University.

Jeremy Hunter, Ph.D., teaches courses on managing oneself and transforming "the executive mind." He holds degrees from Harvard and Wittenberg Universities and the University of Chicago.

Ira A. Jackson is the dean of the Peter F. Drucker and Masatoshi Ito Graduate School of Management at Claremont Graduate University, where he is also professor of management. He has extensive experience in business, government, civil society, and higher education.

Karen Linkletter is a lecturer in the American Studies Department of California State University, Fullerton. She and Professor Maciariello coauthored an article on Drucker titled "Genealogy of a Social Ecologist," forthcoming in the *Journal of Management History*. She received her Ph.D. in history from Claremont Graduate University in 2004.

Jean Lipman-Blumen holds the Thornton F. Bradshaw Chair in public policy and serves as professor of organizational behavior at the Peter F. Drucker and Masatoshi Ito Graduate School of Management, Claremont Graduate University. She is director of the Institute for Advanced Studies in Leadership at the Drucker Ito School.

Roberto Pedace is an associate professor in the economics department at Scripps College. Prior to this, he was an associate professor in the Drucker School at Claremont Graduate University. Professor Pedace's research interests are in the area of labor economics. His work addresses a variety of important public policy issues.

Jay Prag has a Ph.D. in economics from the University of Rochester. He teaches finance, economics, strategy, and leadership at the Drucker School and Harvey Mudd College. Jay has been voted Outstanding Teacher 15 times in his 23 years at the Claremont Colleges. He also teaches financial analysis at Southern California Edison.

Vijay Sathe is professor of management at the Drucker School. He is the author of *Corporate Entrepreneurship* (Cambridge), four other books, and numerous journal publications. Dr. Sathe has taught in MBA and executive education programs around the world and has advised leaders in all sectors of society.

J. Scott Scherer graduated from the executive management program at The Drucker School and holds a degree in economics from Duke University. He is a principal at CoreWorks Consulting and serves as an executive coach. Scott received his training in integral coaching from New Ventures West in San Francisco, CA.

Richard Smith is the Boyd Chair and professor of finance at University of California, Riverside. Before joining UCR, he was associate dean, professor of financial management, and served as director of the Venture Finance Institute at the Drucker School. He is the author of *Entrepreneurial Finance* (Wiley, 2004) and over 35 journal articles.

With a career as social sector consultant and leader, **Sarah Smith Orr** teaches social sector leadership, governance, and resource development. Orr is executive director of the Kravis Leadership Institute, through which she published Improving Leadership in Nonprofit Organizations (2003), "Women Directors in the Board Room: Adding Value, Making a Difference," *Boardroom Realities* (2009).

Professor James Wallace has had extensive private industry and academic experience prior to joining the faculty at Claremont Graduate University. He has worked as an auditor in public accounting, as a division controller for a major health care provider, and as a faculty member at the University of California, Irvine.